T0120365

# Just Say YES

*Chicken Soup for the Soul: Just Say Yes*
*101 Stories about Stepping Outside Your Comfort Zone*
*Amy Newmark*

Published by Chicken Soup for the Soul, LLC www.chickensoup.com
Copyright ©2024 by Chicken Soup for the Soul, LLC. All Rights Reserved.

The publisher gratefully acknowledges the many publishers and individuals who granted Chicken Soup for the Soul permission to reprint the cited material.

Front cover photo courtesy of iStockphoto.com/THEPALMER (©THEPALMER)
Back cover and interior photo of roller coaster courtesy of iStockphoto.com/DNY59 (©DNY59), photo of world map courtesy of iStockphoto.com/mirsad sarajlic (©mirsad sarajlic), photo of fish bowl courtesy of iStockphoto.com/mikdam (©mikdam)

Photo of Amy Newmark courtesy of Susan Morrow at SwickPix

*Cover and Interior by Daniel Zaccari*

Publisher's Cataloging-In-Publication Data

Names: Newmark, Amy, editor.
Title: Chicken soup for the soul : just say yes , 101 stories about stepping outside your comfort zone / Amy Newmark.
Description: Cos Cob, CT: Chicken Soup for the Soul, LLC, 2024.
Identifiers: LCCN: 2024933840 | ISBN: 978-1-61159-114-9 (paperback) | 978-1-61159-349-5 (ebook)
Subjects: LCSH Risk-taking (Psychology)--Literary collections. | Risk-taking (Psychology)--Anecdotes. | Courage--Literary collections. | Courage--Anecdotes. | Change (Psychology)--Literary collections. | Change (Psychology)--Anecdotes. | BISAC SELF-HELP / Motivational & Inspirational | SELF-HELP / Personal Growth / Happiness | SELF-HELP / Personal Growth / Self-Esteem
Classification: LCC BF637.R57 C455 2024 | DDC 158.1--dc23

Library of Congress Control Number: 2024933840

PRINTED IN THE UNITED STATES OF AMERICA
on acid∞free paper

30 29 28 27 26 25 24                    01 02 03 04 05 06 07 08 09 10 11

Chicken Soup for the Soul®

# Just Say YES

## 101 Stories about Stepping Outside Your Comfort Zone

### Amy Newmark

CSS

Chicken Soup for the Soul, LLC
Cos Cob, CT

Changing lives one story at a time®
www.chickensoup.com

# Table of Contents

**❶**

## ~Be Bold~

**❷**

## ~Let Yourself Trust~

## 3
## ~Give of Yourself~

## 4
## ~Trust Your Instincts~

## 5
## ~Take a Chance~

**❻**

## ~Embrace Change~

**❼**

## ~Connect with Someone~

# 8
## ~Do It Afraid~

# 9
## ~Don't "Act Your Age"~

## ~Rise to the Challenge~

**⑩**

# Be Bold

# Steel Toes

*Courage is being scared to death,*
*but saddling up anyway.*
*~John Wayne*

When I was twenty years old, I moved away from my rural hometown to the nearest big city, Phoenix. I was a single mom who had gotten herself into a bit of trouble with the law, and now I was fighting an ugly custody battle for my little girl.

I'd gotten a job working for just a buck over minimum wage at the front desk of a hotel. I wanted to go to college and be a writer. Instead, I was eating ramen noodles and stalking pro bono attorneys from a mostly empty apartment.

Then, a crew of structural steelworkers checked into the hotel.

They came in every day after work all covered in dirt with their hard hats and lunchboxes, laughing, cursing and trying to flirt with me.

I hit it off with one, Damien. He was my age, a wiry redhead with a personality to match. I poured out my heart to him, and he promised to help me get on my feet and get my daughter back. How would I feel about wearing a hard hat?

They were building a Walmart, but when it was done, they'd be on to the next job: a Target in Los Angeles.

The foreman hired me as a driver and laborer.

I'll never forget my first day on the jobsite. My knees felt weak just observing the guys walking around up on the steel, carrying huge

**Be Bold** | —

loads on forklifts and wielding torches spurting fire. The hard hat felt silly on my head, and I'd never felt more like a girl in my life.

What was I thinking?

The skeptical smirks of my new co-workers told me this was no place for me. I had much to prove.

At first, my tasks consisted of filling up heavy machinery with fuel and holding the dummy end of a measuring tape. But, within months, I was driving the reach forklift. A year later, I had earned my first welding certification.

The guys all accepted me when they saw how hard I worked and how eagerly I learned.

It was dirty construction work, but it was glamorous in a way. We lived in hotels and flew Southwest all over the West Coast. On the weekends, the crew played tourists, strolling boardwalks in California, gambling on the Vegas strip. There were no bills to pay, and we ate at restaurants for every meal.

A year and a half later, I was awarded full custody of my daughter and brought her out on the road with me. She was almost five years old.

Life on the road changed a lot with the arrival of my little girl. I filled our hotel room with her things to make her feel at home. She attended daycare in every city I worked in. My foremen were lenient with me and let me have weekends off so we could spend them together. I took her to Disneyland and Six Flags, and the beach every chance we got. Some days she even came to the jobsite and highlighted blueprints in the back of my truck.

By this time, I was learning so much on the jobsite. I was handy with the oxygen/acetylene torch and the chop saw. I could weld flats, fillets and overheads, and I'd gotten savvy at the telescoping boom lifts. I could read blueprints and a measuring tape now.

My comfort on the jobsite grew. I was beginning to wonder how I had ever managed to tolerate a desk job.

I loved working in the sunshine and even working up a sweat. Time passed quickly, and I stayed in great shape.

On every new jobsite, I endured the stares of other tradesmen who were surprised to see a young, blond woman in a pink hardhat on their jobsite. I wasn't fazed by their scrutiny; I was a show-off.

I pushed myself to be bold and work hard, and I earned a place in a trade dominated by men.

And I could walk the iron.

My first steps on the steel are embedded forever in my memory: swinging myself up out of the boom lift and onto the beam. Wearing my fall-protection harness, I tied off to the steel.

There was nothing above me but blue sky. Down below, the hard hats on the crew looked as small as my thumb. The beam stretched out in front of me for twenty long feet. Was it my imagination, or was it swaying a little in the San Francisco breeze?

My heart was in my stomach. I froze.

I couldn't do this.

I knew the crew was waiting for me. I was supposed to bolt up this connection point, something I had done from the safety of a lift many times. Then, I was supposed to head on down the beam about ten feet to connect another beam the rigger was already hooking up to the forklift down below.

My gloved fingers shook as I twisted the nuts from the bolts and shoved them through the holes, securing them with my spud wrench. I turned to face the seemingly endless beam again.

I could do this.

The year before, no one would have predicted I'd be operating heavy machinery and playing with fire. I'd been making a third of my current salary and playing it safe at a boring desk job. The year before, I wore a skirt to work, but now I wore steel-toed boots.

I put one foot in front of the other and I moved toward the second beam. It hovered in the air, suspended from the forklift, waiting for me to connect it. I walked faster to steady the wobble of the beam like the guys said to do.

Suddenly, I had reached my destination and sank to a seated position, wrestling the new beam into place. My thighs gripped the beam I sat on, and my fingers didn't tremble this time, efficiently working my spud wrench through the bolt holes.

As I tightened the last bolt, I felt a grin spread across my face. I was still afraid, but I was also excited and proud.

I was a tradeswoman. An ironworker. It was so far out of my comfort zone, but I was doing it, and it was changing my life. I'd made a career for myself; I was a responsible adult and had gotten my daughter back.

As the years passed, I earned more welding and machinery certifications and grew even more comfortable on the iron. When my daughter got a little older, I traveled much less and took some positions that kept me in Arizona so she could attend school and have her own house. Sometimes I'd still "boom out" (the tradesmen term for going on the road) for a summer.

The iron offered solitude some days as I welded away under my hood. Other days, it was teamwork all day, and whatever the task, my increasing knowledge of the trade made me an asset. The boys wanted this girl on the team!

I miss the iron a lot, and I have it to thank for the college degree I achieved by night, too. Today I am a writer like I always wanted, but like the ironworkers say, "Once an ironworker, always an ironworker."

I'm so glad I said yes to an unconventional and unforgettable journey, in giving that trade a try, and a decade of my life. The confidence and independence I cultivated as an ironworker made me the woman I am today.

— Cassandra Brandt —

# A Perfect 10

*I realized something on the ride. I realized if I wait
until I'm not scared to try new things, then I'll never
get to try them at all.*
~Marie Sexton

I shaded my eyes as I watched a boat pull parasailers high in the sky over the ocean. It looked so easy. I settled back in my beach chair to enjoy the warm sun and fine white sand on Lucaya Beach.

I turned to my husband George and said, "I would love to do that someday."

"Well, here we are," he said. "You're not going to have this chance back in Pennsylvania."

"You know I'm afraid of heights," I reminded him. "I'd have to be half-drunk to try it."

Just then, a man walked by with a cooler. "Cold beer!"

George signaled him. "I'll take two — and come back in fifteen minutes." He handed one to me and said, "Bottoms up."

We were on spring break in the beautiful Bahamas with our two kids: fourteen-year-old Tim and nineteen-year-old Margie. For months, I had looked forward to putting my toes in the sand while enjoying a good book in a tropical paradise. On the other hand, I wanted something exciting as well.

"This oughta be good," Tim said as he nudged his big sister.

I chugged the beer. George handed me the next one.

Margie, a freshman in college, leaned forward and asked, "Mom, do you want a funnel?"

I wasn't quite sure what she meant, but I drank another beer. Then, a lanky man walked up and down the beach to recruit people for a parasailing adventure.

George exuberantly waved his arms. "Over here!" he shouted while digging into his bathing-suit pocket to find his "beach money."

Both kids stood up and gestured toward me. Fueled with liquid courage, I eagerly followed the man to a wooden boat anchored in three feet of water. The man would take me out to a large, square float, beyond the breakers, about fifty yards from shore, which was the staging area for parasailers.

The tide was coming in and the craft bobbed up and down. I grabbed the side of the boat in the trough of the wave cycle and pushed down with my arms while I tried to hoist my leg over the side.

On the next trough, I felt two big hands on my backside. The wave lifted the boat, and the man raised his arms over his head, catapulting me as the craft splashed down into the next trough. I landed — SPLAT — between the seats, flat on my belly, like a beached whale. I could hear George's guffaws and my kids howling with laughter as the motor powered the boat toward the staging area.

We came alongside the float where half a dozen people waited their turn. I joined them, watching all the activity in a semi-detached daze. The next person already had on a harness and was awaiting instructions to stand on the X and get hooked up to the parachute. Soon, I realized there was only one more person ahead of me, a visibly nervous lady. We chatted briefly. I tried to reassure her but found my own palms sweating despite the ocean breeze. As she soared into the sky, I heard her squeals of delight — or screams of terror. I'm really not sure which.

One of the assistants beckoned to me to step up to the X and put on the harness. I did as I was told. I couldn't wait to be able to say that I had parasailed.

My new friend, the one who squealed in delight, was hovering for a landing when those of us on the float heard the motor on the boat cut out. Without power to pull her, she went straight into the ocean with the parachute drifting down on top of her.

I gasped and put my hands to my mouth. "Oh, no! That's not good." I started to have second thoughts about this adventure.

Just as quickly as it had stopped, the motor started up again, and the boat surged ahead, filling the parachute with air and lifting her out of the water. After one more go-round, the pilot assisted my friend to stick a perfect landing.

At last, it was my turn to parasail. Before I knew it, the assistants had me hooked up to the chute, and the towboat took off. I sailed straight up into the blue sky, finally remembering to breathe. It was so beautiful and quiet four hundred feet up in the air. I could see all of Lucaya Beach and half of Freeport. The marina was full of gorgeous yachts. Palm trees swayed in the tropical breeze, and fish swam in the water. I could see fish! That meant they were BIG fish because, by then, I was sure I was at least several miles above the Earth. Then, I saw a school of gigantic rays flapping their big wings as they glided gracefully in the water around the float I'd be returning to.

The boat turned, and my parachute lost some air and flapped, seeking to be refilled. I panicked. *I'm gonna die!* I thought. I reached up to grab above the O-ring where my harness attached to the parachute. I reasoned that if my harness broke, I'd still be able to hang on because I had a death grip on the lines of the parachute itself. To comfort myself, I sang at the top of my lungs, "Jesus loves me, this I know, for the Bible tells me so…" The boat turned again, and we were headed for the postage-stamp-sized float somewhere beneath me. "Oh, Lord, don't let them dunk me in the water," I prayed and continued to sing, "Yessssss, Jesus loves me…"

The captain did not fail me. I landed like a feather on that postage stamp. It was truly an experience of a lifetime. I looked toward the beach where my family waited for me. I started laughing when I saw that each was holding up a sign with the number "10" written in black.

— Nancy Emmick Panko —

# A Leap into the Unknown

*A different language is a different vision of life.*
*~Federico Fellini*

As I sat listening to a woman I didn't know speak to me in a language I barely understood, I began to question my wisdom in applying for a grant to attend a Spanish-language immersion program in Costa Rica. My spirits had been high when I left my home in New York nearly ten hours earlier. I was going on an adventure! I was going to learn! I was going to grow! Now, as fear and exhaustion overtook me, I was going to cry.

But I refused to cry in front of Marta, my host. Instead, I flipped through my English-Spanish dictionary until I found the word I wanted. "*Cansada*," I said. "*Estoy cansada.*" Then, I gave a weak smile and pantomimed putting my head on a pillow. Marta responded with a stream of Spanish words and then led me to the room where I would be sleeping for the next two weeks.

"*Gracias*," I managed before I closed the door, fell on my bed, and cried.

Six months earlier, I had applied for a Fund for Teachers fellowship grant to study Spanish in Costa Rica. I was teaching English Language Arts in a middle school that had a large Hispanic population. I applied for the fellowship for several reasons: I wanted to learn Spanish to be able to communicate, at least rudimentarily, with parents. I also wanted to feel what it was like to live in a place where mine wasn't the primary language.

I was thrilled when I was awarded the fellowship. For two weeks in August, I would be living in Liberia, Costa Rica. I would attend Spanish classes at Instituto Estelar Bilingüe and board with a family that lived near the school.

When I woke that first morning in Costa Rica, I had to force myself to leave my room. It was Sunday, and since classes at the school were Monday through Friday, I would be spending the day with my host family, who spoke no English.

"*Hola,*" I said as I came into the kitchen. Marta was by the stove, and her husband, whom she introduced as Pedro, was sitting at the table. I smiled at him as I sat down to a plate of eggs, rice, and beans.

"*Gracias,*" I said to Marta as I began eating. I stared at my food, hoping to avoid conversation, but Pedro began talking. I was too polite to ignore him, even though I had no idea what he was saying. My anxiety was like bees buzzing in my head. I took a deep breath and managed to catch a few words I understood. *Playa* was "beach." *Bonita* was "beautiful." I began to understand that he and Marta planned to take me to the beach that day. I smiled to show that I would like that.

My hosts took me to three beaches that afternoon. I saw white, gray, and black sand. I saw trees growing almost to the ocean's edge. And I saw beautiful, turquoise waters.

At every beach, Pedro would look at me expectantly. "*Bonita!*" I would say. "*Muy bonita!*"

Marta walked me the half-mile to school the next morning. I wrote down the directions so that I could find my way home.

Anna, the school's director, welcomed me and introduced me to Merlyn, the young woman who would be my teacher for the week. I was the only student in the class, so there was nowhere to hide when Merlyn taught and then drilled me on irregular verbs. I had a newfound appreciation of my students and what it was like to be learning something new.

I spent the mornings in class and the afternoons on a variety of adventures. I walked around downtown Liberia. I took a cooking class and made empanadas. I joined a group that went to a nearby town to teach children English. I went on runs around a nearby soccer stadium.

(This trip coincided with training for my first marathon.) I went home with Merlyn one afternoon and spent the night at her family's farm in the mountains.

I had a moving-up ceremony at the end of the first week. I couldn't have been prouder of myself. It wasn't just that I had learned Spanish; it was that I had become more comfortable with not knowing, with silence, with needing to ask for help.

The first full Saturday, I went on an adventure tour at Parque Nacional Rincón de la Vieja with strangers from Costa Rica and around the world.

We started with two hours of ziplining through the treetop canopy. I'd never ziplined before, and it frightened me, but I was getting used to facing my fears. I took a deep breath and smiled as I stepped off the platform. By the end of the two hours, I was ziplining hanging upside down. I saddled up and rode a *caballo* — something I had rarely done in my life — to our next adventure: whitewater tubing. I'd never done that before either. I ended the day with a hot-springs mud bath.

I shared a new teacher with another student during my second week of classes. Sonia was also wonderful, and it was fun to sneak in an occasional English word with Julia. I continued to explore on my afternoons and evenings.

One evening, I went to a Zumba class with Marta. I had already run eight miles when Marta asked me to go to Zumba with her. I agreed because I could see she was excited to share this with me.

The class was fun but exhausting, and I was relieved when the music ended. Then, Marta turned to me and said, "*Uno mas.*" Did I hear her correctly? I held up my finger and repeated, "*Uno mas?*" Marta smiled. I did my first — and second — Zumba classes that day.

On my final weekend, I took myself to a waterfall I was told I shouldn't miss. I walked downtown and found the public bus that drove to Bagaces, a town south of Liberia. I asked the driver to let me know when we arrived at the stop for Llanos de Cortés. My Spanish must have been good enough for him to understand because, thirty minutes later, he called out the name of the waterfall. I got off the bus and followed a long road until I reached the waterfall. It was breathtaking. I was sweaty from my walk and delighted to drop my bag and swim in the cool, clear water. I swam under the waterfall and just stood there, feeling overwhelming gratitude.

I'd come to a foreign country where I didn't speak the language and not only survived but thrived. I made friends and had adventures. I learned some Spanish, but I also learned about another culture. And I was reminded what it's like to be *la estudiante*.

I wrote this in my journal at the end of my stay: "It's amazing what you can do when you push past your comfort zone." The Ticos say "*Pura Vida.*" It is a philosophy of life as well as an expression of pure joy.

I carried that philosophy and joy home with me.

— Jeannette Sanderson —

# Elmo for a Day

*Elmo loves to learn, learn about it all. The things
that are big and the things that are small!*
~Elmo

My sister Danielle, the children's pastor, stopped by the counter where I waited to check in any latecomers. She glanced at her watch. "The person scheduled to be in costume hasn't shown up yet."

This was the biggest weekend of the year. The children's area of the church had a huge influx of guests. Many of them expected to see costumed characters from the theatrical production that had occurred the previous day. And now, one of them was running late.

"I have an idea. Come with me." She took off down the back hallway to the supply closet.

I knew the look in her eye but followed anyway. No doubt, whatever awaited me in the supply closet would be more than I bargained for when I agreed to be a greeter. She opened the door and walked to a rack of costumes.

"This will work." A furry red costume with a huge Elmo head hung from a hanger. She smiled widely. "Put this on."

Danielle held out the suit, helping me step into the bright, red legs. "Put these on next. You'll have to take off your shoes."

What amounted to huge house slippers flopped on the floor in front of me. I quickly obeyed, sliding my feet inside them. My hands were next, covered with furry, red gloves, which threatened to slip off if I let my hands hang.

"Now for the head."

Before I had time to catch my breath, an enormous head slid over mine. I looked out through a mesh window that was Elmo's mouth. It was hard to see, and I bumped into a table when I tried to walk.

A hand grabbed the back of the suit. "I've got you," said my sister. "Don't worry. I'll lead you around. Now, let's go see the kids."

When I walked into a room full of wide-eyed four- and five-year-olds, little arms flew around my legs and waist.

I spent the next few minutes patting the little ones on the head and offering hugs while trying to remember to keep my hands tilted up so the gloves didn't slide off. Danielle gave the signal and gripped the back of my costume as she helped me leave the room while I kept waving goodbye.

Catching my breath in the hall, she whispered, "Ready for the three-year-olds?"

And so it went, all the way down to the youngest ones. Once back in the supply closet, she helped me out of the costume head. One glance at each other, and we burst out laughing.

Being Elmo for a day sure was a lot more exciting than the greeter job I had signed up for. I wouldn't have traded it for the world.

— Wendy Klopfenstein —

# Going Solo

*Coming out of your comfort zone is tough
in the beginning, chaotic in the middle, and
awesome in the end... because in the end,
it shows you a whole new world.*
~Manoj Arora

had one more call to make. If my friend couldn't go with me, I would miss out on a local street festival that I was looking forward to.

Like my other friends, she wasn't able to join me at the festival. I wouldn't be going.

With my husband Harold working and my kids grown, I found myself lonely on Saturdays. And that was when so many fun events took place. Unfortunately, it always seemed as if everyone had plans.

Moping around my house, I felt sorry for myself. It occurred to me how much I depended on my family and friends for entertainment and adventures.

Harold was a good sport by going with me to watch "chick flicks" when my friends weren't available. I really appreciated his efforts, but when I glanced over at him in the theater, most of the time he'd be fast asleep! So, despite his kindness, I decided I wouldn't ask him to go to those types of movies again. If my friends couldn't see a movie with me, I would just shrug and think, *I'll wait until it's streamed on TV.*

Dining out became another issue. I love to experiment with different types of cuisine. Unfortunately, Harold is a picky eater. Give him a hot dog and a bag of chips, and he is good to go. Asking friends to go out to eat became discouraging. There were food-restricted diets, previous plans and budget issues, which I understood and respected. Like everything else, I would think, *Another time.*

One evening while talking to a friend, I mentioned how I missed outings because everyone seemed so busy. Her answer seemed so nonchalant and simple. "Go by yourself."

I'd never attended a function or activity solo. I hadn't even considered it. After I spoke to my friend, I imagined how uncomfortable I would feel in a restaurant by myself. Sure, I could eat at a fast-food joint alone, but I couldn't fathom the idea of dining alone at a restaurant with table service. I also couldn't imagine going to a festival by myself. Half the fun for me is enjoying the company I'm with. Talking and mingling is part of the experience. I was also insecure and worried about what people would think of me because I was by myself. The word "loser" came to mind.

A few weeks later, when a new movie came out, I thought about calling my friend to join me. But then I remembered the conversation we had had, and her words echoed: "Go by yourself!" After a day of consideration, I decided I would venture out to the movie by myself. My reasoning was to start slow, and a movie was the perfect first outing to try alone. I could slither into my seat, and the lights would be low. No one would see I was by myself.

To my surprise, when I was settled in my seat at the theater, I noticed many people were there alone. Why hadn't I noticed that before?

I felt a huge sense of accomplishment after the movie. Not only did I feel confident about going out by myself, but I enjoyed the movie and time with myself. An added plus was that I didn't have to share the popcorn!

I've come a long way since my solo movie date. I've enjoyed street fairs, concerts and dining out by myself. I don't feel lonely or self-conscious. I still ask family and friends if they would like to join me. However, if they can't make it, I know someone who will always come along: ME!

— Dorann Weber —

# On a Mission

*Trust the still, small voice that says,*
*"This might work and I'll try it."*
*~Diane Mariechild*

The crowd was roaring. There were hundreds of young people, teenagers and young adults, and most were boys. Then there was Tony Hawk, the world's most beloved skateboarder. Tony and his entourage of athletes arrived like rock stars at our local skate park to perform their most riveting moves. Diving off large, arc-shaped ramps called half-pipes, they soared like great eagles suspended in mid-air. They would spin, twist, and toss themselves in circles, only to make brilliantly calculated landings on skateboards that seemed to be part of their bodies.

All the kids worshiped Tony Hawk. They studied his every move and spent hours practicing the masterful techniques he'd perfected.

I was a bystander, a mother who spent countless nights at these skate parks, watching mesmerized as my child and the other kids took to the air. We were a homeschooling family, so time was ours. I watched in awe as swarms of flying children, perched upon magical skateboards, flung themselves up toward the heavens, hoping they might touch the sky.

The weighted, scratchy sound of wheels and boards gliding across ramps was a promise of great speed, height, and a thrill like no other. To this day, those sounds still make my heart soar. This was a place where the excitement was followed by contentment. Those who participated, and those who observed, exhausted from sheer exhilaration, most likely went home to a cozy night's sleep, filled with dreams of soaring through heaven. Even I imagined I could fly.

The night when Tony showed up with his fellow athletes to perform for his fans might be one of the most memorable evenings of my life. Immediately after their riveting presentation, Tony worked his way through the massive crowd as it was the only route he could take to exit the skate park. Screaming children and adults followed him, beckoning him to sign their boards. I noticed this from high up in the bleachers and was determined to get Tony's signature on my son's skateboard, no matter what it took. I held the board, purchased at the start of this event, tightly under my arm. Working my way down the steep incline, I strategically plotted my path. There was no time for errors.

I had to reach Tony for my little boy — my little skateboarder, one of Tony's most adoring fans. I pushed through masses of people; there was no stopping me. It was a tight squeeze, with the crowd screaming for his attention. Finally, utterly determined, I pushed right through (with an inner resolve that seemed to come from a power greater than myself). And as I approached this giant of a man — the ever-so-tall Tony Hawk — I screamed as loudly as my lungs would permit.

"TONY, FOR MY SON!" I yelled as I lifted my skateboard over my head while striding toward him.

Tony turned toward me. In that split second, my eyes locked with his, and I saw Tony the person — a kind, giving man who radiated authenticity. With a marker in hand, he scribbled his name on the back of my board and then turned around to continue his exit from the skate park.

I am usually intimidated by large crowds. But, on that day, I became a warrior. I transformed into Wonder Woman, imagining I was pushing my way through thousands of people to save the planet. I wasn't just a typical home-schooling mom. I was a conqueror. Getting that signature for my son was a feat like no other.

Somehow, I found my husband and son in the crowd. With the signed board under my arm, I hurriedly approached them. And as my little boy caught sight of that swirl of a signature, something magical happened. His young eyes filled with wonder.

We found our way to the exit and walked into the darkness of the night. The crowd had now dispersed, and I was exhausted, lagging behind my two guys. Side by side, arm in arm, my husband and son walked toward our car. They, too, were content and tired, with my son cradling his newly signed skateboard. I watched them from behind as tears streamed down my face. I think that was the happiest day of my life.

—Andrea L. Fisher—

# How Mom Became a Hockey Player

*Somebody gives you an opportunity, say yes to it.*
*So what if you fail? You won't know if you fail*
*or succeed unless you try.*
*~Ann Meyers*

It was time to move, but I didn't want to. My three children, our dog, and I watched from our yard as yet another moving van drove away from our street. Like a child clinging to her worn, moth-eaten security blanket, I stubbornly stayed. So what if the cost of living was skyrocketing? I wasn't ready to leave my youngest's local school, the brief drive to my work, or our home church. The kids and I certainly didn't want to leave our family or friends. Granted, part of me felt that life had become routine, predictable, and to put it bluntly, boring. But staying in the same place with the same people, doing the same things as I had for over twenty years, was *comfortably* boring.

By spring, though, developers owned our house. Costs in the area were beyond our reach and climbing higher. I spent the next several months looking for a home, each month looking farther and farther away from our neighbourhood. Eventually, I found a place edging a patchwork of farms, a few blocks from a tiny town that was Hallmark-movie perfect. It was rural, quiet, and completely different from the hustle and bustle of city life. It even smelled like the country.

"This neighbourhood is great for us," I told the kids as, in the middle of a heat wave, we carried the last of our furniture from the rental truck. "There's a library, three grocery stores, and a bookstore. We'll just drive back to our old neighbourhood for everything else. Home will be nice and quiet."

It sure was quiet. That night, it was sweltering hot and so quiet that I could hear each step the kids took in the fifty-plus-year-old house. Mosquitoes buzzed in our bedrooms, and people chatted to each other outside as they walked past. It was hard to breathe. Grabbing my phone that night, and over the next weeks and months, I checked online for kids' programs, activities, and churches — anything to try to connect. No luck.

I comforted myself. *I still have my way to cope and calm down: my online exercise program.* I had exercised weekly, alone, in the privacy of my old home. Granted, I hadn't started up yet since I'd moved, but surely I would any day now.

Our mornings were swallowed up by the endless cycle of pitch-black mornings and commutes back to the old neighbourhood in the dark. Nights and weekends were a blur of car rides to the old neighbourhood. Exercise receded into the rearview mirror. The ties to my old friends were fraying with the distance and busyness. The new neighbours were friendly, but beyond "hello," I didn't know what to say. By early winter, I was getting squirrelly. I decided I was willing to do anything from hot yoga to cow wrangling to make new friends.

With that determination, I searched again. One activity popped up on Thursdays, the only evening I had when the kids were all busy: a Bible study. Due to the move, we had stopped attending church, and we missed it. Maybe a Bible study could fill the void.

That Thursday after work, I dug deep for self-confidence and cranked the volume for the directions on my phone. With my heart pounding, I found the church. There was plenty of room in the parking lot despite the fact I was late, and the door was still open. The warmth of the people in the group and the decaf coffee they served overcame the draft in the church hall and my own worries about fitting in.

Grateful for their welcome, I decided I would go back.

A few weeks passed until the next Thursday when I could attend. Deciding I better stay in my office clothes after work, I arrived at the church with a few minutes to spare. This time, the parking lot was eerily empty. Where was everyone? Nervous, I headed to the door and tried it. Locked. After a few minutes, a lone car appeared, and a woman got out. "Hi, are you here for the Bible study?" I asked timidly.

"I'm here for floor hockey. The church folks let us use the gym on Thursdays." Looking at the Bible in my hand, she nodded to her hockey stick. "Want to play?"

Normally, I would have said a polite, "No, but thanks," and rushed back to the familiarity of my home. However, I was far beyond "normally."

"Well, I haven't played hockey in a long time," I admitted. More women with hockey sticks and sweatpants joined us. I added, "I don't have running shoes." I looked down at my dress, leggings, and dress boots.

"No problem!" I had offers of a loan of sneakers, clothes, and a hockey stick faster than I could think of another excuse.

I swallowed hard. I considered driving back home to the endless commutes and the sense of isolation. I might as well give hockey a try. Really, what was there to lose?

I tucked the Bible back in the car and found a wadded-up T-shirt belonging to my youngest. Before I could change my mind, I marched into the church.

An hour and a half later, after huffing and puffing back and forth across the gym floor more and more slowly, I was dripping in sweat. I had signed up for hockey, was invited to the hockey Christmas dinner, and found out that I really needed to work on proper stick handling.

That night, as I drove the short distance home, I thought back to the last time I had actually played floor hockey. It had involved an elementary-school gym, red pinnies, and a significantly smaller me. Looking in my mirror as I moved to the turning lane, something else dawned on me. I had just met more people through that one decision to play hockey in snug, borrowed sneakers than I had since the move.

When I got home, I threw open my door. The dog jumped up and down, sniffing at the new smells as I unpeeled my sweaty jacket.

"Guess what I was doing?" I hollered. The dog looked up at me, taking in my disheveled hair, flushed face, and the aroma of post-exercise. "I was playing hockey. I'm going next week. And I think I've found a church!"

I texted the Bible-study leader, explaining I had shown up at the church and seen hockey players, who asked me to play, and I joined them because I couldn't find the study.

My phone beeped. "Sorry we missed you. So many people were sick that we decided to cancel for this week. Did you score any goals?"

"I sure did," I typed in, grinning. The words of the first hockey player who had greeted me at the church door floated back to me: "We've all been through a lot, and we're here for each other. You're welcome to join us."

Now, with my own hockey stick at the front door, a growing ability to chat with my neighbours, and a gym full of friends, I am sure glad that I did.

— Bev A. Schellenberg —

# Stage Fright

*Nothing diminishes anxiety faster than action.*
*~Walter Anderson*

had driven at least three laps around the little farmers' lodge on the corner. After each lap, I pulled into the old, cracked parking lot and willed myself to go in. Each time, just as I was ready to pull the key from the ignition, I lost my nerve and drove around again. Finally, I said it out loud. "Karen Marie, if you don't get out of this car right now, I will never forgive you. This is your chance to do it over again. The worst they can say is no."

That did the trick. Inside the creaky, old 1950s building, down in a basement where I'd never set foot, auditions were going on for a community-theater production. Until the week before, I hadn't even known we had a community theater. The local newspaper ad gave no specifics, just the name of the production: *The Legend of Sleepy Hollow Condominium Association, Inc.* From my terrible fear of making a fool of myself in front of strangers came the idea that this must be a well-known play in elite theatre circles. I had no idea whether I was supposed to know it, have memorized a scene, or be able to take on a character role for my audition. I was charging in headfirst, completely blind, and nearly paralyzed with anxiety.

My love of theatre is boundless. As early as middle school, I was absolutely certain I would become a famous actress. I soaked up musicals and movies of all kinds. For many years, my birthday gift from my parents was a season ticket to the Broadway Across America shows. I could recite all the lyrics to *Mame*, *The Unsinkable Molly Brown*, and *Chicago*. I loved to dance. I loved to sing. I loved orchestrating productions with my sister and our cousins at our family reunions. I simply LOVED the stage.

In high school, I joined a theatre-production class that competed throughout our district. There, I was drawn to dramatic interpretation and original oratory. I won tournaments several times, although all were in a classroom setting. But the stage — the one with the lights and curtains — eluded me. When it came time to audition for the spring productions, which would be performed in front of the entire student body and faculty, I simply seized up and refused to speak a word. I took solace in becoming a regular stage manager in my local community theater. I learned lights and sound and how to manage divas. I was the queen of the backstage, and I loved it.

But, every year, I watched the actors on stage and thought, *That should have been me.*

After high school, I headed off to college far away from home. In my first week, I took my work-study award and sought out the theater. Surely this would be my chance for redemption! I walked into the scene shop on my first day and poured myself into sets and design. In my three years there, I learned the difference between a socket wrench and a screwdriver, how to assure structural integrity of a balcony set, and how to stipple with a paintbrush for interior effects. I could build a set with the best of them. And I loved it.

But while watching each production, I would sit back in the audience and think, *That should have been me.*

Life moved on, as it is wont to do. I had set aside my dream of being on stage in favor of pursuing a family. Then, I realized one day how much I missed the theater. So, when I spied the ad in a local newspaper for auditions, I mustered every bit of courage I had and drove over.

I sat in the basement, at a table with the other performers, nervously chewing on a pencil. The script was in a three-ring binder. The director and the playwright were at the front of the room, calling people up to read various parts and scenes. There wasn't a single familiar face in the room.

Then, suddenly, it was my turn. The director asked me to read the part of Ros, a real-estate agent who moonlighted as a fake psychic. She sounded just quirky enough that I had already begun a relationship with her. I calmed myself just by reading the words on the page, and I let my personality fly. By the end of auditions, I had read Ros against three other characters, and she got more flamboyant every time. When I was done with her, she practiced yoga while walking and spoke with a terribly phony Eastern European accent. Two hours after I bullied myself in the parking lot, I had been cast in my first play.

I went on to perform in a number of other shows. Sometimes, my kids performed with me. Sometimes, they worked backstage. We developed a close-knit group of friends known as "the theatre people." They became our social life, our creative outlet, and our family bonding time. Each day when I walk through our home, I see the shadowboxes we've created for every show, and I think of all the people I've brought to life, all the lines I've memorized, all the songs I've sung, and how many times I've laughed until I cried. Theatre gave me a second family, and that family, in turn, helped me conquer my fear.

It's true what they say: "You'll never know if you don't try." Psych yourself up any way you can. Push yourself beyond your limits. Step outside your comfort zone. And then grab the opportunity before it passes you by.

— Karen Haueisen —

# I Got Swiped

*Have enough courage to trust love one more time*
*and always one more time.*
~Maya Angelou

After forty-one years of marriage, how does one start over again? How do you pick yourself up after the loss of your husband and look for love again? I was soon going to find out — with the help of modern technology. All a person needs is a computer, Internet connectivity, and nerves of steel.

I married young by today's standards — at the age of twenty — and was married for more than four decades. My husband died after a short illness, and my time, after his death, was consumed with completing the house we were building. Thanks to the help of wonderful friends and family, I completed that project in less than two years. I began to look for another project and decided I would spend my time, and a little money, on myself.

My sister suggested online dating. First on the agenda was composing a profile. Have you ever tried writing about yourself? It was my first time. How much should you reveal? You certainly don't want to come off as a "raving beauty" when you're not, but neither do you want to sell yourself short. Luckily, most of the dating sites I visited gave me the opportunity to categorize myself in varying degrees of attractiveness and suitability. I went "middle of the road."

Next was the addition of photos. Oh, boy. Should I include sedate or sexy photos, ones that revealed my intelligence level or just plain good health and vitality? I chose a photo of myself with a simple smile on my face.

I uploaded the photo to the profiles I created on three leading dating sites and held my breath.

Once you've got your profile up, you can begin swiping. It was a new word to me as it relates to online dating. Swiping left, in most cases, is the arduous task of finding your perfect date. The field of wannabe dates is endless and exhausting. He's too short. He's not active or adventurous enough for me. Oops, this one has cats. Too bad. I'm allergic. I settled on a few possibilities and swiped YES.

After a couple of days, I received a few hits from interested prospects, and the "getting to know you phase by way of e-mails and texts" began. That was followed by actual, in-person dates. Scared? You better believe it.

How does one begin to date again after over forty years of not needing to? As I said previously — nerves of steel.

For the most part, I met some very nice men on my journey to finding a companion. We tended to meet for coffee or a simple lunch at a nearby cafe. It was all very innocent, and I didn't have to waste the whole evening to discover how much we *didn't* have in common.

One man I met up with at a public park on the shores of Lake Michigan brought a picnic lunch full of homemade food we shared. That date lasted for four hours. I got home from that date and texted my girlfriend that I had met the most fantastic man. Later that day, I deleted all my online dating profiles. I was sure that something wonderful had happened. I later found out that the man felt the same way. Eight months later, we were married.

Getting out of my comfort zone found me a husband who is my best friend.

— Nancy Hesting —

# Pushing Beyond a Marathon

*Reach high, for stars lie hidden in you. Dream deep,*
*for every dream precedes the goal.*
*~Rabindranath Tagore*

"Ready?" I said to my husband, AJ, as we prepared to step into our first 5K race together.

We were young and had been married for just a year and a half, so we were still learning about ourselves and each other. AJ loved spicy food and eating out; I liked travel and saving money. He enjoyed lifting weights and the gym; I preferred doing sports.

I had always been an athlete. I played every sport growing up: soccer, basketball, softball, volleyball. My dad was a former professional athlete and now ran marathons for fun. For college, I chose volleyball and started all four years at a Division I school. I loved competing and doing everything sports related.

However, I did not enjoy running.

AJ started running to lose weight, focusing on the twenty-five pounds he'd put on since we married. I fully supported him doing what he needed to do to feel good. For the New Year's 5K, AJ wore heavy, black clothes — one of my cotton, extra-large college volleyball warm-up shirts and mesh warm-up pants. We called them "swish pants" in high school due to the sound they make when you move.

They weren't exactly the best or most comfortable running clothes, but we didn't know; neither of us was a runner.

As we waited for the crack of the gun to release us, we bounced up and down at the start line in the bitter January cold.

"You sure you don't mind if I leave you?" he asked. He had started jogging a couple of weeks prior and was running a few times a week.

"Nope," I replied. "Of course not. Do what you need to. I want you to do the best you can."

When the gun erupted, he sprinted ahead. Although I didn't run for fun, I was still in my mid-twenties and regularly walked, so I paced myself with the easy jog of a fast tortoise.

After a few minutes of running, I saw my husband ahead, so I edged up to him. After a mile, I caught him, and we ran together for a bit. Always competitive, I pushed the pace, thinking he would keep up. He fell behind a few feet, then a few yards, and then he was out of sight. I finished the race in a respectable time of just over twenty-five minutes. I felt beyond thrilled, considering I hadn't trained.

AJ was mortified. He couldn't believe that I, untrained and not particularly in shape, had beaten him.

"It's no big deal," I said. "I walk a lot. You just need to train better. I know you can do it."

"Alright," he said. He would have to leave his comfort zone of New York pizza, cheesesteaks and watching TV. He'd need to truly get in shape so he could run a marathon that spring.

I encouraged him to move every day and set goals. AJ called my dad, who had finished the prestigious Boston Marathon multiple times, for tips on how to reach those goals. The two of them ran together when my parents visited. They'd talk about pacing, fartleks, and the art of eating before a race.

They bonded over running.

Then, after AJ did his first marathon while I watched with a college friend and our dogs, he announced that he was going to run a marathon in each state. And since that wasn't enough, and we had not yet started having our four children, he declared he'd do it by the time he was fifty years old — fifty in fifty by fifty. He had forty-nine more races to go, and he'd just started running six months earlier.

By beating AJ in that chilly 5K race, and bringing him into my running family, I had turned my life upside down. Once he decided to do fifty marathons, he moved on to the additional challenge of doing a fifty-miler, his first ultramarathon.

It was challenging, especially as we started our family with a first child who decided she didn't like to sleep, and I was pregnant with our second.

"I need to run four hours tomorrow," he said one night as I began the hour-long process of putting our daughter to sleep.

"Four hours? That sounds awful." Taking care of a one-year-old for four hours when I needed sleep sounded terrible, too. "Can you at least push the baby for part of it?" I asked. He got early-morning duty with our one-year-old since I had her all night.

"Okay. I'll come home after an hour and take her if she's awake." She was, and he pushed her for two hours until she fussed for me.

In rural Indiana for his race, AJ ran on wooded paths through the large hills (small mountains) while I met him at aid stations, pregnant and swollen with our second, carrying our eighteen-month-old daughter on my hip. The November air was cold and smelled of coming winter. It got dark early, and it hailed. He saw lightning, loose dogs, and warning signs to watch for hunters. He hated it.

"I don't know if I'm going to make it," he said as he left the aid station for the last five miles. It was pitch-black with the moon shrouded by clouds. The race director and I stood at the finish line. All the other competitors had either finished or quit.

"This was awful," AJ complained as he crossed the finish line. "This was absolutely miserable."

The race director gave him his medal. I gave him a kiss. Our toddler wrapped her arms around his stinky body to give him a hug. He had given the race everything he had and needed to sit down from the pain and exertion.

"Never again."

Four years later, with four kids: "I want to try a hundred-miler."

"People do that?"

This race was near our house, along the national C&O Canal. A hundred miles — of running!

I took the two oldest children while my parents stayed with the younger two. We watched and cheered. His friends came and supported him, running with him and cheering for him in equal parts.

It was overwhelming to watch him push himself, especially knowing that I had started him on this journey. He had pushed himself beyond what he thought he was capable of. He didn't just step out of his comfort zone; he *ran* out of it!

AJ finished his hundred miles in a little under twenty-four hours. A day of running.

An entire day of running! (And let's be truthful, plenty of jogging and probably some shifts of sleepwalking.)

AJ was hungry and tired. He wanted to give up, but he didn't.

He showed my girls the meaning of grit and pushing yourself to your limit.

When he crossed the line, he certainly wasn't comfortable (the briars and skinned knees from falling saw to that), but he was satisfied. He had pushed himself beyond what he thought was possible and finished.

Time for another goal — and still twenty-five more states to go.

— Kaitlyn Jain —

Chapter
2

# Let Yourself Trust

# 11

# Guests for Christmas Break

*Each of us must confront our own fears,*
*must come face to face with them.*
~Judy Blume

O ur daughter was beside herself. "But, Mom, I have to bring Rocky and Balboa home with me. It's too cold for them to stay in the sorority house for a month. We have to figure out something." We continued the discussion while loading the family car for her to come home for Christmas break.

I didn't mind when Margie brought friends home with her, but Rocky and Balboa were snakes. In her junior and senior years as a college student, she attended classes, worked in her free time, and diligently cared for her two pets. Why did she have snakes as pets? After years of her personal items disappearing, none of the sorority sisters came into her room to borrow clothing or jewelry once she got the snakes.

Snakes terrified me. The thought of driving two hours with two three-foot-long boa constrictors made my skin crawl.

Margie persisted in her argument. I resisted even though she told me that if it got cold enough the snakes would get sick and die.

She had been deprived of furry pets because of her allergies. We introduced fish, turtles, and frogs to her as a preschooler. Fish and amphibians were still in favor, but while in Brownie Scout camp, she was the only one who looked for snakes and wasn't afraid to pick them up.

"Mom, I'll bring my whole aquarium, and they won't get out at home. I promise. Please, I don't want them to get sick. In the car, I'll put them both in a pillowcase and hold them on my lap so they stay warm from my body heat on the way home."

It was a valid plan, or so I thought.

"Okay, let's finish loading. We need to get home before it snows." I shuddered, thinking of my slimy, squirming passengers.

We left the college town in north-central Pennsylvania later than planned. Both Margie and I were hungry. We had to stop for something to eat before getting on the interstate that traversed hundreds of miles through mountains.

Pulling into the parking lot of a family restaurant, I looked sideways at Margie. "What are we going to do with these guys?" I gestured toward the undulating floral pillowcase.

"Uh, we have to take them in with us."

I gasped.

She continued, "It'll be too cold in the car within minutes." She pulled the pillowcase close to her body. "I'll put them under my coat."

We got out of the car and walked into the warm restaurant. After being seated, Margie lay the squirmy, knotted pillowcase on the bench seat beside her. We scanned the menu for something quick and tasty.

The waitress approached and took our order. She didn't notice anything out of the ordinary. Our food came. We ate and paid the bill. As we were getting on our coats to leave, the waitress stopped by to thank us and noticed the pillowcase moving on the seat.

"Uh, what is that?" She pointed at the floral bag. Margie and I looked innocently at each other.

Margie was quick to reply. "Oh, I'm taking home some dirty laundry."

"Dirty laundry, eh?" the suspicious waitress replied.

Margie nervously giggled and said, "Merry Christmas. Gotta run."

We waved, took our heavy pillowcase, and made a hasty retreat to the car. With the heater going full blast, I asked Margie, "How are the boys doing?"

She opened the bag to check. "Settling down, Mom. I can't believe I detected a bit of concern from you, the person who hates snakes."

By the time Margie had to return to school, my attitude about snakes had significantly changed. I learned that each of her pets had a distinct personality. I found that snakes are not slimy. I learned to bathe them when they were shedding to decrease their discomfort. I learned that, after a bath, Rocky and Balboa loved snuggling in the soft folds of my bathrobe.

One evening, Margie walked into the family room to see me watching TV with a sleeping Rocky in my lap. "What's this? I thought you hated snakes."

I gazed up at her and put my finger to my lips. I whispered, "Don't wake him. Let's say I'm warming up to the idea of snakes as guests."

I heard my daughter laugh as she left the room.

— Nancy Emmick Panko —

# 12

# Believe Me

*Fight your fears and you'll be in battle forever.*
*Face your fears and you'll be free forever.*
~Lucas Jonkman

I adjust the camera on my phone for what seems like the hundredth time, trying to find the perfect angle and lighting to capture my face. It isn't working.

Sighing in defeat, I get ready to press the Join button. No one will care what I look like in a chronic-illness support group anyway.

But wait…What if they think I look too healthy? I don't want to be exposed as a fraud.

"Look at her. Who does she think she is joining this meeting with impeccable lighting and glowing skin? There's nothing wrong with her. She's HEALTHY! Out with her!"

Maybe I should tousle my hair and lie down. Yes! I need to lie down. People with chronic illnesses most certainly can't sit up. And I need to get my icepack contraption that covers my whole head and soothes my aching jaw pain. Ohh! As soon as I join, I'll groan too, really selling it and marking my territory that I belong here, dammit. Not an exaggerated groan. Just a whimpering one that says I'm in pain, but I'm trying to tough it out. They'll think I'm admirable. They'll accept me.

I look down at my clothes. Perfect, I'm wearing pajamas. I mean, it *is* after 8:00 P.M., and I just got out of the shower. Sure, they'll think that I've been in them all day, my pain too unbearable to even imagine pulling a shirt over my head and a pair of pants over my legs. They'll have to believe me. I'm sure of it.

Believe. Whew, there is that heavy word again, weighing me down from years of wondering if people actually believe me.

As someone with chronic medical conditions — Hashimoto's, fibromyalgia and, as of recently, acute insomnia, because why not tack one more onto the list — it's commonplace for someone like me to struggle with people believing me since my illness constantly changes, and flare-ups come and go. And to be fair, I don't look or sound sick. My illness is invisible.

Does my doctor believe me after I call her up for the third time this week with new symptoms popping up every day: joint pain, muscle pain, extreme fatigue…?

Does work believe me after I call out sick for the fourth time in two weeks when I appear to be a healthy and fit thirty-three-year-old…?

Do the ER nurses and doctors believe me as I come crawling in on hands and knees, begging them to help me sleep after nearly a week of sleepless nights while swearing to them that I'm not some addict looking to score drugs…?

Does my husband believe me when I tell him that tonight I just simply can't? I can't clean up the dishes in the sink. I can't give our son a bath. I need to lie down….

Do my friends believe me when I change my diet for what seems like the millionth time? Gluten-free. Dairy-free. Soy-free. Sugar-free. And the stringent plans for a night out must fall into my parameters: home by an exact time, limited drinking, and I can neither stand nor sit for too long…

Do I even believe me? I'm exaggerating. I'm being dramatic. I don't belong in a chronic-illness support group. I'm not that bad… STOP!

I smooth out my hair and sit up straight. I smile because I like smiling, and I'm going to be positive because I like being positive despite everything. I belong here because I love myself enough to do this for me and no one else.

Before any other self-deprecating and negative thoughts can even enter the realm of my mind, I press Join. I see a sea of different faces, and after ten minutes or so, a wonderful feeling arises. I feel believed — vindicated for every experience I've ever had related to my chronic illnesses. Why? Because they all have similar stories.

And, for the first time in a while, I sigh with relief.

—Lauren Barrett—

# 13

# Watershed

*The greater the obstacle, the more glory*
*in overcoming it.*
*~Molière*

The five of us — my husband, our three boys, and I — just stood and looked at each other. The harsh overhead light in the shabby railway station in Bratislava, Slovakia, accentuated the weariness on our faces. We were a long way from home and had been travelling by plane and train for forty-eight hours. Now, it was night again, and we were finally at our destination.

As the train emptied, other passengers scuttled off with their luggage. We remained standing on the platform, too tired to even look around.

A fellow passenger who spoke English had helped us retrieve our two overstuffed hockey bags from the baggage department, while we wrestled with six other suitcases. "Can I call someone?" he asked after I explained the situation. I knew whom to look for, though, as I had been there on an exploratory trip a few months previously to scout out the possibilities for accommodation. Then, I spied him!

A solemn face greeted us. Pastor Jan! He paused and took in the mountain of luggage. "God bless you!" he said with feeling. Sighing with relief, we were soon on our way in a taxi and the pastor's small LADA.

For the past year, we had been contemplating the prospect of going to Slovakia to help start a Christian school. It was an exciting idea, but it was also terrifying to think of leaving our comfortable home in a little village in British Columbia where my husband and I had lived for seventeen years.

My husband and I loved travelling and had seen a few places in the world. It was quite another thing to uproot the family, leave my husband's steady teaching job, and venture off into the unknown. Where would we live? How could we afford it? Would our children's schooling suffer? Would my relatives think we were crazy?

The months of waiting were a challenge. The Christian school that the boys attended folded, and we suddenly found ourselves home-schooling. The pastor in Slovakia was still waffling. He wasn't sure if he wanted to sign the contract with the company that sponsored the school program. Accommodations seemed to be unavailable in this post-Communist country in 1991. My mother wrote a fearful letter to me. "It will be so hard to live there." Others confused Slovakia with Slovenia and thought we would be in danger from the armed conflict that was happening there. It was winter, and my chest ached with a respiratory infection. Sixteen-year-old Chris had just met a girl and didn't want to leave. "You're stealing my life away from me!" he complained.

Slowly, our plans fell into place. The pastor signed the contract after all. My husband received permission for a year's leave of absence from his teaching job. My mother resolved to be brave and write positive letters. Even my aunt in that country promised to welcome me and not say anything negative. Chris was quietly resigned to the move.

Only one obstacle remained: We had no place to live in Bratislava.

On my reconnaissance trip months before, prospects had been bleak. I had been so ready to give up and send my husband a telegram: "Accommodation unavailable." My faith was being stretched to the utmost. Alone in the hotel room, I jumped up and stamped my foot. "No!" I cried out loud. "God, You sent me here, and I'm going to trust You!" Somehow, I felt God would provide a place. I had no idea how, but my trust in Him was growing.

As the months inched forward, we still didn't have a place. "Nothing is available," the pastor had said. In a whirlwind of activity, we had rented out our house to a fellow teacher, packed all the furniture and our possessions into one basement room, applied for new passports, lent out our van to another family to use, and packed what we thought we'd need for a year.

I kept wondering where we would stay, as I wandered through the house, its rooms empty except for the phone sitting in the middle of the floor of the study. An hour before we were to leave, the phone shrilled in the empty room.

The excited voice of the pastor described the apartment he had found for us.

A living room. A large bedroom and two smaller bedrooms. A kitchen. A bathroom with a washing machine, bathtub, and the adjacent "water closet." Not only that, but all the furniture, bedding, dishes, pots and pans, kitchen utensils, heat and electricity were included. And the rent was less than we were getting for our house in Canada!

I burst into happy tears.

Looking back, I see how our two years in Bratislava, Slovakia, became a watershed in our lives. From that time on, I had no doubt that we could trust God in all the details of our lives.

— Alice Burnett —

# Flying High

*To change one's life: Start immediately.*
*Do it flamboyantly. No exceptions.*
*~William James*

Our son Thomas had a break from college, and my husband and I decided to take him with us to visit our family living on the Oregon coast. While there, our kids usually explore the beautiful, rugged outdoors. Over the years, they had been rafting, salmon fishing, hiking, skiing, crabbing, and even sand surfing. I thought they had done everything there was to do on the Oregon coast until Thomas noticed a flyer hanging in a local grocery that read: "Beginner-level hang-gliding lessons."

"Are there levels?" I asked.

I had imagined hang gliding was much like bungee jumping, with no skill required, just the will to launch yourself off a bridge and pray. Intrigued, my son called the number on the flyer and talked with an expert hang glider named Doug, who assured him there was a beginning level to hang gliding, and he taught it. Thomas informed me that the only problem was that Doug only taught group lessons.

"Where will you get a group of people who want to throw themselves over a cliff with you?" I asked.

Thomas shrugged his shoulders and grinned. "Dad has to work, but if you go, we will make a group."

"Oh, no! I don't think so," I laughed. I did not share Thomas's enthusiasm, but he assured me there was no cliff, and we would be floating under the hang glider, only traveling a few feet off the ground. After much convincing, I reluctantly agreed, and we drove to the coast the next afternoon to meet our instructor.

I got my first clue that Doug was different from the average instructor, or even your average person, when he zipped his car into the parking spot next to us. Leaping from it, he apologized profusely for being late. Doug explained he had been involved in a minor traffic accident on the way to meet us. He said the helmet and airline neck pillow he happened to be wearing had saved his life. I regarded his strange attire and apparent propensity to exaggerate and debated whether to get out of our car.

Too late, I realized Doug was already greeting Thomas with a hearty handshake and an enthusiastic grin. Doug's hang glider draped comically over the roof of his car like two giant chopsticks rolled in a used paper napkin. He quickly began to pull the rest of his equipment from the car's hatchback. Unfortunately, his trunk hydraulics no longer worked, so the trunk closed on him each time he reached into the vehicle. It appeared the car was devouring him — helmet, neck pillow, and all. I looked at Thomas, and we both raised our eyebrows but glanced away quickly in an attempt not to laugh. I surveyed the beach, wondering if we were actually on *Candid Camera*.

We watched as Doug assembled a large, metal triangle frame with white fabric attached to rope and duct tape. Noticing us eyeing the duct tape skeptically, Doug assured us. "She is older but sturdy," he said gingerly, patting the craft's wing.

"How much older?" Thomas asked.

"Well, It's hard to say. I got it from an army-surplus store, but she is newer than WWII," Doug told us, as if that news was reassuring.

He continued lecturing on the mechanics and history behind hang gliders and shared story after story of his years soaring with the birds. There was no mistaking Doug's love for the sport. Enthusiastically, he proclaimed, "It's as close to an independent flight as you will ever achieve because you control your movement through the air." His description of hang gliding seemed inspired, almost magical. Obviously, for Doug, hang gliding was not just a hobby. It was his life's passion.

The yarns he spun seemed a mix of history, Wikipedia, and his own real and imagined experiences.

The three of us struggled to drag the giant, refurbished hang glider to the top of the dunes. At the same time, Doug enthusiastically recounted how, in Jamaica in 1975, he had landed his glider on a beach, only to discover a herd of wild horses. He claimed one stallion allowed him to stroke its mane before it disappeared into the jungle. Eventually, Doug shared how he learned hang gliding in the army and that Dolly Parton had once asked him for hang-gliding lessons.

It seemed to Thomas and me that our time with Doug had propelled us into a strange new world. *Forrest Gump* meets *Jumanji* on the beaches of Normandy. Reaching the summit of the dune, Thomas held the hang glider steady as Doug strapped his harness to the middle of the frame. We observed as he demonstrated the technique of running down the sand under the belly of the glider. Instantly, it lifted him about eight feet off the ground, and he floated just above the sand like a kite with no strings and landed softly on the beach below.

At this point, I'm not sure Thomas or I knew what to make of Doug. We had never met anyone quite like him. Doug's enthusiasm for people, hang gliding, and the gift of life was refreshing, but he marched to the beat of a different drummer. He was so unconventional that I imagined some people might easily dismiss him. Instead, I reasoned it was their loss; they missed out on the experience of flying and some unbelievable stories.

When it was my turn, I clipped the strap on my harness below the glider and took a deep breath. Doug had promised the glider would not float more than a few feet off the ground, and the flight would be the experience of a lifetime. I ran forward and immediately lifted into the air, sailing about eight feet above the dune. As he instructed, I pushed the bar in front of me from right to left, turning the glider.

Doug was right. The experience was as close to flying as I had ever felt. The feeling was peaceful and exhilarating as the beach appeared to open below me, and the wind danced past my face, catching the glider's wings and holding me above the ground. It was heavenly until I reached the shore, where I pulled back too quickly on the bar, causing the glider and me to careen nose-first into the wet sand. Undaunted, I unhooked myself and hopped up, assuring Doug and Thomas I hadn't hurt anything more than my pride. I couldn't contain my excitement as I stood there, covered in sand from head to toe.

"Did you see me fly?" I asked Thomas.

"Oh, I saw you, Mom," he grinned. We sat down and laughed together for so long that I thought we might never be able to collect ourselves enough to help carry the hang glider back up the dune.

Thomas and I agree we will never forget Doug or our time together that day. We have recounted the story of our hang-gliding adventure many times, and in honor of Doug we always tell it with wonder, excitement, and a bit of exaggeration.

— Kimberly Avery —

# 15

# Courage of Another Color

*When we share our stories, what it does is, it opens up*
*our hearts for other people to share their stories. And it*
*gives us the sense that we are not alone on this journey.*
~Janine Shepherd

I sat in the nail salon, my feet in a basin of warm, swirling, lightly scented water. Cheery Christmas decorations filled the salon and holiday music floated through the air above the quiet chatter of the women in the room. Everyone seemed to be happy and relaxed, and I should have been also, but I wasn't. Even though I was in this salon once a month for my regularly scheduled manicures this would be my first pedicure in years.

Why? I have post-traumatic stress syndrome. As a result of this condition, I have tremors. I'm often embarrassed when a stranger in public not only notices my involuntary shaking but asks about it. I don't want to talk about my PTSD so I usually avoid situations that will call attention to my tremors. Like pedicures.

Sometimes though, we need a bit of pampering. That's what brought me to the salon on that day just before Christmas. Truth be told, I'd been going through a rough time.

In October a lump was found in my breast at my annual mammogram. Months of further testing had been followed by surgery in early December to remove the abnormal tissue. I was not only recovering from surgery, however. Our son's marriage was ending in divorce. I traveled across the country to support him during this painful time.

Then, as I grieved the loss of part of our family, I received notice that a dear friend had passed away unexpectedly. I had endured three months of grief, uncertainty and pain. By December I was feeling overwhelmed and definitely not in the mood to celebrate Christmas. That's when I decided to "treat myself" to a pedicure.

On the day of my appointment, I took my place in the deeply padded chair at the two-person pedicure station. I was careful to avoid eye contact with the woman in the chair next to me, praying she wouldn't notice my tremors.

When I'm nervous my trembling gets worse, so I tried to relax by chatting with the young woman attending me. When I worked up the courage to glance at the customer next to me I discovered that she was shaking too! Immediately my heart went out to her and I determined to put her at ease.

I complimented the woman on her pretty jacket and she turned to me and smiled. We introduced ourselves and began a conversation. Renée was originally from Michigan, where my husband and I had lived for thirty-five years while we raised our children before retiring to Florida. She and I both loved to travel, and we talked about some of our favorite trips. She worked with thoroughbreds and since I love horses, we also talked about horses. For the next forty-five minutes, Renée and I enjoyed chatting and our pedicures, as we trembled away, side-by-side. Even our nail techs joined in our lively conversation. I was thoroughly and unexpectedly enjoying my visit thanks to Renée's company.

With her pedicure finished Renée and I warmly wished each other a Merry Christmas before she left. While Renée's nail tech busily cleaned and sanitized her station I sat back in my comfy padded chair, closed my eyes, and smiled. I was so glad I "forced" myself to take this step out of my comfort zone.

A few minutes later the chair next to me creaked as another woman arrived for her appointment. I glanced over and saw the woman lean back in her chair and close her eyes. While her tech prepared the water for her footbath, my technician showed me some nail colors. I was feeling brave, and I thought the bright sparkling red one matched my mood perfectly!

I imagine it's difficult painting someone's toenails while their feet tremble but my tech was skillful and the layers of pretty color on my toes made me smile. The woman in the chair next to me began a conversation with her tech and when I looked over I was shocked to discover she too was trembling... sometimes violently. I wondered, how could it be? I tried not to stare when the realization came to me. Looking down at the arm of my own comfortable chair I saw massage controls. Each pedicure chair had a set of buttons that controlled the movement of rollers hidden inside its luxurious back. My new friend Renée had not been trembling after all... she'd simply been enjoying a massage in her chair!

With my nails done, I slid my feet into my sandals, careful not to smudge my pretty toes. I checked out at the front desk, paid my bill, and exchanged Merry Christmas greetings before I left. Stepping outside I broke into a laugh I could no longer contain.

I'd found the courage to step outside my comfort zone, made a new friend, and pampered myself, all at the same time.

— DeVonna R. Allison —

# 16

# Asking for Help

*Don't be afraid to ask for help when you need it.*
*Asking for help isn't a sign of weakness,*
*it's a sign of strength.*
*~Barack Obama*

I had just gotten out of the psych hospital when I made the decision to ask my parents to send me to a residential treatment facility. I had spent a total of five days being monitored for self-harm in the form of dermatillomania and agoraphobic tendencies. It was the beginning of my senior year of high school, at least on paper. In reality, I had completed little more than two years of schoolwork as I had not attended consistently for more than a day or two since the beginning of eighth grade. I was depressed, anxious, and stunted in every sense of the word.

Sitting in my room at the hospital, I had realized something. Maybe it was the change in environment, maybe it was talking to people who weren't my parents for the first time in a month, but something in me shifted. I didn't want to be like this forever. I hated feeling this way, feeling trapped by my own mind, a slave to my destructive habits. That night, for the first time since my mental stability dropped off the face of the planet, I asked for help.

I walked downstairs after a heavy picking session and much deliberation on how to go about this and asked my parents to sit down. Surprised that I was out of my room and talking to them at all, they sat on the couch without a word and waited for me to go on. "Mom, Dad,

I need to go to treatment." The vulnerability of that statement opened the floodgates. I cried hard for the first time in a long time. Within two weeks of asking them, I was on a plane bound for Logan, Utah. While I was spending the better part of a year and a half retraining my brain to think and live functionally, my parents were fighting the school district tooth and nail to get them to pay for it.

It was hard. Really, really hard. My eighteenth birthday happened a week after I arrived. I sat by myself in my dorm room opening presents from my family. They had all sent gifts and cards with platitudes like, "You got this!" and "We believe in you!" I felt so alone. There was so much I couldn't do, and the road ahead of me looked impossibly steep. That helplessness coupled with the fact that I wasn't getting along with my new peers made me desperate to call my parents to come and pick me up. I was sure that if they could just hear my voice and see what a terrible decision I had made, they would come. I would go back to school for real this time and get better at home where it was safe.

They don't give you phones in treatment, though, for that exact reason. It's a long and arduous process, rehabilitating your mind so you can join society again, and it takes a degree of force at first before you're receptive to change. I saw so many kids go into the program and get stuck fighting against everyone, not realizing that the only way out was through yourself and your problems. For that reason, I was glad it was my choice to go into the program, not something that was court-ordered or parent-enforced. I was able to get out quicker than most.

It's been about two and a half years since I went, a year since I graduated. The things I learned there have stuck for the most part. I'm in college now just finishing up my second semester. I live in an apartment I pay for with money I make from my job in an accounting department. I'm not cured. I don't think anyone can ever leave depression behind fully once they live through it. Some days, the hardest thing I do is get out of bed and go outside. Some days, I think about how much easier it would be to not try. When the world feels too much, though, and my stress levels are so high I feel paralyzed, I ask for help. My mom, my therapist, my boyfriend, my friends, my study group, my school counselor—I have all these people now I can lean on when I need to. I wouldn't have even met half of them if I hadn't gone downstairs that night. Asking for help is the reason I am where I am—*who* I am—today.

—AJ Peterson—

# You Mean the Problem Was Me?

*Life shrinks or expands in proportion to one's courage.*
*~Anaïs Nin*

I turned the page. There, at the top, was the sentence that changed my life. "When did you get to be such a witch?"

I was reading a book about living with an alcoholic. I figured if I read enough books, I could help my husband become sober.

My husband grew up in an alcoholic home and inherited his disease from his father. I felt sure I could cure his disease. If I could show my husband what joy, laughter, and love were like, he would be fine. He would quit drinking.

My husband never raged, abused us, stayed out all night, came home drunk, or passed out on the living room floor. In fact, I rarely saw him drink. Instead, he withdrew, didn't engage with the family, and always seemed to be angry at something. It wasn't a loud, belligerent anger. It came across in subtle ways: snide comments, stares, walking away, and blaming others.

I spent my days stuck in the middle, trying to keep things running smoothly and make things better for my kids.

Come to find out, I was not making things better or helping my kids. I certainly wasn't helping my husband become sober. Instead, I felt crazy, angry, and out of control all the time.

I kept reading that book. At the end of the page, it said, "Get thee to an Al-Anon meeting." It was not in those exact words, but that's what I remember. What was Al-Anon? Would he quit drinking if I went to an Al-Anon meeting? Would he be nicer to the kids? Would he engage with us and go on vacations with us? Would I learn to love him again?

I kept reading. Al-Anon was for people who were affected by someone else's drinking. That would be me.

Then I read that Al-Anon was about focusing on myself. What? I wasn't the problem. He was. I was fine. He simply needed to stop what he was doing and do what I knew he should be doing. He was the alcoholic, not me. He was the problem, not me.

I kept reading. I learned that his problem wasn't mine, and I couldn't do anything to control it. I couldn't do anything to cure it. The only thing I could do was deal with what was inside of me. Then and only then could I make decisions about what I wanted to do with my life.

Going to an Al-Anon meeting meant I had to break through the veil of denial I carried around with me all the time. "Everything's okay." "I'm happy." "My family is happy." "The kids are growing up strong and joyful." "Really, everything is fine."

All lies.

Breaking through that veil of denial was terrifying. Did it mean I had to admit that I had a problem? Did it mean I had to change? Did it mean I had to let him keep drinking? Did it mean I had to take the kids and leave?

By the time I finished that book, I thought I would check out this Al-Anon thing. Maybe they could tell me what to do with my husband and my life.

Going to that first meeting was one of the scariest things I've ever done. The building where the meeting was held was easy to find. But I sat in my car and thought, *What door do I go in? What if I walk in the wrong room and end up in the AA meeting? What if I have to tell somebody what my life is really like? What if I say the wrong thing?*

But I had three children by three different fathers, all alcoholics. What was it I loved about alcoholics? Why was I attracted to them? Was it because I loved being in control? How could I break the cycle? Maybe in that room I could get an answer. My heart was beating. My adrenaline was rushing. I didn't want to do this. And yet, more than anything, I wanted to do this.

I opened my car door and stepped out, determined to do something that frightened me to the core. And then God stepped in and gave me a gift. A neighbor parked her car next to mine and got out. I didn't know she was married to an alcoholic. I didn't know she went to Al-Anon meetings. I didn't know her life was as messed up as mine. I took a deep breath.

I told her why I was there. She walked me into the building and into the correct room. Someone saw I was a newcomer, walked over, greeted me, and put a book in my hand. "Read this," she said.

I listened as people spoke, told their stories, and shared their lives. When it was my turn to speak, I explained why I was there. I ended by saying, "My marriage has seven seconds, and then I'm leaving."

Someone said, "Thanks for sharing. Come back in seven days." I did.

Driving to the building and getting out of the car were some of the hardest things I've ever done in my life. It paid off. I have now been in those meetings for more than thirty years of seven days.

The people in those meetings didn't teach me how to help my husband become sober. He chose that for himself. They never even told me what to do with my life. But I read that book I was given when I walked in. I listened to people's stories. I began to focus on what was mine, and I learned to stay out of other people's business. I will forever be grateful that I walked into that building more than three decades ago. It changed my life forever.

— Trudy K. —

# Wise But Unwelcome Words

*We must be willing to get rid of the life we've planned,
so as to have the life that is waiting for us. The old
skin has to be shed before the new one can come.*
~Joseph Campbell

I heard the roar of speeding cars passing us. I had to focus on the sound of my uncle's bicycle leading the way. Since I had limited remaining sight, I briefly closed my eyes. I explored the sensation of depending on my hearing.

Uncle Fred pumped with the steady repetition of a mantra. I biked behind, only a few inches away from his rear tire. He shouted out directions at each intersection. Suddenly, his voice rose with urgency, "Carol, stop! A car is turning."

My retinas were dying a slow death from an eye disease. Yet I could not give up the freedom of riding my bike. At thirty, driving a car had become out of the question and giving up my bike seemed like the last straw in my new world.

A second careless driver pushed Uncle Fred to his limit. "You jerk!" he yelled. I prayed that he wouldn't hop off the bike and shake his fist in anger. He could be rough around the edges. Uncle Fred was muscular and would not back down from a fight. His personal challenges were well-known in our family. For many years, he had struggled with alcoholism and had a reputation for being a loner.

My father had been my uncle's rock when they both returned from military service after WWII, but then my dad died. Now my uncle and I exercised together, a way to calm our frustration as both of us had problems to work out.

When we reached our destination, we rested our bikes against our favorite park bench. My shoulders ached from all the concentration during our ride. As I sat next to Uncle Fred, his mood grew somber. He cleared his throat and said, "Carol, why don't you think about getting a guide dog?"

Had I heard him correctly? He knew I was afraid of dogs. Words stuck in my throat while I wiped away a tear behind my sunglasses. Nearby, the rumble of river rapids intensified, and so did my self-doubt. He began again, "I've been reading about those trained Seeing Eye dogs. They can give you independence." His voice cracked, and he lightly squeezed my hand. He continued, "Just think about having a guide dog. Do some research on your own and see what you learn."

We were quieter than usual on the four-mile ride home. But Uncle Fred had planted the seed of an idea. If Uncle Fred had the courage to face the hell of war, couldn't I overcome my fear of dogs?

My world, even my neighborhood, had shrunk as the shroud of my blindness grew worse. Mobility training with a white cane seemed slow and cumbersome to me. Did my stride change? Was my walking more halting now? I couldn't be sure. A strength I did have was a good sense of direction, allowing me to visualize neighborhood routes. This skill could be an asset when working with a dog.

After deliberating the pros and cons, I finally called the guide dog school. The admission application arrived, but I still wasn't sure. One day, I phoned a blind friend, a longtime guide-dog user in my town. He shared his positive experiences in a way that I could not ignore. "These dogs have plenty of training. They will help you, and you will learn to care for your dog." He continued, "It's a partnership. The dog's eyes and your hearing make you a team." Somehow, his words convinced me to give it a try.

During the twenty-eight-day training, the dog trainer encouraged me to take one day at a time. "You don't have to bond with every dog, just the one I choose for you." The dog trainer's coaching and each successful walk bolstered my confidence. As Misty and I bonded, my shoulders relaxed.

When I returned home from the Seeing Eye school, I wanted Uncle Fred to be the first to meet Misty. "I'm so proud of you," he said. Misty sat at our feet thumping her tail. She must have picked up on the positive energy that circled us like a hug.

"Not as proud as I am to be your niece," I said.

Eventually, I shared a tandem bike with another man, Don, who later shared my life. Over those next few years, I often opened my front door to find a large bag of freshly picked apples. *Uncle Fred again,* I thought. He dropped off little gifts for me, but our bike rides had stopped. True to his solitary nature, Uncle Fred bicycled alone and stayed busy. When we did spend time together, his hugs were not as strong, and his youthful frame grew more frail with age.

At a crossroads in my life, I traded two bicycle wheels for four paws. My guide dog Misty shattered my anxiety as I slowly opened my heart to her. Just as Uncle Fred had predicted, overcoming my fear gave me the opportunity for more independence. I've been able to keep my stride. My new confidence came from using a guide dog, allowing me to walk tall. I know that Uncle Fred's advice moved my sense of joy from my bike's handlebars to my dog's harness handle.

— Carol Chiodo Fleischman —

# Only in Paris

*To travel is to live.*
*~Hans Christian Andersen*

After completing college at age nineteen, my daughter applied to the most prestigious culinary institute in the world. The institute is known for rejecting first-time applicants, which was a relief to me as I had already spent the majority of the money I had saved for college expenses to pay for her undergraduate degree.

But there is a first time for everything, and my daughter was overjoyed when she was accepted. In addition to the substantial tuition that had to be paid in full, we also had an enormous amount of other out-of-pocket expenses, including airfare to Paris, housing, food, and local transportation.

The institute found her a place to stay for the first quarter, but then we had to find housing for the remainder of the year. I took thirty days off from work, flew to Paris, and started house hunting. We found her a safe place within the first two weeks, so with two weeks remaining in my vacation, my daughter suggested we go to the south of France.

While it was a great idea, I had already given just about every penny I had to prepay her rent. She told me that since we had the train pass, all we would need to be concerned about was a place to stay. Being a protective mother, that was not a small concern for me, but she confidently told me she had the whole thing figured out.

On the train to the south of France, she told me about a website where people put a profile on the site offering travelers a free place to stay for a night or two. Having come from a large Italian family, I didn't think that was so unusual, but I was in a country where I did not speak the language and I was going to stay somewhere with people I had no connection to?

At the train station, we were met by a young man approximately my daughter's age. He carried our suitcases onto the campus of a large university. We arrived at a dormitory, and the man brought our suitcases to a dorm room, which is where we would be spending the evening.

I am still stunned that I did not realize we were in an all-male dormitory. When I did, panic set in. My daughter assured me that we were completely safe. She suggested that we take a walk around the village to enjoy the sights. I'm not sure if my brain was operating fully, but that's exactly what we did. Upon our return to the dormitory, our "host" blew a whistle, and the hallway cleared so that we could return to our room in safety and comfort.

That night, we slept head-to-toe opposite each other to fit in the bed, but we managed. The next morning, the whistle was blown again, and we were free to use the washroom without interruption. Later that morning, the young man walked us to the train and wished us safe travels. We were off to our next stop.

From Bordeaux, we took the train to Montpellier. We arrived in the evening, and my daughter was getting hangry, so she was quite impatient waiting for our host to meet us. About fifteen minutes later, a young man came jogging up to the station and apologized for being late. As we were walking to his apartment, he said he couldn't phone us because his place had been robbed the previous night, and all his electronics had been stolen. A definite pause in my step was quickly replaced by the thought that the odds of getting robbed two days in a row were slim. We enjoyed a great evening in Montpellier and headed to the train for our next destination.

We arrived in Aix-en-Provence to see an enormous Christmas festival going on in the city. Our host, a male nurse, explained to us that there was a bit of a mishap, but we were welcome to stay. Over dinner, his wife, a Ph.D. candidate, told us that their current guest had been injured in a bicycle accident, so the only place for us to sleep was under the kitchen table on a pile of blankets. I mean, really, could I possibly make this up? Again, it was a wonderful evening with our hosts, and the next day we roamed around and enjoyed the holiday festivities.

In the late afternoon, we boarded the train to Cannes. The host at this location said that he was unable to meet us at the train and gave my daughter directions to his place. We figured out that the reason he didn't meet us was that the route was one winding, uphill road after another. Schlepping our suitcases, we said at every turn, "This has to be the last turn, right?"

It was six turns in the road before we arrived at the very top of a mountain (okay, maybe just a large hill), and we dropped to the sidewalk, hot and sweaty. However, the view of the Mediterranean Sea far below was breathtaking. Our host arrived and walked us up three flights of stairs (had we not walked enough?) into the most exquisite apartment. His former wife was a gourmet chef, so my daughter fell in love with the granite countertops, multiple ovens, and hanging pots and pans. While my daughter and our host were making extravagant meals, I was doing yoga on the porch overlooking the sea.

Our final stop was Monaco. At the train station, a man who looked like a leprechaun carrying a small dog in his arms, announced that he was our host. It was nighttime by then, so we were unable to see where we were going. He dropped us off in front of a church, gave us a key, and told us to go in while he parked the car. Our mouths dropped, and we walked into a century-old rectory that was superbly decorated and spent the evening in a heavenly (get it?) room. We spent the next day touring beautiful Monaco.

In the late afternoon, we boarded the train to start our trip back to Paris. We had one more stop to make: the Festival of Lights in Lyon, France. This international event is renowned for its temporary light installations that transform the city for four days. Innovative, breathtaking, mind-boggling, outrageous, and stupendous can't even begin to describe this festival.

We arrived back in Paris the day before my departure, and we were exhilarated and exhausted. Needless to say, I never thought that stepping outside my comfort zone would provide a lifetime of memories. To this day, I still host travelers and continue to be treated to new people, experiences, and friendships.

—Judith Fitzsimmons—

# The Wild Blue Yonder

*We have to be braver than we think we can be, because*
*God is constantly calling us to be more than we are.*
~Madeleine L'Engle

The side door of the small aircraft was opened wide, and a brisk wind rushed through the cargo hold. Packed tightly like sardines were fourteen silent people. Two of them were my adult children. Holding themselves perfectly still, they stared out at the endless sky.

When we reached an elevation of 14,000 feet, my son's face turned ashen as he cautiously inched next to the opening, leaned sideways, and fell out of the airplane. Something went cold in my heart when I realized he was gone. But, only seconds later, instructions were being barked, and my daughter suddenly appeared in the same space just occupied by my son. Her face, however, was gleeful, and she laughed and whooped, falling away into the wild blue yonder after her brother.

For a quick moment, a desperate fear overcame me, and I wondered if that was the last time I would see them. But the thought soon passed as I felt a strong tug on my pack and was moved into position by my tandem partner.

With a big birthday looming, two of my adult children had chosen to surprise me with an unforgettable way to dive into the decade. I'd wanted to chicken out once we reached the airport, but when a woman celebrating her fiftieth wedding anniversary spontaneously decided to dive, I knew I had to do it, too.

Now I was in the air. I forgot all the instructions I'd received on the ground only minutes earlier. Reminders to scream in order to exhale and to hold our arms out wide were lost as the sheer terror and outrageous joy of freefalling took over. Although it felt like forever, the minute before the parachute opened was unforgettable. The world below appeared in full circumference, and the endless sky above could be seen perfectly without windows or walls.

We drifted in hushed wonder. Adrenaline was still coursing through my veins, but I was surprisingly calm and deeply satisfied. With the earth quickly approaching, I spied my son and daughter detached from their parachutes and running in their blue jumpsuits to greet me as I landed. We had an elated three-way hug.

It was a symbolic moment. In so many ways, I had taken a leap. It was only one small step to leave the relative safety and comfort of the small plane to throw myself into the wind, but something transformative happened in those suspended moments. Learning to let go of what appears safe helped me understand how to overcome fears that hold me back. I could have refused to leave the plane, missing both the extreme thrill of the descent and the unique beauty of the viewpoint from the sky. Clinging to the appearance of safety no longer felt like the only option.

I had grown up in suburbia. Life was predictable, comfortable and sheltered, and I had absolutely no intention to ever live otherwise. But not long after my skydiving experience, I was surprised by a job offer requiring a move to Chicago. It seemed ludicrous to leave behind what was secure for the unfamiliar. Cities are loud, large and difficult to maneuver. They didn't feel safe or manicured. Yet, my experience skydiving had taught me that seeing things from a new perspective can be life changing. I took the leap and accepted the job.

Now, the sound of sirens and airplanes are background noise. There is traffic and energy, and people of every variety living in close proximity. I buy my groceries at little local markets, ride my bike by the beauty of Lake Michigan, and face new and surprising challenges every day.

Within five miles of my new home are restaurants featuring the cuisine of dozens of countries. The sights, sounds, tastes and smells are unfamiliar, exciting, and mirror the delight and wonder I experienced when skydiving. Just like the panorama unfurled from the mile-high experience, urban life has revealed that the world is so much bigger and broader than I could have imagined. The views in the city are much different from those outside my suburban window. Now, I am embracing the chance to discover how to press beyond the comfortable, let go of the known, and overcome the fear of what might lie ahead.

— Diane Lowe MacLachlan —

# Give of Yourself

# Sharing My Spare

*We cannot live only for ourselves. A thousand fibers*
*connect us with our fellow men.*
*~Herman Melville*

"Who wouldn't want a piece of this?" read the woman's T-shirt in an online photograph. She was a living kidney donor. I laughed and marveled that any person would dare donate a body part. I understood the important after-death organ donation — the "If I can't take it with me, let it help someone else" donation. But while in the midst of your own life? When you are actually using your organs? Enduring a surgery you don't need? Who would do such a thing?

I dove into my research for a writing assignment on the National Kidney Foundation of Arizona for DesertLeaf, a local publication. I listened to living kidney donors share their stories on YouTube as part of The Erma Bombeck Project. Bombeck, the beloved humor columnist, had kidney disease. Her family created the project in her honor.

The experience of one bright-spirited donor stayed with me. Karny Stefan had been immersed in a TV movie when her BlackBerry sent a notification. She turned her attention to a group e-mail from an acquaintance urgently seeking a kidney for her husband, Jeff. Karny turned back to her movie just in time to hear an actor declare: "Well, I was close to your grandfather — I do have one of his kidneys."

"You've got to be kidding me, God," Karny recalls thinking. "You did not just tell me to do that." She struggled internally for three minutes. Today, one of her kidneys, nicknamed Sydney, lives on in the body of her now flourishing good friend, Jeff.

A soft thought circled my heart: *Why wouldn't you do it? If you were healthy, if you could thrive with one kidney and someone would die without the transplant, why wouldn't you donate? Why wouldn't I?*

It was a strange thought. I was supposed to be a mere tourist in the land of living kidney donations. I am not a go-to-the-doctor kind of person. I had too many needless allergy shots as a child and too many doctor visits for a mere cough or a 99-degree fever. Dental appointments made my heart jump. Mammograms panicked me. I felt overwhelmed by women's wellness appointments even with my compassionate naturopath. Crinkling in the paper gown, feet up in the stirrups — no, thank you. Fortunately, at age sixty-three, I had never needed major surgery. I took no prescription drugs. I hiked, danced, and gleefully engaged in a kickboxing exercise program. I had no idea what it was like to live with a failing organ.

During my interview with Leslie McReynolds, CEO of NKF of AZ, that gentle *Why wouldn't I?* strengthened. It wasn't pushy or bossy, just a possibility floating in my consciousness. *If my body was up for the task, why wouldn't I?* Curious, I did not swat it away but let it hover in the periphery as I learned more.

In my career, I have read and reported hundreds of distressing stats. Numbers can feel like a mirage shimmering in the distance, eliciting momentary pangs of empathy. But you can't hug a number. Feel a number struggle to breathe. Listen to a number's pain or help-lessly witness it lose its life force and then almost immediately revive again after a transplant.

Somehow, these numbers pierced me: One in three people in the U.S. are at risk for kidney disease, and most do not even know it. One-hundred thousand people are currently waiting for a kidney transplant. Three thousand new patients are added monthly to the kidney waiting list. Thirteen people die each day due to a shortage of kidneys. The last number haunted me the most.

After a month of holding *Why wouldn't I?* in my heart, I could not contain it any longer. I filled out the online National Kidney Registry application to explore becoming a living donor. A day later, heart pounding even faster, I filled out my medical history, vowing not to tell anyone until I could make sense of what I was doing. I liked that Karny only told a few people about her plans to donate. "I didn't want them to think I was crazy or holy. I'm neither."

Two days later, I was on the phone with Patty, an enthusiastic donor mentor ready to answer any questions — for me, not for an article. She was a teacher who had donated a kidney five years earlier to a stranger and had no regrets. In fact, Patty and other Kidney Donor Athletes climbed Mt. Kilimanjaro to demonstrate that having only one kidney won't keep you from being healthy and active. She said her life had completely changed in a positive way. Most of her friends were also donors — normal people, not heroes, living normal lives.

I sit here now, unafraid after a few preliminary medical tests and interviews with a social worker, a living-donor nurse coordinator, and a living-donor advocate from my potential transplant center. Will my kidneys and I qualify to move forward? Will I be able "share my spare," as they say? I'm eager to know. But at least my wait won't kill me.

— Jan Henrikson —

# I'm OK with RAOK

*Carry out a random act of kindness, with no*
*expectation of reward, safe in the knowledge*
*that one day someone might do the same for you.*
~Princess Diana

The first time I heard the phrase Random Acts of Kindness (RAOK), I was running my own successful small business in Flagstaff, Arizona, as a locksmith with a walk-in shop and a fully equipped service van. I stayed so busy that I would often catch lunch on the go by swinging through whichever fast-food drive-through had the shortest line when I caught a break between service calls.

Most evenings after work, Jenny (my future wife) and I would snuggle up together and watch an episode of *The Oprah Winfrey Show* that Jenny had recorded earlier in the day with her VCR. I was not all that enthralled with Oprah, per se, but I was always eager to spend time with Jenny, doing whatever she enjoyed doing with me. One memorable Oprah episode that stuck with me was the one where Oprah was interviewing the author of a book about random acts of kindness. Oprah's producers were intrigued enough with the concept that they sent a film crew to sit at a highway tollbooth to capture people's responses when they were told that their toll had been prepaid by a previous driver. Most of the drivers that the film crew interviewed were pleasantly surprised but chose to pay their toll anyway to pass the free ride along to the next car that came along.

The next day, Flagstaff got hammered with a heavy snowstorm. As I made my way to pay for my lunch at the drive-through window, I found myself musing about *The Oprah Winfrey Show* I had just seen the previous night and internally grumbling that there was no way to do such a thing as pay someone else's toll because we did not have toll roads in Arizona. When the cashier stuck out her hand to take my money, it dawned on me that there was a perfect stranger out of sight around the corner at the ordering window doing what I had just done when I ordered my lunch.

I paid for my lunch and that perfect stranger's lunch. It was the first time in my life that I had done something nice for someone because it felt good, with no expectation of appreciation from them. As a seasoned cynic, I had been raised with such platitudes as, "There's no such thing as a free lunch!" and "Unconditional love does not exist!" Thus, when we do something nice for someone, the hidden-agenda expectation or condition is that they will at least say, "Thank you," as our reward. The whole free-ride-at-the-tollbooth example turned that truth inside-out for me.

There was no way that the receiver of my kindness could thank me. By the time they got up to the pay window, I would be long gone with an ear-to-ear grin, just imagining their joy.

Later that same day, after a busy day at work, I was driving cautiously downhill on a snow-slickened mountain road. I was anxious to get home before nightfall so I could shovel the wet and heavy snow from my steep driveway where I parked my service van. As my wipers sluggishly cleared the snow from my windshield, I saw the emergency flashing lights on the car stopped dead in the middle of my lane on the road ahead. I managed to stop my van, set the emergency brake, and turn on my own flashing emergency lights before tapping on the window of the stranded motorist ahead. The young mother in the car quickly apologized that she had just run out of gas while trying to get to the closest gas station just two more blocks away at of the bottom of the hill.

Our bumpers lined up perfectly, so she agreed to let me push her the rest of the way to the gas station while she steered her car along the snowy road as our flashers warned others of our slow but steady progress. As she coasted up to the pumps at the gas station, I waved goodbye and got back into traffic, eager to get to my driveway shoveling.

As I turned toward home on my street, my headlights lit up my freshly shoveled driveway. Nobody in the neighborhood knew who had cleared my driveway or when it had happened!

— Art Prennace —

# When Life Changes in a Moment

*Dare to reach out your hand into the darkness,*
*to pull another hand into the light.*
*~Norman B. Rice*

Before October 19, 1991, I was happily married, raising two children — Brian, eighteen, and Christie, fourteen — on horse property surrounded by mountainous deserts in Phoenix, Arizona. I was a stay-at-home, daycare mom at the time. When our family needed additional income years before, I had decided this was a good alternative in order to stay home.

A doorbell ringing to the tune of "Hush Little Baby" that fateful October night shattered my world forever. A police officer informed us that Brian had been robbed and shot while walking his girlfriend home from the bowling alley in our neighborhood. Losing a child to anything is catastrophic, but losing a child to violence transcends absolutely devastating. Our world suddenly made no sense. We were thrust into a scary and confusing judicial process that eventually failed us, allowing the killer of our son to serve only seven years in prison.

It took us many years to begin truly living again and not just go through the motions, living like robots. In those days, I smiled simply because my mouth knew how to; emotionally, my smile was broken. I cooked meals and took care of my family while thinking, *How dare the world keep going on as if nothing happened.* It took a lot of hard work to eventually accept and redesign our lives, which had been forever changed by two bullets to our son's chest for his wallet. But the beginning moment for me, which guided me on the course of my new life, was going home for Christmas mere weeks after Brian was killed.

My mom had asked us to come home to Kansas that year, knowing how difficult the holidays would be for us. I reluctantly agreed simply because the alternative of being in our home without my son was worse than making the trip home.

On Christmas Eve, in my mom's home, I was sitting at the kitchen table with her when the phone rang. It was my brother Jim who was in the Navy and could not get leave time to visit. I could tell by my mother's end of the conversation that my brother had asked how I was doing. My mom replied, "Pretty good considering she will never get over this." At that moment, it was as if my mom had slapped me in the face with the truth.

For the past weeks, after Brian was so cruelly taken from me, I had been giving myself little goals for my survival. If I could just make it through the funeral… If I could make it through Thanksgiving and my wedding anniversary… If I could make it through that first Christmas, I would be okay. This horrific, god-awful pain would end, hopefully, as I knew I could not endure it much longer. But what my mom said to my brother was a wake-up call. It caused me to admit something I could not face before this point: I was never going to get over my son's murder. I ran to my bedroom and cried the entire night. But before dawn that Christmas morning, I realized that if I was never going to get *over* this, then how was I going to get *on* with it?

Part of learning how to get on with life happened soon after those holidays when my husband, daughter and I sought help in a group, Parents Of Murdered Children (POMC). Fifteen months later, I became the leader of the Phoenix chapter, somehow instinctively knowing that helping others would allow my healing, at least whatever measure of healing was allowed me. It gave me a purpose while living with the unending pain and relentless sorrow of my son's loss. I had to truly step out of my comfort zone to run the organization, and I remained its leader for the next twenty-eight years.

Transitioning from daycare mom to leading a group that needed so many things, such as funds, brought me out of my cocoon and allowed my wings to spread in places I never knew I could. I learned to write grants, put on major fundraisers, host conferences, do public speaking and media interviews, meet with professionals, and ultimately teach them how to better assist crime victims. I learned to go to the legislature and fight for new laws for the rights of crime victims or oppose stupid ones. I also learned that, while I could hold the hand of our members in need, I could not fix this for them. I could, however, provide them with much-needed support, compassion, and information, and help them navigate the confusion and frustrating maze of the criminal-justice system. Thus, our support group allowed a safe place for families to vent their emotional pain and assist them in regaining some of their lost control.

It was a great struggle at times to leave my protective cocoon. I realized somewhere along the journey that if God came to me and said I could have my old life back, of course, I would take my son back. I would not, however, want to give back all of my new life. The lessons and places my wings have taken me in order to give meaning to my son's death and sing his silenced song are too important to lose. I have met some of the most courageous people who have been through unspeakable tragedy. They forge on, shakily and lost for a long time, but eventually they redesign their lives, forever changed by the aftermath of what murder leaves behind. They become better people despite tragedy, and they make a profound difference in our world.

The second moment when I realized that something would drastically change my life again was in August 1996, nearly five years after Brian's death. I stood in a hospital delivery room, trembling with absolute tears of joy, as my newborn daughter, through a special adoption, was placed into my waiting arms. It was an amazing moment of transformation. After Brian was killed, I truly felt I would never experience true joy again. Here I was, though, reveling in the awesome miracle of this child's birth and the renewal of hope she was giving to my wounded family. I knew I had healed just enough to open my heart to another. A few weeks later, while blissfully caring for the newest addition to our family, I had a rough patch of feeling guilty for feeling so much joy, as if it somehow diminished my love for my son. In my heart, though, I know nothing ever will. Sometimes, we have to quiet our head and listen to our heart.

Leaving my comfort zone literally saved me. I could easily have ended my life to end the pain, and it did cross my mind at one time. But I am a survivor and proud of my journey to healing.

—Beckie A. Miller—

# Grandma Joins the Fire Department

*Remember that the happiest people are not those
getting more, but those giving more.*
~H. Jackson Brown, Jr.

By nature, I'm a shy person. I don't like to be front and center, am uncomfortable in unfamiliar situations, and dislike being the "new kid" in a group of people. I am the poster child for the term "introvert." But sometimes even an introvert gets bored with her own company, and that was me several years ago.

My retired husband and I had moved to California to be near our daughter and family, bought a distressed house, and spent our first three years gutting and fixing it up. With the project complete, I felt restless and somewhat lonely. I needed something — not more books or more alone time — but something.

When I told my elderly (but incredibly outgoing) neighbor that I still didn't know anyone, she said, "Nobody's going to come knocking on your door. Get out there and look for them."

Me? I didn't want to get out there. What if I was rejected? What if I went to a group where everyone knew everyone else — and I was the odd one out? Nope. Not for me. Instead, I wanted to be magically included in a familiar group of people who already knew and accepted me. Unfortunately, I also knew that magic wasn't the answer.

One afternoon, I noticed a small ad in our local newspaper asking for Support Volunteers to help out at the fire department. Hmmm. Maybe I could do some filing or other office work.

I called and was told they were starting a class to train new volunteers. When I realized that everyone was going to be a newbie at the same time, I smiled. Now, that was more like it!

I was interviewed, and had my fingerprints taken and my background checked. I passed.

I was nervous the first day. But as soon as I met the other new volunteers, I discovered what a great group of people they were.

Volunteers, in general, are special because they are donating their time and energy, but this particular group was made up of retired people with interests similar to my own. They wanted to be active. They wanted to be connected. And, most of all, they wanted to be of service to the community.

The Support Volunteers — or SVs, as we were called — came from many different walks of life. Before they retired, some were business owners or former military. There was a man who had installed high-tension wires across the desert. Another had been involved in creating the first space satellites. Several had been teachers or school administrators, and one had been a trauma nurse. Together, we made up an efficient, knowledgeable, capable team.

When the academy was completed, we were issued fire-department dress uniforms. To my delight, we didn't file or answer phone calls. Instead, each of us was on duty for twenty-four hours, one day a week, with a partner. While on duty, we transferred mail and equipment to and from the city's seven fire stations, city hall, and fire/police headquarters. We also taught businesses and the public how to use — and how *not* to use — fire extinguishers, helped monitor school fire drills, installed free smoke detectors in the homes of seniors, and handed out fire-prevention information at community events. I became certified in CPR and learned how to direct traffic around an incident and how to operate a generator for nighttime emergencies.

The group's main function, however, was to maintain, drive, and set up the Incident Support Van at fires. Our specially designed vehicle held folding chairs, canopies, chilled water and Gatorade, cool towels, and other items firefighters needed when they spent extended time at a fire. We had misters for when the temperature soared, and we always kept the coolers fully stocked with ice. Essentially, our job was to take care of fire personnel while they took care of the flames.

Although I initially joined the volunteers to meet people, I continued my satisfying work with the SVs because of something that happened a few years ago.

Southern California was in the middle of a severe drought, and the brush-covered hills were brown and tinder-dry. Added to that danger were the powerful, hot Santa Ana winds that blew in from the desert with a force that approaches a hurricane. Any spark — from a lawn-mower blade striking a rock, to a hot tailpipe, to a fire purposely set — can be fanned by the wind to become a roaring blaze. Then, gusts pick up embers and carry them a mile or more away to start new fires.

On one stifling afternoon that May, seven large wildfires were burning simultaneously in the county. The department where I volunteered had been called out of the area the day before.

My daughter's family in the neighboring town was at the store when they got a cellphone alert to evacuate their home. The newest Cocos wildfire was spreading rapidly. They raced up their long driveway with only time to grab the cat and their laptops before the road officially closed behind them.

The family came to our house. While my two grandchildren stayed with my husband, my daughter, son-in-law, and I joined others on the top level of the library parking garage (the highest structure around) to watch the fire's progress.

As we watched, the wind suddenly shifted. Huge flames raced toward their house, hidden behind a hill. Helicopters and planes dropped water and fire retardant as fast as they could, but they seemed terribly small as they flew in and out of the billowing smoke.

Television stations showed fire personnel on the ground doing what they could to save houses. The air was hot, the wind was hot, and the flames were even hotter, yet these men and women continued to fight for someone else's home, someone else's memories.

It was four days before my daughter and her family were allowed to return home. When they did, they discovered that a fire department unknown to them had been there, directly protecting their property. A flowering bush that climbed a wooden pole had been chopped down, saving the porch above it, and the barbecue's propane tank and the porch cushions had been moved away from the building. Flames had scorched palm trees in the yard, turned wooden plant barrels next to the back door to ashes, and melted the electrical wires hanging from the nearby poles, but their house was untouched.

During my years as a fire-department volunteer, not only did I lose my shyness, but I became more confident and wasn't afraid to put myself out there. I also learned what it felt like to be on the receiving end of services provided by a totally different but fiercely dedicated group of firefighters.

I'm glad I had the courage to make that original volunteer phone call. I learned that if I can be on call for twenty-four hours at a time and get up at 3:30 A.M. to respond to a fire, I can do almost anything!

— Michele Ivy Davis —

# 25

# A Kick in the Pants

*As you begin to live according to your own guidance*
*and your own daring everything changes completely.*
*~Leonard Willoughby*

One day, I was leaving the grocery store with both arms full and a heavy purse over my shoulder. I noticed some customers and store employees were laughing at a homeless man who was trying to transfer his purchases from the store's cart into his personal cart. His dog's leash had wrapped around his legs, and he was so skinny that his pants had fallen down to his knees, exposing his lily-white butt.

I looked back at the store employees and said, "Help him!" They just stared back at me. I looked around, and no one was doing anything. The little dog seemed scared and was looking up at all the onlookers as if to say, "Help my person, please."

I ran out to my car parked close by, threw my bags and purse inside, locked the doors, and rushed back into the store. By that time, the homeless man had made it the few feet outside the entrance/exit doors with everyone still standing and watching as if they were in San Francisco watching a street show.

I said to the man, "Here, let me help you."

He replied, "Oh, thank you, thank you."

I was not afraid to touch him or his clothes. I pulled up his pants from behind, but they caught on his knees and then "elsewhere" in front. Things began to fall out of the pockets. He dropped the dog's leash, and again a crowd of onlookers began to assemble. I kept my cool and said to the man, "You pull up the front, and I will pull up the back at the same time. Together, we will get them up." I told him not to worry about the fallen items. I would pick them up later, and the dog was staying put.

Finally, he was ready to go, thanking me again and again. I asked him where he was headed and if he needed a ride. He was so ready to get out of there that he said, "Thank you. I am just going someplace quiet and cool." (We live in Yuma, Arizona, and it was very hot.) I bade him farewell and went home.

Once home, I stewed over the gaggle of store employees and customers standing and watching, not helping that poor man. I got madder and madder. I had to do something. I called the store manager and explained the situation, of which he was aware. I understand that store clerks cannot touch customers by law. However, I said to the manager, if it happens again, at least try to keep your staff from standing in a group and laughing. Or, better yet, help the man transfer his purchases from one cart to the next. They could have done that, at least! The store manager told me that the homeless man frequented the store regularly, and they would try to be more courteous next time.

I felt better after venting to the manager, but I wasn't finished. My heart told me I had more to do. I was embarrassed to be human if humans were like those I had witnessed. Was I, a sixty-plus-year-old woman, the only one willing to do something? I vowed I would find the homeless man again and bring him some things he could use.

I bought a dozen bottles of water, a couple of bags of dry dog food, a belt, underwear, T-shirts, jeans, a jacket with a hood, a hat, and a backpack to carry everything. Then, I set out to find him. I drove around the area and looked where I would want to be if I were homeless, such as shady, out-of-the-way places. In the early mornings and late afternoons, I asked other homeless people who might know him if they'd seen him.

A week later, I was on my way home and decided to swing through the parking lot of the grocery store where this all began. Out of sheer luck, I saw the man hobbling through the lot with his dog.

I obediently stopped at the stop sign and then barreled across the parking lot with my tires splashing through puddles of water (we had had a rainstorm) and pulled up alongside him. He was surprised, but I was pleased that he remembered me as the lady who had helped him a week earlier. After we talked and I gave him his new things, I asked him where he was going as he was headed in the opposite direction from before. He was headed to Walmart to get a disposable phone. I said I would give him a ride.

We exchanged names. He said his name was Michael and his dog's name was Rowdy, after Clint Eastwood's Rowdy Yates in *Rawhide*.

I can't begin to express how wonderful it felt to find Michael and Rowdy and give them those things. I am going to look for him again in another week or so and keep him going for as long as I can. I have been very fortunate in life, and this is just one of my ways of paying it forward.

— Karen Lorentzen —

# 26

# Listening to the Inner Voice

*Somewhere inside, we hear a voice. It leads us
in the direction of the person we wish to become.
But it is up to us whether or not to follow.*
~Pat Tillman

our years after my daughter Lily was born with Down syndrome,
I found myself in a hospital auditorium surrounded by medical professionals. A woman on stage was explaining the proper
way to deliver a diagnosis of Down syndrome to new parents.
She shunned common stereotypes and told sad stories of new parents
who were given grim outlooks for their baby's future. She explained
about the immense love that families have for their disabled children
and the great potential that exists with early-intervention therapies
and medical advancements. She shared her own experience and said,
"If I only knew then what I know now, I wouldn't have cried so hard
the day my daughter was born."

I was not in that audience to learn anything new. I'd lived everything
she was saying. I had been volunteering as a support parent since Lily
was just six months old, encouraging mothers and fathers who had just
learned of their child's diagnosis. I'd heard the firsthand accounts of
nurses asking mothers if they had done anything during their pregnancy
that could have harmed the baby, as if falling down the stairs or having
a glass of wine before they knew they were pregnant could cause an

extra chromosome. I'd listened to a mom's tearful account of a genetic counselor telling her that her two-day-old son might one day grow up to "put things in boxes" as his job, as if anyone could possibly make a prediction about a child's future at that age.

I was in that audience to watch my friend dispel the outdated opinions and information about Down syndrome and have a visible effect on the medical professionals in the room. But, as I sat there, the same thought repeated over and over in my head. An inner voice that I did not want to listen to said, *You can do this, too. You need to do this. You can make a difference.*

For days, I tried to silence that voice. I countered it with other repeating thoughts. *You have three small children, one of whom has a disability. They need all your focus and attention. You do not have time for this.* But the other voice seemed to only get louder and more persistent. *You can make a difference.*

Six months later, I found myself in the same hospital, presenting to a group of obstetricians and pediatricians. I had completed training for public speakers and had presented to small classes of nursing students. This was my first time in front of a larger audience of doctors. They had been practicing for years and believed things were meant to be done a certain way. Before going in, I paced outside the room and talked on the phone with a friend, getting last-minute words of encouragement. As I finally stood at a podium and rubbed my sweaty palms on my legs, I thanked the audience for making the time to be there and started to tell them my story.

Because it was my lived experience, the words poured from me effortlessly. I detailed the hours I spent on my back when I was twenty-one weeks' pregnant while an ultrasound technician pushed and pressed a probe over my belly, only to tell me that she needed to get a doctor. The fact that my baby was in a breech position would be "the least of my worries," she said. A few doctors gasped, and I knew I had their attention.

I confidently recounted the alarming stories I'd heard from other parents. And I told them about all the mothers who had shared with me that the day their baby was born was not a day of celebration but a day full of tears, fear and grief. Looking back on that day as they now hold their baby in their arms or watch their toddler play, they are filled with regret and shame for having been so sad.

And then I told the doctors that they could change that. I reminded them that they are the medical experts, and how they deliver the diagnosis can determine the way a parent responds to the news. I asked them to try saying "Congratulations" rather than "I'm sorry" and to give examples of all the things people with Down syndrome can accomplish rather than the things that might never happen. I asked them to imagine being on their deathbed. Would they wish that they had learned to read at a higher level or had earned another degree? Would they say how glad they were that they had worked in a certain career or made a good salary? Or would they look around at their friends and family and see the love that they had put into the world and feel content with the love they had received in return?

I told them how, during my pregnancy, I had cried to a family member and said, "I just want her to know and receive love." And then I described how, earlier that day, my daughter with Down syndrome had beamed when I told her I was going to talk to doctors about her. She'd hugged me and said as clearly as possible, "Good luck, Mommy. I love you." I assured them that there is one prediction they can make accurately: the ability for someone with Down syndrome to love. And I asserted that to be on the receiving end of that love is truly an incredible gift.

I watched a doctor brush a tear from her cheek. Another wrote down notes. One came up to me afterward and said, "I wish I'd heard your message years ago."

Public speaking definitely took me out of my comfort zone, but I'm so glad that I listened to that inner voice. It's been fifteen years since I started giving presentations about Down syndrome to medical professionals. I've received cards from medical students thanking me for changing their perspective. One even told me she was going to focus on working with the disabled community because of what I had shared. I hear fewer stories of negative experiences and more stories of doctors and nurses congratulating new parents and immediately providing them with resources for support.

These days, I speak mostly to students and teachers in elementary schools about how to accept and include anyone with an intellectual disability. As my children grew, I witnessed the need for these presentations firsthand. And as much as I tried to silence the voice again — because talking to an auditorium full of fourth-graders can be terrifying — I felt compelled to listen.

I've presented to thousands of people over the years, and I still get nervous before every talk. Then, I wipe my sweaty palms on my legs and tell myself again: *I can do this. I need to do this. I am making a difference.*

— Nancy F. Goodfellow —

# 27

# Life-Changing Decision

*Not flesh of my flesh, nor bone of my bone, but still*
*miraculously my own. Never forget for a single minute,*
*you didn't grow under my heart — but in it.*
*~Fleur Conkling Heyliger*

had been on my own for a couple of years, and life had settled
into a comfortable pattern. One night, I sat in front of the TV
watching *The Dying Rooms*, a documentary on the horrific plight
of many baby girls across China. Two English reporters had gone
undercover across the Communist country and filmed infant girls
being tossed away like useless garbage.

Some were left in parks, in stairwells of buildings, and in alleyways.
Others were drowned in buckets of water. Those in orphanages who
were weak and sickly were placed in a dark room. These were called
the dying rooms, where the babies were given no food, affection, or
compassion. They were considered a burden, unworthy of life and left
alone to die an agonizing death.

Those images played in my head for weeks afterward. One morning, my sister called from Israel to chat. I told her about the show and
how I felt.

"Go," she said. "Go and bring at least one home."

"Are you crazy?" I replied.

"You love kids," she said.

I turned my sister's words over in my mind. It was ridiculous, I
thought. My life was good, full and very busy. I couldn't do anything

other than send money to some organization.

But the thoughts and images persisted until I finally picked up the phone and called the government to find out more information.

The first step was to complete a home study. These were done by a specialized social worker who would evaluate if I was suitable to parent, especially a racially different child. I decided to schedule the home study and then determine afterward whether or not to go through with the process.

In early February 1996, I met with the social worker four times. We hit it off from the start. Every time we met, she encouraged me to adopt. She even called an agency in Stratford who called me to tell me they had a baby girl from Guatemala they would love to place with me.

"What? No!" I told them. I wasn't ready to adopt. Besides, it was the baby girls in China who had captured my heart.

During that time, a local Shoppers Drug Mart held a contest. I filled out the ballot and won. The prize was a full box of items to make a home baby-safe.

They had another contest. This time, it was for a toddler's Little Tikes rocking horse. I won that, too. Were these signs?

And then I met a woman who had recently come back from China with her adopted daughter. She slipped a card with a name and phone number into my hand. "Call this person," she said.

At home, I stared at the paper. It was the name of a Chinese woman living in Ottawa who had helped with adoptions of the discarded babies. What was I thinking? I couldn't do this.

Yet, I soon found myself talking with Li. She sent me a package of information, and over the next few months, she walked me through the process to adopt internationally. I went through the motions, collecting all that was required yet still telling myself, *I can't. I'm nuts for thinking I can do this.*

One morning, I read an article in the newspaper about how many Chinese orphan girls grew up and became caught up in the sex trade because they had no one to look out for them.

I thought back to my own life when I had been kidnapped and

held for eight months before I escaped. No one had helped me at the time, but now I could help one girl avoid that kind of life.

From that moment forward, I began to tell myself, *I can do this.*

I was still afraid and worried about whether I could manage financially or whether I'd be able to handle the changes in my life.

But, despite these concerns, there was now a strong determination in me to bring a child home and give her a safe, loving environment to grow up in.

My doctor was a big support, and so were many others. To help pay the high cost that was involved, I sold many items around my home that I would never have parted with previously. I asked myself, *What is the life of a child worth?*

Nine months after I first met with the social worker, I was on a plane to China. It was a long flight, and I was grateful for the young businessman sitting next to me. I poured out everything to him: what I was doing, my fears, and also my faith.

We arrived in China. I felt overwhelmed and worried that I had gotten myself in over my head. But when the seven-month-old baby girl was placed in my arms, my heart melted. She was tiny for her age. She whimpered, cried and threw up. I couldn't help but think she would have been one of the babies placed in the dying room. All day long, she twirled her little fingers in front of her face, a sign, I was told, that something was wrong with her.

Li noticed her frail, sickly condition. "We can change the baby for a healthier one," she said.

I shook my head. This baby was the one God wanted me to bring home. I held her close, sang to her and thanked God for her life.

When we arrived at the airport to return home, the man I had sat with on the flight over ran up to me. "I prayed I would get a chance to see her." He held up a stuffed panda. "I know you'll take good care of her," he said.

That baby is now twenty-three years old. She is healthy, strong and brilliant, and completing her master's degree on a full scholarship. I discovered that those little, twirling fingers were not a sign of something wrong but rather her only stimulation at the time.

My life did change dramatically—all for the better. Three years after I adopted Shel, I returned to China to bring another baby home.

— Nikki Rottenberg —

# 28

# Opening My Heart

*Love is not something you protect.*
*It's something you risk.*
~Gayle Forman

*'m flying in a shoebox.* The thought raced through my mind as we ascended through the clouds.

Two weeks earlier, I had told my boss that I needed time off to go help the survivors of Haiti's earthquake. I'd been overwhelmed by work, and I just needed to do something different, hence this out-of-character decision. Me, the one in my family with the least interest in travel, was on the way to a place with no electricity, a military-ration food plan, and temperatures in the nineties.

After a six-hour train trip from Orlando to Miami, I was several miles up in the air on a Cessna that held only twenty-eight people. The plane was so small that I was sure a flock of birds could have knocked us over. Around me, I recognized most people from church, but I knew no one personally.

With every gust of wind, I froze, grabbed the armrests, and wondered what I'd gotten myself into. Fortunately, it was a short flight.

We landed a thousand feet from a nondescript, gray building. Soldiers with guns slung over their shoulders lined the tarmac.

As she stood to disembark, our team leader reassured us that the military were there to ensure that all relief help made it safely into the city. We followed behind and took the stairs down to the tarmac. Feeling panic rise within me, I took measured breaths and quickened my pace to keep up with everyone. After the inspection of our bags had been completed, we convened outside the front doors.

"Stay together and don't take anyone's offer to carry your bags," ordered our team leader.

It seemed an odd instruction, but then we started across the road, and the immediate swarm of islanders brought with it an understanding of her instruction.

"Miss, miss, your bag, your bag."

"Carry your bag?"

"Help with bag?"

"Need bag help?"

"Take bag?"

Within seconds, I was surrounded. I could hear my peers ahead but couldn't see them. Lowering my head to avoid eye contact, I grunted and dragged my overstuffed bags across the dirt road. With the bus in view, the crowd dispersed, and I caught up with the rest of the team. The last one on, I found a seat in the back next to a woman who looked to be in her early fifties. I introduced myself and quickly shared that I was an introvert who did poorly in big groups. My new friend Christy shared that she was also a "small-group person," but this was her ninth mission trip, and she'd help me through the experience.

At base camp in Port-au-Prince, we met our host and a group of Haitian college students who'd agreed to help with translation. Each had a genuine smile and warm personality. They'd been through so much loss and yet showed remarkable interest in helping us unpack and get comfortable. They even stayed and ate dinner with us. I did my best not to stare at the broken windows and camp-style bunk beds in the large room.

A few students noticed how shy I was in the large group. They came over individually, reintroduced themselves, and managed to make me laugh about what they called our "exquisite accommodations." Worn out from the train and plane rides, I was one of the first to say goodnight and head to bed. With a mosquito net in place and my arms slathered with repellent, I fell sound asleep within minutes.

The next three days took my heart to some of the highest and lowest places it's ever been. The hugs from orphans we met — I would sleep outside in the dirt to get more of those. The stories of loss retold to us with help from the translators — my chest ached with the heaviness of grief. At night, our group prayed for divine showers of comfort to blanket the thousands who had lost someone to the earthquake.

I've never been one to lead a prayer, but on the third night, when the team coordinator asked if anyone wanted to say a prayer, I spoke up.

I stumbled over my words and had to stop and pause. *I don't deserve to be leading a prayer,* I thought to myself. *I came on this trip for selfish reasons.* The lump in my throat got bigger until the person sitting next to me reached over and put a reassuring hand on my shoulder. It was so quiet that I could hear the wind outside. Raising my chin, I continued. Later, from across the room, our Orlando team leader gave me a reassuring nod and smile. With just her smile, I understood that it was okay to have come with uncertainty. What was important was that I was keeping my heart open to every experience before me.

Despite long trips in the back of a truck to remote places, my energy grew. Being with the group lifted me emotionally (especially when I started missing my daughter). Using my nursing skills outside the typical hospital setting made me thirsty to stretch myself even more. By the last day, when we prepared to leave, I let the tears come. They weren't tears of sadness. I was overwhelmed with joy. I felt like my heart had literally expanded in five days.

I understood what it meant to have unconditional faith, to know that everything happens for a reason. I no longer let anxiety shadow my days. Taking a trip in a tiny plane to a devastated island had a profound impact on who I am, what I believe, and how I love.

— Susan Bartlett —

# 29

# The Simulation

*We cannot always build the future for our youth,*
*but we can build our youth for the future.*
~Franklin D. Roosevelt

I had just retired from nursing when the director of Cherokee County First Steps approached me about becoming a VISTA (Volunteers in Service to America). She was adamant I was the right fit. I was sure I wasn't. I had finally reached a position to do what I wanted when I wanted. I wasn't about to give that up. "No" was going to be my answer regardless of her sales pitch. But when she said I would be helping children rise above poverty by putting free books in their homes, my heart skipped a beat. Memories of my childhood flooded my soul.

I didn't know children's books existed until I started school. The only book in our home was my mother's big, black Bible. Our family was "po," not poor. The "or" means you have an option. We didn't. It was hard for Daddy to keep a roof over our heads, food on the table, and a few clothes for five children.

I am sure if I had had books at an earlier age, it would have made a huge difference for me in learning to read. It took me a long time to successfully read and understand *Fun with Dick and Jane*. Reading opened new worlds to me. I was captivated.

As a school nurse, I saw too many kindergarteners pretending to read as they held their books upside down. It was obvious they were not used to books. If being a First Steps' VISTA meant I could help prevent children from suffering the way I had when starting school, I was all in.

As a First Steps' VISTA, I would attend community functions and health fairs. My main responsibility was registering children, up to age five, to receive books free from Dolly Parton's Imagination Library. Each month, an age-appropriate book would be mailed to them in their name.

All was well until it was time for a poverty simulation. My stomach churned as the VISTA leader said five of us would take part in the process. The coordinator said we would get a better understanding of the people we were trying to help if we experienced seven hours of their day. We would not be allowed to use our cars. We would receive bus tokens. We were to walk from the office and catch a bus to our destinations. I cringed. I didn't want to be chosen. I had signed on to help children, not to be reminded of my years of poverty. I whispered, "Please, don't let my name be chosen." It was. I could barely contain my emotions. I had spent the past forty-three years making sure I would stay out of poverty. I felt I was being forced to live in it again.

In the simulation, I was assigned to live as a single mother, working two jobs while caring for her two children. They were supposed to ride the bus to school after I left for my first job as a waitress. The rent was due, and the electricity was going to be turned off if the full amount wasn't there by 5:00 P.M. If I paid the power bill, there wouldn't be money for groceries. I made ten dollars too much to receive food stamps.

With each step toward my first job, the pain of my childhood grew. I had to put it out of my mind if I was going to make it through the assignment. Waiting tables turned out better than I thought. I received some big tips. I was getting comfortable with the staff when I was called to the phone. It was a neighbor.

"A police car just pulled away with your kids," she said as part of the simulation.

"What! They were supposed to be at school. If they missed the bus again…"

The neighbor continued, "You will need to get down to Child Protective Services and see what is going on."

"Thank you. Do you know the address?"

This would be my first time riding public transportation. My daddy always had a shabby car to take us where we needed to go. My destination would be the fifth stop. A lady with groceries boarded, and some spilled as she took her seat. She scrambled to pick them up. At the next stop, an older couple got on. The woman was frail and pale. It was summer, and she had on a coat and hat with a scarf around her neck. The man gently laid her head on his shoulder. I thought, *She is sick.* At the stop before I was to get off, a foul-smelling man took a seat across from me. I wasn't sure if it was body odor or the alcohol causing my waves of nausea. It took all I had not to vomit. I was glad when the bus finally reached my stop.

At the Department of Social Services, I met with Agent Dawkins.

"Ms. Sarratt, the school officer brought your children in because they were home alone. They are too young to be left unattended. They have also missed twenty-five days of school. There will be an investigation to see if they can remain with you."

That was part of the simulation, of course, and thankfully the last part of it. I breathed a sigh of relief and gratitude that it was over, and I realized my environment growing up was completely different from the twenty-first-century working poor.

In my childhood, most families in our area were sharecroppers like us. We lived in rundown houses without indoor plumbing. We had electricity. Ours was never disconnected. We had to work in the fields to help with basic survival. We would be out of school for weeks. No one came to see why. Children weren't taken from their parents for missing too many days.

That simulation awakened the wounded, insecure, nine-year-old girl living deep inside me who started third grade with only three dresses her mother had made from flour sacks. The experience scoured away the shame that had made her a prisoner of poverty. She was free, and I was no longer her slave. I was unleashed from her!

A fire was lit in my spirit. I became passionate about getting free books to as many children as possible. I started carrying registration forms in my purse. I didn't want to miss an opportunity to sign up a child for the program. First Steps' book enrollment increased from eight hundred to twelve hundred families by the end of my twelve-month service.

Afterward, I got involved in poverty prevention. I volunteered for First Steps as their Outreach Specialist. I became a mentor for an alternative school for troubled students.

Four years later, I received Cherokee County First Steps' Oscar Fuller Education Achievement Award. It is given for outstanding contributions to education and supporting First Steps' mission to get children ready for school.

Being uncomfortable led to one of my greatest rewards. I was freed from my childhood shame, and I had helped empower our youth for the future.

— Mae Frances Sarratt —

# 30

# The Delightful Life Detour

*Our greatest fulfillment lies in giving ourselves to others.*
*~Henri J.M. Nouwen*, Life of the Beloved: Spiritual
Living in a Secular World

I have read many times that we don't meet people by accident; they are meant to cross our paths for a reason. This was most certainly true when several years ago, my life took a bit of a delightful detour when I met the most wonderful eighty-nine-year-old long-term care resident, Ms. Ruby. I am firmly convinced that our paths were meant to cross so that we could share a special friendship.

Our initial introduction occurred while I was teaching a nursing clinical course at the care center where she lived. "You need to meet our new resident, Ruby! She is in room 618 and you will love her," the charge nurse shared with me one day at the beginning of our day. I simply poked my head in her room to say hello and five years later we are what Ruby refers to as BFFs (Best Friends Forever).

Over the years it has occurred to me that in an intergenerational friendship such as ours each generation has so much to learn and teach each other. During my frequent visits we shared our life stories and I learned that she was a widow, had no children, and had few family members close by.

Ruby was also a nurse and had trained as a United States Cadet Nurse at the end of World War II. I loved to hear about her nursing practice in the 1940s and she was always eager to hear about today's advances in healthcare. She would regale my nursing students with stories of retrieving babies from the pediatric wing of the hospital and bringing them to their dorms while they studied. She explained that they had to sterilize needles back then — no single-use syringes for them. It was a very different type of healthcare than we know today.

During one visit, Ruby shared with me that she once taught Sunday School and really missed being around children. This prompted me to think of my own precious grandchildren and the possibility of another generational friendship.

That Christmas I arranged for my grandchildren to meet Ms. Ruby in a most inspiring way. One day at the beginning of December I picked up all four of the children and sprung a surprise on them. For several years, I had bought their Christmas gifts in different categories, such as something they wanted, something they needed, something to read, or something cozy. But that year I gave them gift cards in a new category: something to do for others. They voted to use the money to buy holiday decorations for Ruby's room at the care center. We went shopping and they purchased a small tree with meaningful ornaments and then surprised her with these gifts. The next intergenerational friendships were born.

Over the next few years, I witnessed the joy that the children and Ms. Ruby shared with each other. They developed a mutual love for each other that I wished we could recreate for other seniors. I just needed to figure out how to plant the seed to make this happen. This thought stayed with me until I retired from nursing a few years later.

That was when I figured out how to promote my idea of intergenerational friendships. After a thirty-three-year nursing career, I became a children's book author. The story of Ms. Ruby and the children's extraordinary relationship with her was the catalyst for writing a book that encourages children to befriend older adults.

I took on the challenge of self-publishing this mission-driven book and spent the next eight months creating *Ms. Ruby and The Gigi Squad: Friendship Comes in All Ages*. This labor-of-love book chronicles the many fun events the children created for Ruby over the years. They held surprise birthday parties, tea parties, took her to school musicals, and made her a "bonus grandma" necklace. These events each made for beautiful illustrations that tell the story of a group of children (the Gigi Squad) and their grandmother (aka me, Gigi) who became an active part of an older adult's life. What a wonderful life lesson for children to know that they possess the power to make a difference for someone, just by showing up!

This book has taken my life by storm as it has received multiple awards and brought many opportunities to publicly speak about intergenerational friendships. I have given interviews on podcasts and YouTube channels.

To say it has been a lot of work would be a huge understatement. I had no idea what I didn't know about self-publishing a children's book, but quickly found out that it was a very large undertaking. I thankfully had many individuals who steered me in the right direction. The day my first copy of the book arrived in the mail was indescribable. I seriously felt like I had given birth to it and in a way, I had! Recreating myself as an author at my age was exciting yet scary, and is one of my favorite life accomplishments.

A few highlights of the writing process for me have been first and foremost giving the book to each of the grandchildren, as it was a special legacy for each of them. Secondly, sharing the process with Ruby as it unfolded. She not only proofread the book but helped critique the illustration process. I would excitedly bring the illustrations to her as I received them, and she would hang them on her door for bragging rights.

Lastly, my vision for the book was originally on a smaller scale and written to encourage families with children to visit an older adult. I was in awe when entire schools began approaching me to use the book for service projects. One activity that I included in the book titled The Sunshine Bag Project took off and children began giving seniors these special bags that included letters, cards and small treasures. It had not dawned on me until this happened that the book would be successful at encouraging large numbers of children to befriend large numbers of older adults.

It was quite humbling to realize that my mission of promoting intergenerational friendships was being fulfilled through this labor-of-love book. It was also a joy to know that in this next chapter of life I could continue to make a difference for others, all because I had the nerve to step out of my comfort zone and take a delightful detour to authorship.

—Vickie G. Rodgers—

# Trust Your Instincts

# 31

# Time to Go to a New Hello

*If you're brave enough to say goodbye,*
*life will reward you with a new hello.*
*~Paulo Coelho*

After fourteen years as an office worker in corporate America, my boss made me cry. I do not cry easily or often; I think my most recent jag had been after losing one of my dogs a year before. But when my boss lit into me for something I had done to try to help a customer, I let fly with tears and sobs of frustration that all my hard work and creativity could not change the company.

I liked the job okay, but I was in a customer-support role, and the company had made it clear they cared more about the bottom line than the people they had already sold to. The reprimand felt like a betrayal when I had tried so hard to please our clients. I didn't think I could do it anymore since I am not the type to just do a job without caring. Deeply.

This episode happened on a Friday. I shook with adrenaline for a long time after the confrontation and closed my office door to shut out my co-workers. I didn't get much done for the rest of the day.

Over the weekend, I spent some time feeling sorry for myself and then discussed the situation with my husband, who agreed it was time for me to go. We decided we could make do if I got a part-time job and worked on my writing career for the rest of each workday.

It was a scary decision but wonderfully freeing! I hoped to find a job that would be fun, not just provide a paycheck. And if I could make a positive difference for someone, that would be a big plus. I had no idea what kind of work to seek, so I searched the job boards with an open mind.

I wound up applying for jobs that had never been on my radar before: midday dog walker and pet sitter. As a lifelong dog owner with experience handling both dogs and cats from previous work in a veterinary vaccine clinic, I knew I could do it and enjoy it! By Wednesday, I had secured a position with a small pet-sitting and dog-walking company, and I put in my two weeks' notice at my corporate job.

The new job was a perfect fit! Every day, I went to five or more households, walking dogs of all sizes and temperaments, feeding and playing with cats, and learning about exotic critters like lizards, birds, and guinea pigs. My new customers had fuzzy faces and soulful eyes, and they never complained! It was a constant learning experience, too, as I discovered how to handle dogs that lunged at cars or other dogs, plus where to look for hiding cats. I found I was a natural leader of animals. Who knew? And I easily got in my 10,000 daily steps. It was a new lifestyle, not just a new job, and I had found my passion!

Fourteen years later, I run my own pet-sitting business. I enjoy every aspect of the work, from interacting with the pets and their doting parents to managing my team of enthusiastic sitters, to the accounting and administration. And I know I make a difference in the lives of my human clients and their pets because they tell me so! I often say I have the best job in the world, and I mean it.

Yes, when my boss made me cry, it was time to leave my long-time corporate job and say hello to a new one I could be passionate about!

— Kim Sheard —

# 32

# An Adolescent Adoption

*Taking risks doesn't mean shirking responsibility,*
*but embracing possibilities.*
*~Vick Hope*

A t age twenty-five, with a degree in social work, I was on a mission to change the world. Excited to be working with people in need and to help change lives, I possessed the idealistic, energetic attitude that anything was possible. Little did I know that ambitious drive was about to be put to use in a very real way in my life.

One evening, sitting in my little, one-bedroom apartment, I received a phone call from my aunt. I was living in Indiana, she in Arizona. I sensed the concern in her voice as she explained to me that my ten-year-old second cousin had been removed from her home and placed into an emergency foster-care center. I tried to offer advice and get some information on the situation, which sounded dire. I contacted the social worker in Arizona, who filled me in on the situation.

Maia had been removed from her home, and it was unlikely that she would be able to return, given the situation. The social worker was thrilled to hear from me and said that Maia would likely remain in foster care unless she could move in with a family member. To further complicate things, she needed to be in a home without men.

I fit the criteria. My heart jumped, swirling with emotions. Would it be possible for me to raise a ten-year-old girl? I was still a graduate student. Were there other options? Could I live with myself if I did nothing, and she became lost in the foster-care system?

At that point in my life, babysitting was the extent of my experience with caring for children. I consulted with my mother, who is wise, reasonable, and realistic, always guiding me to the right thing to do. We had a heart-to-heart talk and decided to travel to Arizona together to assess the situation.

Upon arrival in Arizona, we met with the social worker, who took us to see Maia. By then, she had been moved to a foster home. She was living with a kind woman but in a very different environment from what she was used to. Not only had her home changed, but everything had changed for her—her home, her parent, the religion of the home, the race and culture of the household, her room, her rules, her siblings, and her school.

Tall for her age and thin, with huge bluish-gray eyes and short brown hair, Maia looked shell-shocked. She hugged us tightly and begged us to take her home with us. We attended a meeting with the social worker, the lawyers, and the state prosecutor. After realizing that we were left with only two other choices—either Maia stayed in foster care until she was eighteen, or she went to live with family in Indiana—I decided to take on the task. With my family's support, I started the process of getting custody.

Before we left Arizona, I was interviewed by a gruff man who worked in child welfare. He grilled me on how I expected to manage school, work and a child; what support I had; how I didn't know what I was in for; and how I had better be sure because he didn't want me calling him to ask for her to be sent back after I had failed. My stomach churned, but I sat in the old, wooden office chair and didn't budge. I assured him that, no matter his doubts about my age or status as a student, I would figure out a way to do this. I was resourceful, determined, and stubborn. I wouldn't give up.

My mother and I had to say goodbye and leave Maia behind in Arizona while we returned home. It was a difficult, tearful goodbye. I took a semester off from school and took foster-parenting classes, got my certification, moved from my apartment into a two-bedroom rental house, and had the home inspected by social workers, all within several weeks' time. Indiana had to work with Arizona and vice versa to hash out the custody agreements, and it was a grueling process. Paperwork, interviews, home inspections and certifications took up most of my time.

Eventually, everything was worked out, and I returned to Arizona to collect Maia. We took what belongings we could and hopped onto the plane to head to our new home.

I raised Maia for ten years, eventually adopting her. I got side-eyes from people when I registered her for school — a twenty-six-year-old with a ten-year-old daughter — as they did the math in their heads. I hired babysitters so I could attend study groups while my friends went to parties, and I called my mother for advice on how to deal with the pre-teen mood swings that I had suffered myself not so many years before.

Raising an adolescent is certainly not for the faint of heart, but in the end we managed to live together, thrive together, love each other and, in many ways, grow up together.

—Jennifer Starr—

# Outside the Box
# and Down the Road

*Once we accept our limits, we go beyond them.*
*~Albert Einstein*

y husband and I unexpectedly acquired my dream retirement home in the country several years before retirement, but that caused a commuting nightmare. I kept my dream job as a breast-cancer navigator for a large, metropolitan hospital, but the commute kept me from seeing my country home during daylight. So, a couple of years in, I reluctantly sought a job nearer to home and landed a healthcare-educator job at the nearest hospital. The transition was a bit of a shock, but I believed I was there for a purpose and intended to fulfill it and learn to love it.

Even though my job was as an educator, my background as a breast-cancer navigator proved valuable to the women of the community and the hospital as well. I was encouraged by management to be involved as a volunteer navigator. I coordinated meetings where the diverse medical group met to discuss cancer cases and brainstorm treatment options. I fielded calls from women who needed help navigating the confusing world of cancer care and many who needed to find financial help to get a screening. The recession had impacted the rural community much harder than urban areas, and the pool of unemployed and working poor was large. I took calls from women who had only enough gas in their car to drive to work but not enough to also drive to the hospital for a mammogram. So, another year or two went by without them being screened and potentially getting an early diagnosis and easier, more successful treatment.

One businesswoman in the community had started a Bras for the Cause campaign a couple of years before I arrived, and it was so well-received by the community that it became a big event with tremendous participation. Money raised had doubled each year, so now they had a dilemma: What to do with the money? They had bought post-mastectomy supplies for a resource room and provided other small-ticket necessities, but the room was full. For once, supply exceeded demand. Yet, the number of women who were diagnosed with late-stage cancer had not improved.

I was invited to a round-table planning session to discuss what to do with the upcoming event funds. The group tossed out buying more gowns and more of same. But when it came my turn to speak, I told them I think much bigger and introduced the idea of sponsoring a mobile mammogram program. I expected to be shut down, but the group unanimously approved the idea.

Over the next several months, I was assigned many tasks I had never done before. I had to find a suitable vehicle, prepare an operating budget, and work with a committee of in-house department heads and a CEO who were much less enthused about an idea that would require them to do more work. The radiology-department director had the mistaken idea that we would just move existing patients to the van and take away "their" patients. Unfortunately, the CEO listened to him and voiced that concern often.

We finally found a slightly used mobile unit for sale from an out-of-state cancer center. The Hospital Foundation launched its first-ever employee fundraiser, and it was a stunning success, raising nearly $10,000. The Bras for the Cause group pledged financial support, so the hospital only needed to provide the mammography machine and staff it with existing mammographers and a newly hired bus driver with a CDL license.

Community churches and businesses sponsored mobile mammogram days, which solved the transportation problem for many women, and employers welcomed having their employees take a fifteen-minute break during a workday to get screened.

Ten years later, the numbers were astonishing. Rather than taking "their" patients and moving them to the van, the mobile unit had become an extra mammography room, increasing radiology's patient numbers by thirty-three percent and making a screening mammogram possible for women who had never had one. Some hadn't had one in over fifteen years! Some were insured, but for those who were not and couldn't afford a mammogram, I still had my resources to find grant funding, and many churches and businesses stepped up to sponsor mammograms for women in their groups.

After a good ten-year run, the old van started having mechanical issues, and the mammogram machine that had already been replaced once was facing its normal replacement years. So, once again, Bras for the Cause stepped up and agreed to sponsor a new one. They raised enough money to pay it off in full, just months after the new van hit the streets for a robust schedule of mobile clinics. They also added a bone-density machine so women can get early screening, leading to early treatment for bone loss as well as possible breast cancer.

It was frustrating to bring a novel, progressive idea to a rural area. I won't sugarcoat that at all. But when I see the impact on women's lives, I know it was worth it!

— Judith Quan —

# 34

# Switching Gears After Twenty-five Years

*The path from dreams to success does exist. May you*
*have the vision to find it, the courage to get on to it,*
*and the perseverance to follow it.*
*~Kalpana Chawla*

I have always loved school. I played school with my younger sisters from the time they were old enough to talk. I even tutored my mom when she went back to school to get her GED. I wrote in my high-school diary that I would be an elementary-school teacher and write books for kids someday.

When I was in fifth grade, I won a schoolwide writing contest. An author had come to our school for a visit, and she called me up to claim my prize: an autographed copy of *Can't Catch Me, I'm the Gingerbread Man.* Up until that point, the bulk of my writing had been in my diaries. It was the first time I had viewed my writing as something that others could enjoy.

My high-school job was working in the children's section of our local public library. I LOVED that job. I could preview all the new books before anyone else got to check them out. I got to read to kids and help them find books they might enjoy. I thought about how amazing it would be to write a book that could end up on one of those shelves someday.

Being a teacher was the more sensible of my two goals. Becoming an author seemed more like trying to make it as a musician or an actress. Ordinary people from tiny towns surely didn't get to do such things.

I graduated from college and started teaching first grade. I loved it. Teaching is what I was meant to do. But, one day, I learned about an opportunity to apply for a teacher creativity fellowship.

I spent weeks preparing my essay and application. I gathered letters of recommendation and sent everything in. The fellowship was for teachers who wanted to pursue a passion of some kind over a summer. I had to come up with a six-week plan to learn or explore something I was passionate about. My plan was to learn all about writing for children. I proposed to take online writing classes and attend two week-long writing conferences.

After a long wait, I got the fellowship! I spent that summer learning how to write for kids. I started working on manuscripts during any spare minutes I could steal. Just two years after receiving the fellowship, my first picture book came out. *I Am Not a Pirate* is about my younger daughter, who had to wear an eye patch. I was hooked. I began to do author visits on my fall and spring breaks and kept writing. More books came out.

In my twenty-fifth year of teaching, I thought about what it would be like to write and do author visits full-time. It seemed incredibly silly and selfish. It would cut our income in half. My older daughter was in college and getting married the following summer. My younger would be in college before too long. How could we afford to do that? I was supposed to teach for at least another ten years. Still, I couldn't shake the thought.

I prayed about what to do. I got the idea to take a sabbatical leave for a year to test the waters. Even if it flopped, surely we could recover after just one year without my income. In January 2020, I turned in my request to have the next school year off. I started booking author visits and events for the next school year. It was going to be amazing.

You may know where this was going. In March 2020, schools everywhere closed and went virtual. Covid was shutting down everything in its path. I started receiving cancellation emails for all my bookings. I went to my principal and asked if I could wait a year to take my sabbatical, but it was too late. They had already hired my replacement.

My sabbatical was nothing like I had planned. There were no live events, which meant very little income. I did get a lot of writing done. At the end of my sabbatical, I had to make yet another tough decision. Would I go back to teaching or try again to write and speak full-time?

I figured if we survived the pandemic without my salary, surely it would be better when things returned to normal. I turned in my resignation to pursue the second half of my dream, which I had written about in my high-school diary. Although scared to death, I took the leap of faith.

In the meantime, my daughter graduated, got married and was hired as a first-grade teacher. I was excited for her and happy to pass the torch, along with my classroom contents. We set up her room that summer, and she was ready. I could not wait to hear how her first day of teaching went. I called that day after school, and she was crying.

"Oh, no. What's wrong?" I asked.

"I found out today that Jon has Covid. I have to stay home for two weeks and miss the beginning of my school year. I don't even know what I'm doing yet. How am I supposed to write sub plans for two weeks? And, on top of that, you told me how important the first two weeks of school are for bonding with your students."

I couldn't believe it. I ached for her. So, I did what my mama heart told me to do: I cleared my schedule and filled out the paperwork to be her substitute. After all, I had helped her set up her room and knew where everything was. Most of her classroom was filled with my stuff. It only made sense for me to do it.

Since she lived two hours away and I couldn't stay with her, I stayed in a teacher friend's basement for two weeks while I taught my daughter's class. I Zoomed Emily in when I could so she could see her students, and they could see her. She was able to see what I was teaching and interact with the kids to ensure a smooth transition.

Having this opportunity to help Emily was the first time I knew for sure that I did the right thing leaving my classroom. If I hadn't, I wouldn't have been able to do this for her. It was an incredible bonding experience for us. The rest of the year, I knew exactly who she was talking about when we talked about school. I knew her kids and her staff.

Since that time, I've had the chance to come to her school to do author visits and share my books with her kids. Although it was really hard to leave my own classroom, I now get to travel to classrooms all over the country and keep creating books. And you know what? Some of my books are now on those shelves in the library where I worked in high school.

— Shannon Anderson —

# 35

# It's My Art

*And the day came when the risk to remain tight in a
bud was more painful than the risk it took to blossom.*
~Anaïs Nin

At a recent community gathering, an acrylic-art class for adults
was offered on the agenda. Since I do card making and journaling as a hobby, I thought it would be fun to add a little more
art knowledge to my repertoire.

I'm an introvert. While I love people, I don't like to be in crowds.
This class was filled with ladies of all ages, and none of them had a
familiar face. I felt more than a little intimidated. I found my spot
at the back table and perused the supplies I was provided: a small
canvas, a paintbrush, paper towels, and a cup of water. There were
four drops of paint on a paper plate — green, blue, white, and brown.
A photocopied sample of the project depicted a green hill with a tree,
a pale blue sky, and a barn with a fence. It looked plain.

The teacher was a bit stiff and serious. She picked up her brush
and demonstrated how to apply the paint for the blue sky in straight
lines across the canvas. She applied the simple green with a little flick
and swish to make it appear as a rolling hill. I tried to mimic her
movements on my canvas, but the plain blue of the sky was boring.
I mixed a small amount of paint on my plate and applied a more
abstract, stormy sky. I did the same with my rolling hill but didn't
make it monochrome green.

The instructor strolled around the room looking over her students' shoulders. I heard compliments such as, "Nice job," "Well done," and "Yes, that's the way to do it."

Then, she got to me. She looked over my shoulder and said, "Well, there's a little problem here. It's supposed to look like the sample." She took the brush out of my hand and swished it on my canvas, and the perfect, plain, green hill reappeared. She toned down my stormy sky until it resembled her sample. I was quickly becoming the bad student, and self-consciousness and doubt about my abilities started to set in.

We progressed to painting the tree. My tree trunk came out perfect like the sample, but the branches were wonderfully wonky. I mixed the colors to apply the leaves, and I loved the final product.

The instructor came around again. "The sample has green leaves, not fall leaves," she said. Her frustration with me was becoming apparent.

I was starting to get a little miffed. *I'm sixty years old, not in elementary school. This is my painting, isn't it?* As she walked away, I reapplied my stormy sky and added a little more depth to my rolling hill. When it came time for the barn, I again did not follow the precise instructions. I went off-script and made my abstract barn match the imperfect sky, tree, and hill. She looked over my shoulder one more time and simply walked away.

At the end of class, a lady at the table in front of me gushed, "Oh, I absolutely love yours." I received many compliments. It wasn't because my painting was good; it was different.

We had to gather as a group for a photo. Twenty of us held our paintings. Nineteen were similar to the sample, but mine was not one of them.

It felt wonderful to go off-script, get out of my comfort zone, and paint and create the way I wanted — a reminder to simply be me.

— Dawn Smith Gondeck —

# Help Me Get Ready

*The only way out is through.*
~Robert Frost

The nurse walked out of the room, and I sank onto the cold, vinyl couch, my head spinning. I dropped my head into my hands and fought back tears as my anxiety started to build. Had I heard her right? Did she say we were being discharged?

The past nine days had been some of the hardest of my life, and I wanted nothing more than a real shower, a decent cup of coffee, and my own comfortable and warm bed. The emotional roller coaster after the diagnosis had exhausted me, but now the idea of facing this on my own replaced the exhaustion with fear. I started to pace the floor beside the tall, metal crib.

*What are they thinking? They can't send us home; I don't know enough yet. There is so much information. What if I get it wrong? I could kill him!*

My breath started to shorten as the doubts weighed upon me. I looked into the crib at my twenty-two-month-old son hiding newfound toys under his hospital blanket. After all he had been through, he sat there playing as if the world had no troubles. He looked up at me as I approached and smiled. He reached his hands forward and pulled himself up to the metal bars that suddenly looked like a baby prison.

"Ookie," he said as he grinned. It had been his first word, and since then his favorite, and he was constantly waiting for the possibility of a sweet reward every time he uttered it. But this time the only response was my tears hitting the floor as I wondered if he would ever get to have another cookie. I may have been clueless about what to do, but I knew enough to understand that cookies and type 1 diabetes did not mix. I knew enough to understand that everything in my life and his was about to change forever.

I leaned my head against the bar, and he half-patted and half-pulled my hair. I looked up as I heard the nurse come back into the room and saw her carrying several stacks of paper. The panic returned, and my head started spinning. I was not ready.

I interrupted her before she could speak. "Look, I know you said this is protocol, and I am sure a hundred other moms have this all figured out, but you can't discharge us. I am not ready."

"It will be fine," she said. "We have all this material for you to read, and you will have a follow-up appointment in three weeks, and—"

"No, you are not hearing me. I can't. I am alone. I am a single mom and doing this alone. I could kill him if I mess up. You said so yourself!"

"Now, that is not exactly what I said," she said in a huff as she straightened the papers. "You can do this. You had two days of training."

"Two days? You are going to send me home to do things doctors go to school for years to learn with two days of training? I am telling you that I am not ready."

I kept going as she tried to get a word in to dismiss my fears. "I haven't even given him a shot by myself," I said, looking back at my son. His chubby face almost appeared to reflect my concerns. "All you have let me do is poke at an orange. I am telling you that I am not ready. I have no idea what I am doing, and you have to help me make sure I can take care of him." I walked away and plopped firmly back down on the couch. "And I am not leaving until I am."

She probably thought I was crazy. But this was more than just anxiety. I knew for sure I was not ready for this.

The nurse sighed in exasperation and laid the papers on the plain, white counter. "I will send the social worker," she said flatly. She turned and walked out of the room.

I walked over and carefully lifted my son over the bars and sat in the brightly colored vinyl chair beside his crib, pulling him close, careful not to bump the IV in his foot. "I don't know what to do next, kiddo, but whatever it is, we will do it together." I sat holding him for what seemed like forever and watched his face as he eventually drifted off to sleep. I felt the tension drain into weariness as his heartbeat seemed to sync with mine.

After what seemed like hours, a social worker came and listened to my concerns. At the end of the conversation, she smiled, put her hand over mine, and said, "It is okay if you are not ready, and it is also okay to say so." She looked back at my son in his crib, expectantly waiting for her attention. "You are going to have to be his voice and advocate a lot in the days ahead, so it is good to know you are not scared to say what you both need. It is okay to ask for help. Let's do whatever we can to get you feeling comfortable enough to get you and your sweet boy home."

The nurse changed her tune and became a huge help to our little family. She and the diabetes educator let me handle his care under their supervision over the next two days until I felt more prepared to handle it alone. They stood beside me and answered hundreds of questions as I learned to navigate a journey I never imagined I would take.

That was twenty-one years ago. Today, I watch my son as he studies for his master's degree, learning hard things as he prepares to step out into an unknown world, unsure if he is ready. As I recall many days when I had to reach out for help from an unsure place, I hope in those uncomfortable moments that he will also be brave enough to ask for what he needs and reach out for help.

In a hospital room long ago, I stood as a young mom and learned what it meant to be out of my comfort zone in a big way. I also learned that there is nothing wrong with speaking up about my needs. It is okay to not be ready. It is okay to need a little time. It is okay to ask for help, even when I am uncomfortable — *especially* when I am uncomfortable. I may not get there right away, but with a little help, I can be ready.

— Shannon Leach —

# 37

# The World Is My Classroom

*The best education does not happen at a desk, but
rather engaged in everyday living—hands-on,
exploring, in active relationship with life.*
~Vince Gowmon

The note read, "Mrs. Hoy, your son was sent to the office this morning because he refused to sit still. He did cartwheels down the entire hallway on his way to the office, disrupting every classroom along the way."

Ugh! That was just one of the daily notes I'd been getting from my kindergarten son's principal at school. I remember thinking, *He's only there two and a half hours a day!* This was the turning point that got me thinking about something that was way out of my comfort zone: homeschooling.

To back up a bit, this was one of our two adopted sons. We also have two slightly older biological children. Our younger adopted son was preschool-aged. Our adopted sons had not lived with us very long, and school hadn't gotten off to a good start.

The afternoon I received that note, I had a heart-to-heart discussion with my husband. "I'm getting notes about his behavior at school every single day. He's a young kindergartner. I think we need to pull him out of school and give him time to settle into our family." He agreed, but we were both concerned that if we waited a full year, he'd fall behind academically.

This was way before Covid made homeschooling popular or acceptable. Despite my unfamiliarity with homeschooling and the lack of confidence in my ability to pull it off, I told my husband that I could try homeschooling our son in hopes it would better prepare him for public school. He agreed.

I knew that more than a few mothers at our church were home-schooling their children. Before that time, I couldn't fathom why anyone would want to keep their kids at home when they could free up hours in the day to do other things while the kids were at school. Now, I was curious.

I called a few of them and asked lots of questions. Why do you homeschool? How do you do it? Where do you get the materials? How much does it cost? How do you manage your day? How do they graduate? To say those phone calls were enlightening is a complete understatement!

When voicing my concerns about my teaching ability, one mother asked me an unexpected question, "Do you love your kids?"

I answered emphatically, "Of course, I do!"

She then told me that loving them was all it took to be an effective homeschooling parent. That simple statement gave me the courage to try.

Upon the advice of my fellow homeschooling mavens, I mustered up my courage and ordered a preschool/kindergarten phonics program that centered around singing.

I sat my son on my lap and said, "As of next week, you are not going to school. Mommy will be teaching you right here at home."

His enthusiastic response greatly surprised me. "Just me? Not the other kids? Just me and you, Mom?" he repeated over and over.

"Yep, just you and me for a whole hour every day."

I found the curriculum very easy to teach. Surprisingly, it was a lot of fun! What was also very surprising and a little mind-boggling was that this kid who couldn't sit still for a minute at school was all ears during his teaching time. I started to realize the problem wasn't that he couldn't pay attention; he just needed attention. When he got my undivided attention, he suddenly became calmer than ever before.

I took him back to the school a couple of months later for speech therapy, and the teachers were beyond shocked to learn that I had taught him to read in that space of time.

Homeschooling also brought about some other unexpected benefits.

His biological brother, who is fourteen months younger than him, was listening to the lessons I was teaching and started learning right along with his brother. It wasn't long before he was reading, too.

Around the same time, my husband took a job as a traveling carpenter, and he'd be gone nine to ten weeks at a time. That's not what a mother of four young kids who are five years apart wants to hear!

Then, I had a brainstorm. What if I homeschooled all four kids, and we traveled with him some of the time? It was a crazy idea, but it would help us spend more time together, and it might just work.

We bought an older motor home with all the amenities: full kitchen, bathroom, and more. It even had bunk beds for the kids. Over the next few years, we traveled everywhere my husband went for work. I learned how to put together unit studies that worked for all grade levels. I taught science, social studies, and language arts to all the kids at once. I doled out assignments according to their grade levels.

Whatever we studied in the morning, we went to see in the afternoon. We studied the Revolutionary War in Boston and went to see the battlefields of Concord and Lexington later that day. Forest rangers taught the kids about trees, plants, and wildlife in Michigan. In Alabama, they learned about the birds and marine life on Dauphin Island and a lot about the Civil War. We got to spend lots of time together, and we all enjoyed it.

When someone asked our kids where they went to school, they said, "The world is my classroom!"

If they disliked anything about homeschooling, it was that they never got a snow day!

When it came time for our oldest child to go to college, we talked about her experiences with school. She said, "In Christian school, I learned about character. In public school, I learned what to think. But, in homeschooling, I learned *how* to think." She thanked me for never giving her the answers but always showing her how to find them.

How did things turn out? Each of our four children took their own paths as adults. One went to college. One went into the military. One is in trade school, and the other works in the building trades. Each of them is successful in their own way.

As a mother-turned-teacher, I created a thirst for knowledge in all our kids. I have no regrets and I cherished every single minute I got to spend with my kids.

—Toni Hoy—

# 38

# Sweet Emily

*Adoption is complicated, but it is also rich with*
*narratives of strength.*
*~Jillian Lauren*

She looked like a chubby, little puddle, forlornly sitting in the middle of the floor. The adoption caseworker had counseled us that little Emily had several serious health concerns and was developmentally delayed.

It is hard to say what caught our eyes at first. Her jawline was blemished with a huge, red hemangioma. Her crossed eyes looked huge through her thick eyeglasses. Even at thirteen months old, she had very little hair and was toothless.

The foster mother told us that Emily was not very interactive and had not yet learned to crawl. She explained that with several other special-needs children in the foster home, Emily did not get much attention.

We learned that Emily had been born three months prematurely. Her breathing issues necessitated steroid treatment and use of a nebulizer several times a day. Her life, thus far, had alternated between the special-needs foster home and the children's hospital.

"Would you consider taking Emily home with you for the night... just on a trial basis?" the caseworker pleaded. I looked at my husband, and I could tell he was as scared as I was. I have never considered myself a "nurse-type person." Taking care of this child was definitely outside of my comfort zone. I was afraid that I would not be able to keep everything straight for little Emily's care, medication and treatments. It seemed overwhelming.

Several years before, within a few months of each other, we had been blessed through adoption with two healthy sons, now seven and eight years old. I treasured all the tasks of motherhood: bottles, cloth diapers, rocking, cuddling, story time, swimming and skating lessons, pre-school, kindergarten, elementary-school programs and more. I knew I was made to be a mother. I loved it!

My husband and I always wanted a daughter, too, but I gave up on that idea when I turned forty years old. In my head, forty was my cut-off age for becoming a mother again.

But then, we got a call from the adoption agency about this little girl who badly needed a loving, caring home. "You were only thirty-nine when she was born," my husband reminded me. "Let's go meet her."

Now, we were in a dilemma. We had been introduced to Emily and made aware of her needs. "Should we take Emily home for the night," we wondered, "just to see if we can handle it?" We offered a quick prayer to God and gave a feeble "Yes" to the caseworker. We accepted the responsibility of this fragile, little girl for one night only.

The foster mother packed up some bottles, diapers and clothes. She gave us the meds and nebulizer with instructions on how to administer them.

I was so nervous about giving Emily her treatments. Her health was fragile. I was afraid I would forget what I was supposed to do. That evening, I had questions but was unable get in touch with the foster mother. It was a long and stressful night. The weather was cold and damp, which made matters worse. Little Emily was not doing well, I could tell, but we made it through the night.

By the next morning, we were exhausted and stressed-out. We dropped Emily back off at the foster home and sighed with relief. We had not made up our minds about adoption.

Later that day, we were dismayed when the caseworker called to let us know that Emily was back in the hospital. Had we done something wrong, or was it the cold and damp weather that affected her? I was beside myself with fear. The thought plagued my mind that we did not have what it takes to care for little Emily.

"Let's pray about it," my husband said, "and then let's go visit her at the hospital."

When we got off the elevator at the hospital, we could hear the sound of a baby screaming. *Wow*, I thought. *Don't the nurses hear that poor baby screaming? Aren't they going to do something?* I dismissed that thought, and we made it to the nurses' station to get Emily's room number.

As we looked for Emily's hospital room, we realized the screaming was coming from Emily! We entered her room, and the screaming halted. She looked at us and immediately reached out her arms for me to pick her up. Just as quickly, she turned to my husband with outstretched arms, then back to me, and then back to him. Over and over and over, she claimed our arms and our hearts.

The next two days were packed full. The crib was set up, and her room was decorated. Friends showered us with little-girl things. We picked up our little darling from the hospital and made our way home, anxious for Emily to join her brothers.

The weeks to come were precious. She came into our family and made us whole. With the attention of two big brothers, she was crawling within a week and running soon thereafter. She got three teeth in the first week and beautiful, blond hair soon after. She never had to go back to the hospital for her breathing issues. And, as I learned, her frequent screaming gave her weak lungs needed exercise.

As she matured, we were able to wean her off the steroids, which had made her face and upper body so puffy. Before she entered kindergarten, she had surgery on her chin to remove the unsightly hemangioma. A couple of years later, eye surgery corrected the crossed eyes.

In time, our beautiful Emily's health stabilized, and she became the most athletic member of the family. Throughout her school years, she loved participating in basketball, volleyball, horseback riding, and cheerleading. She was amazing to watch as she relentlessly trained our Golden Retriever through her homemade obstacle courses. Emily starred in school plays and sang in school and church choirs. She matured into a gregarious, beautiful young lady.

It has been more than thirty years since I noted that the nurses in the hospital let Emily scream. That observation diminished my fear. Little Emily wasn't as fragile as I thought she was. God nudged my husband and me to welcome her into our home. Emily needed a caring, loving family. I became the mother she needed, and she became the daughter I so desperately wanted.

—René Ashcraft Sprunger—

# Shopping Therapy

*As we work to create light for others,*
*we naturally light our own way.*
*~Mary Anne Radmacher*

"**D**o something just for you," friends said, trying to cheer me up and help me relax. "Have a pedicure, get a massage, or treat yourself to a little shopping therapy."

But the way I saw it — shopping and self-care could only go so far. So instead, I pursued a different kind of project — a special kind of shopping trip that brings me joy every time I think of it.

I'd never really done anything like this, so I was nervous about asking for permission, but I am so glad I did.

It all started when my four-year-old son's bloodwork showed elevated tumor markers. We had to do an MRI, and it was a truly nerve-racking experience as the date approached. As if the fact that doctors were checking for tumors wasn't scary enough, they explained that they would have to sedate and intubate my son for the procedure. They would have to pause and restart his breathing to get the pictures they needed.

When the big day came, it was even worse than I imagined. My little boy clung to me tightly as nurses instructed me to lay my baby down on the hospital stretcher. He screamed and desperately reached out for me while they put him to sleep using a mask. It was a hard day to be a mother.

I could barely see through my tears as the nurse escorted my mother and me to the waiting room. She explained the procedure would take two hours. Like a zombie, I walked straight to the restroom to bawl my eyes out and catch my breath, feeling hopeless, worried, and guilty for the way I had to help hold him down.

My little boy already suffered from breathing problems when he was sleeping, and I was terribly afraid of how the sedation and intubation would affect him. And of course, the gravity of the future test results was weighing heavily on me, too.

I was a wreck. I knew I didn't want to sit in that waiting room. But how else could we get through those next two hours?

We went to the elevator and got off when we saw the cafeteria, where I got a hot cup of coffee — my thinking juice. After a cup of coffee and a few minutes of biting my nails, I got up and told my mom, "Let's go shopping."

I think my mother was caught off guard as I snapped out of my zombie-like state and started speed-walking toward the hospital gift shop. She followed closely behind, carrying all our bags.

"Do you need a little shopping therapy, honey?" she asked with a confused smile, and I just nodded as I walked. I was on a mission to make the next two hours count, doing something worthwhile instead of sitting there worrying. As I was browsing the gift shop, looking for toys for my son, an idea came to me.

So I walked up to the front counter, still teary-eyed, and explained (or babbled) my plan to the young girl working the cash register.

"My little boy is getting an MRI today. So we are just hanging out and waiting here for the next two hours. Would it be okay if we purchased a whole bunch of gifts and sent them upstairs to kids in the hospital?"

"Of course, we can send gifts upstairs," she said. "Who would you like to send it to?"

The young girl was not fully understanding me. She was confused and I was a little embarrassed. I struggled to find the words.

"Wait, do you mean you want to send gifts to, like, random kids?" she asked.

"Is that allowed?" I asked, praying she'd say yes. "Can you just give them to the nurses and let them give it to the kids who need them the most?"

She smiled and gave me a thumbs-up.

Over the next hour and a half, I filled up all the extra counter space in the store, stacking gifts. I know I looked like a crazy person, and I must have asked her to blow up a dozen balloons, but she didn't complain. In fact, she seemed excited and there was a spring in her step as she took each balloon back to fill it.

And something truly magical happened. As I picked out gift after gift, my tears began to dry and my quivering lips began to smile. A happy peace came over me as I stopped worrying and started doing something worthwhile. I was helping other kids, and their moms, get through their own tough days.

It wasn't long before I let my mom in on my little secret, and she immediately joined the fun. For every gift I had picked out, I tied a "get well balloon" on top, and she picked out cuddly stuffed animals to go with the gifts. When we went to check out, the young lady handed me little cards to go with all the gifts. I struggled to find the right words to write to perfect strangers... kids and parents I didn't know. So, on most of them I wrote one simple thing: "I hope this brings you a needed smile."

As we went to check out, my angel of a mother pulled out her credit card and paid for the whole thing. Hospital gift shops don't have many bargains, but that was money well spent.

Before I knew it, my phone started ringing. It was my son's nurse calling to tell me that everything went okay, and my son would be in the recovery room soon. We were just finishing up the last few cards. Two hours had gone by, and they were not wasted. Not one bit.

I thought that MRI was going to be long and miserable. Helping others while I was falling apart was certainly not what I expected to do when I walked into that hospital. Hopefully I will remember this shopping trip the next time I find myself in the middle of a breakdown. When I shifted my focus to doing something for others, it lifted me far above my own troubles and fears.

When I was down and out a few years ago, my daddy was the

one who reminded me that the greatest joy is found in helping others, in giving somebody else a needed smile. Time and time again, I find that to be so true.

I'll admit, a nice pedicure, or buying a new dress at the mall can bring a smile to my face after a hard day. But shopping in the hospital gift shop brought a thousand needed smiles to my heart. The next time I find myself needing some "shopping therapy," I'll know exactly where to go!

— Kayleen Kitty Holder —

# Chapter 5

# Take a Chance

# 40

# Meeting One New Person Every Day

*Scared is what you're feeling;*
*brave is what you're doing.*
~Emma Donoghue, Room

After a lifetime of living on the East Coast, my husband and I decided to retire and move to the San Francisco Bay Area of California, almost 3,000 miles away, where our daughter and her family were living. I was concerned that I wouldn't fit into this unfamiliar new community. So, I decided to make it my mission to meet one new person every day. It wasn't necessary to have a long conversation with the new person, just make a connection.

Soon, I discovered there was no shortage of open and diverse people to meet, if only I had the courage to make the first move. By looking the person in the eye, smiling, and at least saying, "Hi," I found that most people were open and willing to respond with a smile and a "Hello" back to me.

Sometimes, I would never see my new acquaintance again. Sometimes, the encounter would result in discovering we had something in common, and we subsequently became friends. I would often tell someone, "I have a mission to meet one new person every day, and today you're my person. Thank you!"

Here is just a small sampling of the people I met:

- A renowned chef and former dean of a culinary school
- A woman who survived the Jim Jones cult mass suicide in Guyana
- A young couple with two daughters, ages four and six, who walked from Honduras to Southern California to escape violence in their country
- A teacher at the local school for the blind
- A physician who is director of a free clinic in San Francisco
- An attorney in a law firm representing employees in workplace-discrimination cases
- A Japanese man who now works as a highly successful chef in a New Orleans-style restaurant
- A professor of medical anthropology at San Francisco State College, originally from Florida
- A former priest from Ireland, now a counselor in a local high school
- A woman from Israel who relocated to California to teach Hebrew to school-aged children
- A woman of Chinese ancestry who managed several political campaigns in New Jersey before retiring to the Bay Area
- A formerly homeless woman with a drug addiction, who is now happily housed, working, and sober
- A man who worked in Army Intelligence as a linguist and decoder during the Vietnam War

By meeting new people with different life experiences and interests, I discovered I was enriching my own. I found myself trying new things like my newfound friends were doing: exploring local biking and hiking trails, seeing plays in San Francisco, trying out new ethnic restaurants, and even exploring Buddhist philosophy. I also found I was sharing my own interests and experiences with the people I met. When I told some of my newfound friends about my family tradition of making homemade ravioli, they were very interested. That prompted me to host a ravioli-making party at my house. It was loads of fun, and we made more than 400 delicious ravioli to share.

One of my newfound friends is first-generation Chinese American. She invited a small group of us to explore Chinatown in Oakland during the Chinese New Year. She introduced us to a dim sum restaurant where the locals go, as well as several grocery stores. For one day, we were totally immersed in Chinese culture, which was a fascinating and rich experience.

There is no doubt the Covid pandemic made this mission more challenging. Face masks, lockdowns and social isolation really tested my resolve. I had to be more inventive and persistent.

Meeting one new person every day has been a rewarding endeavor. It makes me happy, pushes me to step out of my comfort zone, and enables me to experience new things. In the five years since we moved to California, I have met over 1,500 people. But that's not enough. I'm having too much fun, and I don't want to stop. At first, people laugh at me when I tell them about my mission, but they quickly come to understand how valuable an experience it has been. Several people who initially laughed are now adopting this mission for themselves. I encourage everyone to try it for a month, regardless of where they live. You never know, the next person you meet might just become a lifelong friend!

— Alice Facente —

# 41

# I Used to Live in a House

*It's your place in the world; it's your life.*
*Go on and do all you can with it,*
*and make it the life you want to live.*
*~Mae Jemison*

Several years ago, my husband and I sold our house, divided up our worldly goods between the kids, a garage sale and the trash, and moved into a ten-year-old Monaco Dynasty. This Dynasty was not Chinese, porcelain, Ming, or covered with fine art. It was solidly American, made of steel and covered with designer fabric. It was a motor home. And it was going to be our one and only home for the foreseeable future. By today's standards, it was fairly simple. It was thirty-eight feet long with a clean paint job and none of the slides (those big sections of wall that move out when the motor home is parked to give added living space) that all RVs have today, but it ran like a top.

We had made the decision to chuck the traditional life at a pivotal point in time. After working one and frequently two jobs at a time most of our lives, we were finally retired. Our children were educated and on their own. The nest was empty, and the calendar had a predictable feel to it. After having lived disciplined and productive lives for decades, we were seemingly at loose ends but kept coming back to the idea of a life on the road. Why not take a chance? We could always go back to a *Leave It to Beaver* life later on if we didn't like it. A smaller house was in our future anyway.

Weeks of research and some on-site investigation led us to a used Monaco at a good price. We were in love. Our first trip was to Cape Canaveral, Florida from St. Louis, Missouri. It was brief but proved that we could move across the country, eat, sleep, live and be happy in an RV. I even learned to drive the machine — a piece of cake, but a big piece of cake.

When we got back from our shake-down cruise, we let the family know that we were hitting the road. I can only imagine the bets that were taken on how long we would last. At least one person said they thought we wouldn't go longer than two years. They were right in one respect. We kept our first motor home only that long before deciding it was time to upgrade to a bigger and better unit. We had sampled the lifestyle and knew we were in this for the long haul, no matter how the bets at home lay. So, we traveled to a rally in Rayne, Louisiana, and bought a brand-new Monaco Windsor. It had two slides, push-button conveniences, and wheels that take us anywhere we want to go.

There are some people, however, who are not convinced that I really have a home at all. The questions are always the same. Don't you get cold? We have a furnace. Don't you get hot? We have air conditioning. Do you cook? We have a double-wide refrigerator, ice maker, oven, microwave, and stove. I have cooked a Thanksgiving dinner in my motor home. I have a washer/dryer, a shower with a skylight, a lovely bathroom, and even room for a limited number of knickknacks. We have a comfortable living room with a fold-out table that becomes a usable office area.

It is true that two people must enjoy being together, *really* together, to live full-time in an RV. You also have to be able to downsize effectively. The result of all this downsizing, by the way, means that our carbon footprint is quite low. When we are parked (as we are for six months of the year when we stay at our winter resort), our magic number is only seventeen tons of carbon dioxide. (The national average is twenty.) That is because our small size makes us easy and efficient to heat and cool — not to mention our ability to physically move our home to milder climates during the cold of winter and the heat of summer. When we are on the move, our diesel engine boosts our carbon footprint up to twenty-one, but we are still in the ballpark.

Of course, there is nothing free. We give up some things while gaining others. We miss the ease of seeing friends and family on a casual, even spontaneous basis. But we relish the times we are with them all the more. We have little room for keepsakes and souvenirs, but there is refrigerator space for the grandchildren's artwork. There are no large dinner parties given in a motor home, but if the weather is good, we can have as many people as we want in the front yard outside our door. And what a front yard that can turn out to be.

Some people only dream of having a beach house or a mountain cabin, a winter home in the desert or a vacation bungalow on the Great Lakes. Well, we have had all of those. Our home is any place we park.

We have eaten meals while watching pronghorns herd up for the night on the high plains of Wyoming. We have grilled steaks while watching ships go up the St. Lawrence Seaway. We have toasted the setting sun on the Pacific coast and sunrise at Kitty Hawk. We have followed the path of Lewis and Clark from Clarksville, Indiana, to Fort Clatsop, Oregon, and still slept in our own bed every night. We spent one magical night at the toe of Matanuska Glacier outside Anchorage, Alaska, and listened to the glacier growl and grumble all night long. Our Windsor has been our home in the desert, the mountains, across the Great Plains and through much of Canada.

The friends we have made and the places we have seen are so dear to us that when people ask us which adventure was our favorite, we have only one answer: "All of them."

— Louise Butler —

# Trust

*He who is not every day conquering some fear*
*has not learned the secret of life.*
*~Ralph Waldo Emerson*

love America. Thus, every summer, I do a bicycle tour of some part of this great country. To escape the heat and humidity of my home in South Carolina, I always explore a northern or western state.

In early 2020, I decided that my summer bicycle adventure would be a counterclockwise loop through South Dakota's Black Hills. To get there, I decided to do a one-way rental of an SUV from Hilton Head Island to Rapid City. There was only one requirement: The SUV had to have ample room in the rear for me to put down the seat and take my Trek touring bicycle.

On Friday, June nineteenth, Enterprise Rent-A-Car came through with a Chevrolet Excalibur that had only sixteen thousand miles on it. Nice! I arrived in Rapid City on Tuesday, June twenty-third, where I removed my Trek and turned in the Excalibur.

Then, in a maxed-out comfort zone, I declared, "Let the games begin!"

The highlight of my South Dakota adventure occurred in Custer on Sunday, July fifth.

I had spent the Saturday night prior at Custer's French Creek Campground. I crawled into my sleeping bag early at 7:30 P.M. with an alarm set for 4:00 A.M. in anticipation of the next day's big event.

But it didn't matter... I woke up anyway at 3:47.

I rolled out of my sleeping bag, having slept in the clothes that I intended to wear that day. In the darkened campground, the only light available for eating breakfast was in the bathroom. Thus, I ate an energy bar while standing next to the toilet.

Then I walked to a 5:00 A.M. meeting in downtown Custer at Black Hills Balloons.

There, I met other sleepy-eyed tourists who were present for the same reason. After filling out the required paperwork and making our payments, we found ourselves packed into vans going to a grassy field west of Custer. We were followed by four pick-up trucks towing trailers containing piles of colorful material.

At the grassy field, I exited the van, and watched the process of setting up and inflating four multicolored, hot-air balloons.

Minutes later, I climbed into the gondola beneath one of them. It was divided into four compartments surrounding the pilot in the center. That particular morning, it held eight passengers consisting of two couples, a family of three, and me.

Then the pilot jockeyed a pull-down handle that shot four-foot flames into the balloon, and the gondola slowly escaped the Earth's bonds. Four hot-air balloons slowly climbed as the sun was rising over the Black Hills.

It was spectacular! For an hour, we traversed the Black Hills.

I especially enjoyed a gizmo that was mounted in the corner of my compartment where the pilot could see it. It was an electronic placard with digital readouts of our flight data: the air temperature, wind, height above the ground, air speed, and climb or descent rate.

But, alas, all good things must come to an end. In eavesdropping upon our pilot's radio communications, I learned that the four balloons were to land on the grass at Custer County Airport.

So, I checked the placard, noting our descent rate. In accordance with my gut feeling, it seemed to be fast. I also happened to notice that our pilot appeared to be wrestling with the wind.

Then, as we continued our descent, he said what no balloon passengers ever want to hear: "Guys, I need you to sit down, face backward, and cover your head."

Uh-oh.

We followed his instructions as our balloon continued its descent. Suddenly, THUD!

We hit the ground, and everyone hung on as the wind tried to drag our gondola across the grass. Meanwhile, ground crews scrambled to stop it. With the gondola eventually halted, everyone climbed out and walked away uninjured.

Whew!

Minutes later, Black Hills Balloons treated us to champagne, cheese, and crackers. They also presented each passenger with a certificate of completion. What a class act!

With both feet firmly planted back upon Mother Earth, I was back in my comfort zone. And I had learned that there are times when you just have to trust those in charge.

— John Scanlan —

# 43

# A New Coat of Me

*Don't fake it till you make it. Fake it till you become it.*
~Amy Cuddy

The moment I saw the for-sale sign, I knew I had to have that mid-century classic in northeast Portland, aka "1955 little blue house." I'd looked at a lot of houses but never experienced love at first sight until then. Never mind what greeted me when I went inside. No first date is perfect. The diversity of the neighborhood, the proximity of two parks for dog romps, and the floor plan of the house that would allow for family gatherings and overnight visits were exactly what I wanted. Its fixer-upper condition made it affordable on my tight budget. How hard could it be to give it a makeover?

"The house needs too much work," the home inspector told my son. "I wouldn't let my mother buy it." But he told me it had good bones, so I bought it.

In my over-the-top enthusiasm, I failed to consider that makeovers require money and skills. I was using most of my savings to buy the house, and changing a light bulb was the extent of my handywoman skills. I was oblivious to reality.

The electrician and plumber submitted their bids. I picked out colors for painting inside and out. A friend volunteered to help me pull up the reeking carpets. I thought that would pretty much cover it.

Then, I walked through the house with another friend who had built homes and did a more careful inventory. In the kitchen, contact paper that couldn't be painted over covered the kitchen cabinets. The stove was filthy. A new Samsung refrigerator filled a quarter of the kitchen, rendering the doorway to the dining room impassible to all but the slimmest cooks and guests.

A good soak in the bathtub after a long day of work would have been lovely — if the tub had held water. The fireplace was filled with debris, and the living room drapes were irreparably stained.

I could go on, but you get the idea. Details make the home. This house had lots of details, including holes in doors, damaged moldings, and a nauseating, unidentifiable smell.

Those of you who can already fix things can't possibly understand how overwhelmed I felt as I looked around my little house with a clearer eye. I grew up reading a book a day and writing A-quality papers for school. Think how an arborist can look at the trunk, branches and leaves of a tree and see the entire system all the way to the roots. They can then determine health or disease. A bookworm like me looks at the trunk, branches and leaves and sees "tree, pretty tree."

With a move-in date six weeks out, I used the remainder of my savings to hire two very handy friends: Karen, a painter, and Virgil, a carpenter and handyman. I traded dog sitting for help from a contractor friend, Ken. I watched carefully and helped where I could. Initially, "helped" meant running to get coffee and pastries for my little crew. Gradually, I learned to use a screwdriver, hammer, and paintbrush. By the time my friends needed to move on to other jobs, I was ready to set my jaw and tackle more on my own. Every time I picked up a tool, a voice in my head said, "You can't do it." But my determination somehow spurred me on.

I had initially thought I would pry open a can of paint filled with a yummy color, dip in my brush, and transform a dingy room into a vibrant living space in a day. Now, I knew I needed to clean the walls, fill numerous holes, caulk, sand, tape, texture, prime, and then, for dessert, paint that yummy color.

What products cleaned walls best? Home Depot had a whole shelf of options. Diluted bleach is good for removing mold, I was told. How diluted? Did it matter the brand? Different-sized holes required totally different treatments. I bought a caulking gun and cartridges. Fortunately, there was a YouTube video on how to load and unload said caulking gun. I'd been a teacher and graded papers for a living. Who knew sandpaper came with grades, too? Which grade did I need? What kind of paint? How did one "cut in" corners?

Shocking everyone familiar with my skill set, I did finally transform every room. Can you imagine how I fumbled while trying to change electric receptacles? Yes, I watched the YouTube videos, but they might as well have been tutorials on performing cardiac surgery. Not to mention how long it took me to assemble a shelving system. Did they throw in those extra parts for good measure? Gazing at the leftover pile of screws, my thoughts teetered between proud and nervous. I refinished doors, hung curtains, and even put together a second pesky Swedish shelving system.

Becoming handier has been a life-changing adventure. When something more complicated needs to be repaired, like the furnace that inconveniently went out during the first cold spell in my new home, I call for help. But when a screw fell out of a kitchen chair and the seat began to wobble, I simply turned the chair upside down, got the right screwdriver for the job, and replaced the screw, tightening the other screws while I was at it. Why is that a big deal? You didn't know me before I became a handywoman. My handy son, just two miles away, is liberated to care for his own home. I invite my friends to lunch on my little patio as an opportunity to talk and laugh, not as a bribe to help me yet again fix something that is broken.

— Samantha Ducloux Waltz —

# 44

# What Am I Missing?

*Ask yourself the question, "Will this*
*matter a year from now?"*
*~Author Unknown*

"**D**o you notice anything different?" I asked my daughter one sunny spring afternoon.

"Not really," she responded while glancing around the living room and into the kitchen. "What am I missing?"

That got the wheels spinning in my head, paving the way for me to eventually take a big step out of my comfort zone.

For as long as I could remember, I'd never believed my house was clean enough to invite friends over. So, whenever we were expecting company, I exhausted myself to make certain the house was spotless. Whether friends were going to stop by for a quick visit or planned to spend a week or two with us, I cleaned so thoroughly that I ended up too tired mentally and physically to enjoy their company.

A great example was the time I offered to host a baby shower for my granddaughter and her husband. Realizing we would be inviting guests from both sides of the family, I was fearful as to how people might view my house. Although we had built our home thirty years prior, it was actually quite lovely. But, I was still obsessed with having everything flawless.

Of course, I wanted my textured linoleum kitchen flooring to look as bright and clean as possible. So, disregarding the fact that all the windows and doors in the house were shut, I mixed a concoction of ammonia and bleach, got down on my hands and knees, and scrubbed away.

Within a matter of moments, my eyes, nose, throat and lungs became irritated, and I felt rather short of breath. Slightly worried, I called my daughter, who told me to open all the windows immediately because that combination of cleaning products had likely released toxic chlorine gas, which could be extremely dangerous.

Taking her advice, I opened the windows but continued cleaning the floors until they were gleaming. There was no way I was going to leave the job half-finished; that would be less than perfect.

As time passed, I realized I was caught between a rock and a hard place — no unnecessary anxiety or exhausting housecleaning, but also a lovely home with no visitors.

It had to be fate the day my daughter stopped by and said, "What am I missing?"

I'd just finished up a week of vigorous spring cleaning that included washing all the windows, both inside and out, shampooing the carpet, scrubbing the kitchen floor, polishing the furniture and appliances, and making certain all the counters were cleared of unnecessary items. To me, the house sparkled with springtime cleanliness.

When I realized my daughter didn't notice anything out of the ordinary, I began to wonder if others likewise didn't pay much attention to how spotless my house appeared after I'd worked so hard to prepare for their visits.

I thought about the times I'd visited friends. Although we always had a good time, not once could I recall how clean or messy their homes looked. We were more interested in talking and laughing — actually enjoying ourselves.

Eventually, with the encouragement of others, I began to feel more comfortable that it wasn't my house my friends were coming to see; it was my family and me.

I took a big step and started inviting friends to stop by. Surprisingly, I looked forward to their visits. Of course, I tidied things up a bit when company was expected, but I definitely did not exhaust myself by trying to surpass what was already perfect.

What a blessing it was to finally accept that we had a lovely, welcoming home where everyone could have a good time — and nobody appreciated that more than me.

— Connie Kaseweter Pullen —

# 45

# Worth a Try

*Once we believe in ourselves, we can risk curiosity,*
*wonder, spontaneous delight, or any experience*
*that reveals the human spirit.*
*~E.E. Cummings*

Each morning, I faced the tyranny of the blank page. Everything was in place — business cards, a new computer, and dreams of a runaway bestseller. Unfortunately, my underdeveloped writing muscles refused to cooperate.

A fellow writer said, "You need to shake up your life."

Creating an oasis of calm had been one of my retirement goals — a reward, or so I believed, for surviving three decades of teaching adolescents. I enjoyed my luncheon dates, yoga sessions, and uninterrupted blocks of reading time. Did I really want to shake up my life? I was stuck, though. So maybe it was worth a try.

Friends offered several suggestions, including signing up for kickboxing, running a marathon, and joining a local theater group. While considering the kickboxing option, I noticed an invitation from Royal City Toastmasters in the local newspaper. I sent a quick e-mail informing the contact person that I would be attending their next meeting.

Several times, I contemplated canceling but talked myself out of it. A bit apprehensive before arriving, I relaxed when I saw twelve people in the boardroom, most of them women. We chatted for a few minutes, and then a gentleman called the meeting to order.

I watched as two members rose to share the word and joke of the day. A third member introduced the Table Topics section of the meeting. I gathered from her brief description that impromptu speaking was involved. And then the woman turned in my direction and smiled. "Joanne, would you like to participate?"

Taken aback, I could only nod as I stood, awaiting the prompt. My heart pounded. I couldn't recall a single circumstance where I had to speak off-the-cuff. I forced myself to focus on the Table Topics presenter. Thankfully, she delivered a general prompt, alluding to the days of Indian summer we were experiencing in Ontario.

I took a deep breath and shared an anecdote about my first Indian summer in retirement. Glancing around the room, I noticed many encouraging nods and smiles. Feeling more confident, I added details about a recent trip to San Francisco. At one point, everyone started clapping.

Was I that good? That articulate? I could recall only one example of students clapping during my classes: I had canceled a test.

When I sat, the woman next to me whispered, "You went beyond two minutes. That's why everyone clapped."

I could feel myself reddening as the other members chuckled.

The following week, I returned for a second visit and joined the club. As I paid the fee, I made it clear that my attendance would be sporadic. I wouldn't be hopping on the leadership track or working toward any designations.

During that first month, I accepted only minor roles. I steered clear of committing to anything that would require too much preparation. At the beginning of the second month, one of the members gently nudged me to present my Ice Breaker speech. Reluctantly, I agreed. My speech was scheduled for two weeks later.

I looked over the first lesson in the manual, focusing on the Ice Breaker. Its aims were clear and straightforward. It provided an opportunity for the new member to introduce herself to the group. It also established a baseline of the member's current strengths and weaknesses. I could speak about any aspect of my life: job, hobbies, interests, or family. And I could use a cheat sheet!

On the day of my Ice Breaker speech, I felt confident about presenting.

All that changed as soon as I entered the boardroom. Over three dozen people were in attendance, many of them middle-aged men sharing golf stories. My mentor approached and whispered, "Our president invited another club to visit."

I panicked, worried about my choice of topic, "Seasons of My Life." While most of it centered on my teaching years, I also included my cancer journey. Would that be too personal to share with male golfers?

Thankfully, my worries were short-lived.

As I spoke, I glanced around the room and noticed everyone listening attentively and nodding in approval. I received many compliments during the break, and afterward I read the written evaluations several times.

"I really liked how you organized your speech around the theme of seasons. You looked very confident, and I enjoyed learning more about you."

"Very brave to share your life experience. You spoke very well and clearly."

"Your personal story is touching."

More importantly, I enjoyed the adrenaline rush — something I had missed since leaving the teaching profession.

In the months that followed, I pestered the Education Vice President for more speech opportunities. I also joined a second Toastmasters club. I was now attending six meetings a month and on my way to completing the ten speeches in the Competent Communication Manual.

At home, a writing practice slowly emerged as I wrote more confidently and prolifically. I was delighted to see my articles and book reviews appear in newspapers, magazines, and online publications. Buoyed by this success, I penned a novel. Five more novels followed and, after many queries, six publishing contracts.

On the Toastmasters front, I achieved the Competent Communicator, Competent Leader, Bronze, and Silver designations. I won and placed in five speech contests and held three executive positions.

Shaking things up had been amazingly transformative!

— Joanne Guidoccio —

# 46

# Make Cookies

*If you can't change the world with chocolate chip
cookies, how can you change the world?*
~Pat Murphy

"This is Lizzie. She's going to start working here," John said, introducing me to the foster-care teen in front of us. Looking me over briefly, she quirked an eyebrow. "Just try not to cry," she said.

It wasn't exactly the welcome one expects on their first day on the job. But it wasn't bad advice considering that I was completely out of my element.

Applying for a job at an emergency children's shelter where I'd primarily be working with at-risk teens had surprised everyone, including myself. Up until now, I'd had what I considered relatively "safe" jobs: a nanny, an assistant preschool teacher at a private school and, most recently, a receptionist at a dance studio.

But when a friend invited me to volunteer at a local children's shelter, I spent days afterward thinking about the experience. And when I found myself sitting in the lobby of a daycare with an application in my hands, I watched as a father came to pick up his little girl, kneeling down so that she could throw her tiny arms around his neck. And just like that, another image came to mind: that of a little girl at the shelter with the cutest freckles across her nose, too afraid to come near me.

It was as though God Himself sat next to me, and I heard the question ring within my heart: *Lizzie, all your life you've taken care of* children. What makes these children in front of you any different from those at the shelter, other than those at the shelter have no one? What's keeping you from applying other than fear?

I left my application on the chair and walked out the door.

Now here I was, my first day on the job, and my first greeting was: "Just try not to cry."

That boded well.

As sure as I'd been about taking the job, exchanging cuddly newborns and tiny ballerinas for "troubled" teenagers was a drastic change. By the end of the first week, I was already convinced I'd made a terrible mistake.

Knowing I'd be working with young victims of abuse and trauma, I'd expected challenges. But nothing could have truly prepared me for the realities of what that actually meant as teenagers cussed me out to my face, children destroyed rooms, and every other day seemed to find me trying to break up a physical altercation.

The real test came one night when my supervisor informed me that I would be conducting my first intake alone, meaning I would receive children into the shelter by filling out their paperwork and helping them get settled.

That alone made me nervous, but what she said next was hard to fathom.

"They're siblings, eleven and fourteen, and their mother was murdered in front of them yesterday by a family member. We've actually never had a case where a death was this recent."

I wondered how I, a total stranger — and a very inexperienced one at that — could possibly comfort them after such a horrific tragedy.

Seeing the siblings, hearing their story of how their own mother had been ripped from them in such a violent and senseless way, watching them go to their rooms that night still in shock… I sobbed that night in prayer, asking God, *Oh, Lord, I want to help! But what can I possibly do? I just don't think I'm cut out for this.*

His answer was surprisingly simple: *Make chocolate-chip cookies with them.*

*What, God?* I asked.

*Make chocolate-chip cookies with them. It's something they used to do with their mom.*

It wasn't exactly an earth-shattering answer, but it was such an unusual thought that I figured it must be the Lord and went to sleep.

A couple of weeks later, speaking to the room at large as kids lounged on the living-room couch, I remembered what the Lord had said. I asked, "Would anyone like to make chocolate-chip cookies?"

Out of the entire room, one youth sat straight up — one of the siblings who'd lost his mom.

"I do!" he exclaimed. "I used to do that with my mom."

Together, we preheated the oven and dropped dough onto the sheets, perfectly spacing each cookie as he shared memories of his mom.

"These are for her," I told him as we pulled them out of the oven. Swallowing hard, he nodded, but for the first time I saw a small smile emerge as he proudly handed out his mom's cookies to the other kids in the shelter.

It was just a small moment of comfort in a sea of grief, but from then on I knew two things: 1) It didn't matter if I was qualified or not. And 2) even when I felt as though I had nothing to offer, I could offer love.

I spent almost five years at that shelter, and today I am a passionate advocate and educator for both youth in the foster-care system and young victims of abuse and trauma. The sheltered, small-town girl I once was became a leader with a voice, and now I encourage others. All it takes is a little bit of courage and compassion to make a difference.

And all because God asked me one day to be brave enough to do something I'd always done, just in a new way: to take care of children and make cookies.

— Elizabeth Veldboom —

# 47

# Substituting Courage

*If you want to achieve a high goal, you're going*
*to have to take some chances.*
*~Alberto Salazar*

After decades of self-doubt, I told myself to take a chance and risk failure, even public humiliation. Following a divorce from my son's dad, I dabbled in community-college courses, always avoiding classes that might reveal what I believed were learning challenges. My biggest fear was Statistics. I had convinced myself very early in life that I was unable to conquer math. But I needed a four-year degree, at the least, if I was going to be able to support myself and my son.

Thus began the daunting task of facing the math monster. I realized the best place to begin was at the beginning: Basic Math Review, followed by Algebra I and II. My teacher, Mr. Nichols, made me believe I could conquer this hurdle, and I did. Straight A's. Statistics did challenge me, but I still pulled off a B. Never in my life had I ever been so proud of a B.

Following the completion of required, transferrable college units, I applied to a nearby state college. Soon, I began the pursuit of my degree in Organizational Communication, graduating at the age of forty-one with a 3.8 GPA. What I didn't expect was tough competition with a younger generation for positions in my field.

Months turned into years, and still none of the job interviews yielded anything except rejection letters. I was discouraged and doubted

I would ever find a position. It became apparent to me that I had to reconsider my career aspirations.

At the time, there was a shortage of teachers. For someone who had always doubted her ability to learn, I wondered how I could possibly consider this career path. I decided to first try it out by becoming a substitute teacher. I soon realized I could do this, at least as a substitute. I took the test required, barely passing the math portion. I was in.

I returned to college with the goal of obtaining my multiple-subject credential. Between college courses, I substitute taught in my city's school district. I quickly learned which ages I enjoyed and those I didn't. Middle-school age students scared me. Still do.

Toward the end of the credentialing program, I applied for a teaching position in the same district where I had substitute taught, but I was not called in for a district panel interview. Apparently, there was a glut of applicants. My self-doubt returned, but each day I earnestly fought against it.

On the last evening of one of our credentialing classes, we had a guest speaker: a school principal from my city's school district. He was there to present on how to interview for a teaching position. I earnestly took notes. At the completion of his presentation, he asked for a volunteer to participate in a mock interview. As afraid as I was, I realized this was my chance to meet a principal, someone who could potentially be my boss. So, I raised my hand, hoping no one could tell how terrified I felt.

Following the interview exercise, Mr. Renwanz commended me for my responses, boosting my confidence. I wondered if I would ever see him again, maybe even substitute teach at his school.

After completing my courses, I resumed substitute teaching in my city's district, which happened to have a year-round schedule.

In mid-June, I got a five-day assignment for a Resource Class at a school where I had never worked. The aide in the class and I were excited to see each other again. She had transferred from another school where we had done a two-week assignment together a year earlier. Little did I know that she had mentioned me to the administrator at that school, recommending me for a fourth-grade opening.

One day during my week there, I went to the teachers' lounge to eat my lunch, but they were having a farewell luncheon for their beloved PE teacher who was transferring to a different school. There, in the buffet line, stood Mr. Renwanz, the principal with whom I had done the mock interview the month before. I wondered if he would remember me. I decided to find out.

With my heart pounding, I approached him. As we began to talk, he let me know he remembered me and even commended me for how well I had done. He asked me where I would be teaching when the new school year began in a few weeks. I informed him that I had no teaching assignment yet. I had no idea he was interested in hiring me for his school. Later that afternoon, the school's vice-principal came into the Resource Room and asked me if I would be interested in interviewing for a fourth-grade position. Not only did I interview, but I got the position and began my teaching career two weeks later, at the age of forty-six.

Over the years, I had many students who reminded me of myself, filled with self-doubt. I realized I was the perfect fit for them. I could encourage them because of what my life's history had taught me. My past insecurities became one of my greatest strengths as a teacher.

After carrying decades of insecurities with me, I had overcome them and earned a degree and a job where I could make a difference. I taught for fifteen years, retiring from the school where I began. Although I had several school principals, Mr. Renwanz was my favorite, because he was a great leader but also because he's part of my story of stepping outside my comfort zone.

— Karen Anderson —

# 48

# Need a Date for My Mom

*Dating should be less about matching outward*
*circumstances than meeting your inner necessity.*
*~Mark Amend*

"**N**eed a Date for My Mom." That was the title under the picture of a beautiful, blond, blue-eyed lady, a daughter looking out for her mom. I was going through a divorce. On a whim, I answered the online dating ad.

I am from a very traditional Chinese family, with two brothers and no sisters. My ex-wife was Chinese, chosen by my mom. When we parted ways, I expected to find another Chinese mate. Three days after answering the ad, I got an e-mail with contact data for Dana Lynne.

We went to the zoo in Washington, DC that weekend. I was anxious because she was the first non-Chinese woman I had dated, and I remembered my mother's admonition, "You bring home a foreign girl, I will disown you!" But man does not live by rice and water alone, and Mom was in New York while I was in Washington.

Everything went well on the first date, and we were together for the next thirteen years. Having previous marriages was a plus; we learned from our experiences to compromise and accommodate each other's feelings. We shared a lot of mutual interests. Dana and I both worked with the U.S. government. We were scuba divers and seafood gourmands. It became a game for us to outdo each other with kindness and care.

The only trouble that we had came from my parents. Mom and

Dad did not approve of having a "foreign devil" for a daughter-in-law. They did not disown me but they did refuse to come to our wedding. Mom wanted to arrange another "nice Chinese girl" for me, but I told her, "You picked the last one; this time, it is my turn." In the end, my daughter Kimberly came and gave me away and was the witness at our wedding.

In time, I was able to bring Dana to family gatherings and meet my parents. Their frosty relationship with Dana thawed quickly. Dana always treated Mom and Dad with respect, which earned many points in her favor. The tipping point came when I was having an argument with Dad, and Dana interjected with a Chinese slang, "Ni go pi." Dad's jaw dropped, and then he laughed until tears ran down his cheeks. From then on, Dana became Dad's favorite daughter-in-law. "Ni go pi" in Chinese translates to "bullshit."

Then, while bidding goodbye at the end of our visit, Dad told Dana, "Next time, you don't have to bring him with you."

Everybody in my family loved Dana, especially the younger generation. Prior to my marriage to Dana, the no-dating-with-the-non-Chinese rule applied to my children, nephews, and nieces. Well, I broke the ice with Dana. So far, three out of four marriages of the younger generation have been with non-Chinese spouses, and there is one more to go.

Dad did not do things in half-measures. He is an avid gambler and especially enjoyed going to Atlantic City casinos with Dana. It was a sight to see a short, old Chinese man, under five feet tall, limping slowly on a cane with a beautiful, blond, green-eyed young woman on his arm.

During our thirteen years together, we did not have a single fight; we were soul mates. One October morning, Dana Lynne passed away due to an aneurysm. For three months, I was a zombie. My parents, my brother Tom, and my daughter Kimberly took turns caring for me. To this day, I have little memory of those three lost months. That was eleven years ago.

Dad passed away three years ago, and in his final days, he still recalled fondly his foreign daughter-in-law. Last month, Mom was over for a visit. She is suffering from Alzheimer's, yet she still talked about her non-Chinese daughter-in-law.

I maintained regular contact with Jennie, Dana Lynne's daughter. Every time we met, I made it a point to thank her for bringing me out of my comfort zone and giving me a chance at love and happiness. She thanked me for doing the same for her mom.

—Long Tang—

# For My Daughter

*We cannot become what we want*
*to be by remaining what we are.*
*~Max De Pree*

It was a lonely, sometimes scary childhood. We were poor. My mother was not well. I was too quiet to make many friends.

My stories were all I had. I wrote all the time, indulging in stories I wished I lived. My writing was my escape and therapy. Sometimes, my mother would read a story and smile. But when she got angry with me one day, she took all my writings and threw them in the trash, calling them garbage. After that, my writing was just for my eyes.

I put myself through college, got married, and had my daughter. I felt a little safer and was more social, but writing was always there. If someone asked what I liked to do for fun, sometimes I would mention that I liked to write. But if their questions persisted, I shied away. The thought of letting anyone read my work was overwhelming. It did not fit into my safe world.

At times, it was frustrating. I was consumed by the other worlds I created, but I could not describe them to anyone without more questions being thrown at me. I had created a life outside that turbulent childhood, and I wanted to protect it.

My beautiful family helped in healing the childhood wounds. Parenting my child with the consistency and love I had been without was everything to me. And as my daughter became older, she showed immense talent in art. Her paintings drew praise and won awards. My husband and I were in awe of her creations, and I encouraged her to keep up with it. After all, how could you be given a talent and not put it to use?

She started college and began to express uncertainty about majoring in art. What if she was not good enough? What if she failed? It was heart-wrenching to witness my daughter's doubt. I wanted her work to shine, to be displayed in front of crowds. But she needed to take that step out of her comfort zone to make that happen.

Then, it hit me. How could I expect my daughter to pursue her dream when she had watched me shy away from mine? I was forty years old and had never taken a chance. It was too scary to think of the rejection or, worse yet, to expose people to my work, only to have them ridicule it.

But, for my daughter, I had to do this. The safe world I had constructed to escape and heal from a traumatic childhood was about to be destroyed.

That first short story received two rejections before it got accepted. I was thrilled. I remember sitting at the dining room table staring at that e-mail.

By the third acceptance, I recognized that this might not be just a fluke. And I promised myself that after twelve accepted short stories, I would send my book to publishers.

When I announced my fifteenth acceptance at work, my boss leaned against the wall and said, "So, that is more than twelve. When are you going to do it? Send out that manuscript!"

I had to step even further out of that comfort zone, but I knew my beautiful daughter was watching. She was learning. She was witnessing her mother take that leap and believe in herself. How could playing it safe ever compare?

And I learned something in this process. She was not watching for my success. She was watching the risks I took. She was taking note of how I handled failure. While I did sell the short stories and the book, there were many rejections in-between. My daughter learned that rejection did not tear me down. It did not stop me.

Today, I am the author of eight novels and over 200 short stories. And, in a couple of days, my daughter will be graduating college with her art degree. Last month, she had her first art exhibit, filled with charcoal drawings, photographs, and paintings that depict a traumatic experience in her own life. And she will be attending grad school to continue this story.

And it's all because she watched her mother take a risk and pursue her passion.

— Trisha Ridinger McKee —

# No Motorcycles; No Cats

*Never apologize for having high standards. People who
really want to be in your life will rise up to meet them.*
~Author Unknown

When I was smugly married, I said I would never do it, no matter what my future held. Too risky.

Flash forward to me squinting at my laptop as I struggled to compose an online dating profile that would sound confident yet humble.

John's prolonged illness and death had left me shattered and exhausted. I vowed to remain single for the rest of my life. Just walking to the mailbox felt like slogging through quicksand. I didn't want to deal with anything beyond the bare minimum. Besides, no man could measure up to my husband of twenty years.

Eventually, I stumbled into my sixtieth decade feeling scarred yet on a path of healing. John had told me many times that he didn't want me to remain alone. That sentiment began to pierce my consciousness, and I admitted to myself that I missed coupledom.

My semi-retired single life included a part-time job, good friends, and several hobbies that brought me joy. But it just didn't feel like enough. I wanted someone to snuggle on the couch with and to share day-to-day stuff with, like, "Guess what I saw today? Fuzzy ducklings crossing the road behind their mama!"

As a member of the AARP set, it seemed unlikely that I would meet someone "organically"—a recently coined dating adverb that was beginning to get on my last nerve.

So, I found myself staring at the screen, conjuring up a list of my superpowers. Images of past job interviews floated through my brain. After years of feeling cherished, I would be evaluated by strangers. I felt in turn elated and resentful. Was I crazy to do this? Perhaps.

After assembling my virtual self, I proceeded to drill down and specify what I was looking for in a partner. Next, I made a list of dealbreakers for my eyes only and stuck the hot-pink Post-it to my computer:

*Motorcycles*
*Cigarettes*
*Geographically undesirable*
*Separated, not divorced*
*Baseball caps*
*Bathroom mirror selfies*

And those were just the first six entries.

For a while, the online dating game was exciting. Each morning, I'd boot up my laptop to see who had messaged me. I weeded out anyone who said only, "Hey" or "What's up?" They were not exactly age-appropriate greetings in my book.

A few weeks after signing up, I ventured out on my first date. He was a smart, handsome, age-appropriate engineer. So far, so good. But as he droned on about his career designing nuclear subs, I fiddled with my wine glass and noted a distinct lack of sparks. He paused long enough to order himself an appetizer, neglecting to ask whether I wanted anything to eat. That clinched it. My search for a true gentleman was on.

Two days later, someone hacked into my account and posed as me, sending messages to a number of potential suitors, demanding their phone numbers. Talk about embarrassing. Worst of all for this English major, the missives were laden with hideous grammar and punctuation. I wrote an apologetic it-wasn't-really-me note to each of the recipients.

After that calamity, I lost momentum. Time to take a break. But as my index finger hovered over the "hide my profile" button, a message popped up. *Maybe one more peek before I put this whole project on pause,* I thought. I clicked to view the sender's profile.

Hmmmm.... This fellow was awfully cute. And he had been widowed for two years. He might empathize with the turmoil of losing a loved one. Further piquing my interest was the fact that he listed his occupation as a semi-retired photographer. Since I'm a writer, I guessed we could make a creative match, or at least form a friendship. I scrolled down to peruse more photos.

That's when I saw the motorcycle.

There was Greg astride a red and black Yamaha. "No, no, no!" my inner voice screamed. But something kept me gazing at his page, bemused. One of the pics showed him peering through the lens of a camera, with half his face hidden. I glimpsed animation, creativity, and a zest for life.

Muttering that I'd surely regret this, I responded to his message. This quickly led to some friendly correspondence. Greg suggested we talk on the phone the next day. "Let's be bold," his message read, bringing a smile to my face. What a turnaround from the men who messaged relentlessly but never suggested a phone call or meeting. I envisioned them pulling up five profiles at once, briskly copying and pasting "personalized" messages.

That first phone conversation felt strange yet good. Greg suggested we meet the next day at a nearby coffee shop. "This will never work," I assured myself. I don't even drink coffee. My contrary heart hoped that I'd take an intense dislike to him and never worry about motorcycles again.

When I walked into the coffee shop, I spotted him immediately. He exuded the same sparkle I'd seen in his photos. He presented me with a single pink carnation. I ordered a juice and so did he. *Uh-oh, a gentleman.* My resolve to dislike him started to melt.

As we chatted, he asked me about my two cats with a barely perceivable wince. I had posted a prominent photo of my kitties on my profile page, leery of attracting an anti-feline man. I channeled nonchalant as I inquired about his motorcycle and watched his face light up even more. A definite spark seemed to be ricocheting back and forth across the table.

He told me later he'd said "absolutely no" to cats. I admitted that I had said "absolutely no" to motorcycles. Yet, as one date led to another and then another, we said yes to so many other things. Yes to laughter, yes to adventure, and yes to love.

"You're turning me into a cat lover!" Greg often accuses with that mischievous grin. I just look at him and laugh as Smokey nestles in his lap and Posey sits regally at his feet, gazing at him worshipfully.

I can't honestly say that he's turned me into a motorcycle lover. But I have ridden on the back a few times, feeling the rush of freedom sprinkled with danger. I admit it is rather exhilarating to lean into the curves of a country road with my arms securely wrapped around Greg's waist.

Any man who listens raptly to my duckling stories and brings me flowers can have all the motorcycles he wants.

— Kim Johnson McGuire —

# A Chance to Be Brave

*The brave man is not he who does not feel afraid,*
*but he who conquers that fear.*
*~Oliver Wendell Holmes*

If I could do it again
I would be brave

I would trust
I am here for a reason
and honour
the path that I'm on

I would cherish
the people I meet along the way
and recognise
our time together as precious

I would bask
in the wonder of everyday miracles
and stay open
to unfolding possibilities

I would champion
those whose voices have been silenced
and acknowledge
those too often dismissed

I would stand
in the discomfort of my becoming
and defend my awkwardness
as part of my charm

I would rest when weary
knowing I had tried my best
and rise with a full heart
to embrace each new day

For I would see each new day
as an opportunity

I would see each new day
as a chance to be brave

—— Florence Niven ——

Chapter
**6**

# Embrace Change

52

# Full Circle

*It is the long history of humankind (and animal
kind, too) that those who learned to collaborate
and improvise most effectively have prevailed.*
~Charles Darwin

I was a salesman for a steel warehouse for over ten years. Market
fluctuations and foreign steel dumping made it hard to sell, and
my income from commissions went way down. My money problems and mental stress contributed to the failure of my marriage.

I had just moved out of my house and into a cheap rental when
I got the word that my company would be closing soon. I was out
of my job the following month. The divorce was in process but still
several months away. I started a mad scramble to find another steel
sales job through my business connections. A great weight came off
my shoulders when I was offered a better-paying sales job. I could
even work out of my apartment.

I had been with the new employer for two months when I landed
a big account. The first order was about $30,000, and my commission
would be over $4,000. I felt much better about the future, even though
the divorce was still hanging over my head. The new job seemed like
a blessing.

I got a call from my new boss to come to the main office and
pick up my commission check. I'd been with the company only four
months, but I could see good things ahead. When I arrived at the
office, the sales manager praised me for my success. The owner was

also there and shook my hand. After handing me the check, he started talking about cheap steel imports and high interest rates. This was sounding all too familiar. It floored me when he said the company had to make cuts. He wasn't even sure if his company would survive. I was suddenly out of a job again.

Within six months, I had lost two jobs. It was a wake-up call. I had to rethink my life choices. My thoughts ran from "You're in the wrong business" to "Selling is not your strong suit."

I decided I'd have to leave the steel industry and also had doubts about staying in sales.

I was depressed and didn't know what type of work I wanted to look for. I decided to take time to visit an old friend from high school, hoping to raise my spirits before I started my search.

Joe and I had grown up in the same neighborhood. As we talked, I mentioned my job situation. He said the strangest thing to me. "You were pretty good at fixing and building things when we were kids. Have you thought about fixing appliances?"

"Appliances? Wow, no. I don't know. I've been in sales for over ten years. I don't think so."

"Well, if you change your mind, I know a guy who needs a summer helper. He'll teach you and pay you while you learn."

The thought of learning a new trade scared me but I thought about what Joe had said. I remembered taking aptitude tests in school, and my highest aptitude was in engineering and mechanics. I scored pretty low in sales aptitude. How did I even get into sales in the first place?

I called Joe the next day. He set up a meeting with the repair guy. It was very informal. Paul had a full red beard, wore grease-stained pants, and drove a beat-up van with no company name on the side. I had misgivings, but I needed a job. I decided to try it for a week.

In that week, I made several discoveries. Paul was much smarter than he looked. He knew his stuff and was quite personable. He also had a one-man business that made a lot of money. The biggest discovery was that I had nearly total recall on every new repair he showed me. Within two weeks, he was sending me out on repair jobs alone.

Within a month, I knew what the most common repairs were and started carrying extra parts in my trunk. It saved me the time of making a trip back to the office to pick them up. Time lost was money lost.

I made good money the rest of that summer and fall, but I didn't know that the repair business was slow in the winter. I was surprised when Paul let me go in late fall. I sat idle through a lean winter. I decided not to go back to work with Paul because his territory was too far from my home. That spring, I found another independent repair company with an office nearby. I worked in the appliance-repair business for about ten years but then I decided I needed a job that didn't have a winter slowdown.

That's when I found my dream job, which utilized every skill I'd learned over twenty-five years of previous employment, including my steel knowledge. I became a supplier's rep to steel mills. It wasn't exactly a sales job but required sales skills. I was at the steel mill every day. My company supplied firebrick and high-temperature ceramics used in steelmaking. I kept track of materials used and how they performed while working with steel-mill managers and engineers. The thing that solidified my new position was the ability to repair specialty machines that fed chemicals into the steel furnace. I attended a three-day crash course on how the machines worked and was able to repair anything that went wrong with them from then on. That job lasted fifteen years until the steel mill went out of business.

Still another business closure shook my world, but this time it didn't matter. I'd managed to build up a substantial retirement fund over those fifteen years. I took Social Security early and I retired.

— John Marcum —

# 53

# Solo

*A woman who knows what she brings
to the table is not afraid to eat alone.*
*~Author Unknown*

I wasn't going skydiving, bungee jumping or climbing Mount Everest. What I needed to do during the biggest transition of my life was bigger than all those adventures put together: I was going camping.

I'm an outdoorsy kind of girl, so camping wasn't new to me, but what was new to me was camping *alone*.

My thirty-year marriage was over, so I was processing countless thoughts, feelings and emotions. I was exploring the world on my own terms. I owned all decisions, personal strengths and independence.

I needed to mark the one-year anniversary of the separation and all I had overcome by doing something I loved but within my financial means. I love the outdoors and had camped many times during my younger years. We had camped a bit when my two sons were younger, and the camping bug never left me.

But camping alone? Was I as tough as I thought? What would other campers think of me? What if I got scared? What if my tent broke? Was I really cut out for this? What if...? What if...?

More and more women were camping alone, and I had always been envious of those who did. Doing anything like that would have been out of the question for me during my marriage, so I had to be content with admiring those brave and free women from afar.

Now was my time. I had to try.

My temperamental, fifty-year-old back was not meant for air mattresses anymore, and my hatchback was too small to sleep in. I borrowed a tent from a friend and came up with the crazy idea to sleep on my couch cushions. I bought a burner and sleeping bag. With thrift-store finds and generous support from others, I was ready to go.

I made reservations for two nights and then promptly made a few deals with myself. If I stayed for the day and left before nightfall, that would be okay. If I stayed for one night and left the next morning, that would be okay, too. And if I stayed the two full nights, then it would be a bonus.

The big day came, and I headed out. Excitement, independence and freedom urged me on, yet uncertainty and self-doubt had me white-knuckle the one-hour drive to the Bamberton Provincial Park campground in Mill Bay, B.C. — far but not too far away.

As I rolled into the campground, I let out the breath I had been holding. I had gotten this far. I had to keep going.

I found my site, set up my tent with my couch cushions and sleeping bag inside, and even hung a tarp all by myself. I was ready!

As I sat under the pines drinking coffee I had brewed over my single burner, I again remembered the compassionate deals I had made with myself. If I lasted only a day or only one night, that would be okay....

But, right then, I was sure I could do at least one night.

That first day, I hiked, read, and journalled. I had ramen noodles cooked over my burner. Evening came, and lanterns lit up the quickly darkening campsite. No fires were allowed given the dry season, but that was fine by me. I wasn't exactly a lumberjack, skilled at chopping wood.

I read by the light of my little lantern as moths danced around the glow. I was content and warm, happy to be by myself. But I still had to get through the first night — if I did at all, doubt reminded me.

As evening became night, I secured my food and valuables in my car. Don't keep food in your tent! I brushed my teeth in the bushes and then trekked to the outhouse. I was watchful for glowing eyes peering through the dark, but I wasn't afraid. I zipped myself into my tent and sleeping bag. My excitement and pride of self-reliance kept me warm. The cushions were comfy.

Lanterns flickered out, and the campground quieted. A breeze skittered leaves over the gravel. They scratched at the sides of my tent and landed on my tarp. Even though I knew they were leaves, my imagination threatened to get the better of me. It was *very* dark and *very* quiet.

Yet I wasn't afraid.

Despite my heightened awareness, exhaustion must have taken over because I was later startled awake by the snarling, growling and tumbling of creatures fighting at my site. I didn't move a muscle; I barely breathed. Gravel hit the side of my thin nylon tent. They were that close.

And these were not raccoons or dogs or squirrels.

I kept still. I didn't even dare to blink in the dark. I counted my heartbeats and breaths. I focused on staying calm and rational. The creatures eventually quieted and, with the snapping of twigs under their feet, moved on.

Lanterns from curious campers flicked on. I checked my phone: 3:00 A.M.

What were the creatures? Would they come back? Should I pack up and go home?

Before I could get ahead of myself, I realized how badly I had to "go."

Stillness and dark settled over the campsite once more, but I *really* had to go. My heart picked up speed once again as I slowly unzipped my tent. I peered out into the darkness; my eyes strained against the dark.

Nothing.

I was brave but not brave enough to trek to the outhouse at 3:00 A.M. I ducked near some bushes beside my car and then crept back to my tent. Could I go back to sleep?

Before I knew it, I woke again to morning sun and sounds of the campsite. I had gone back to sleep despite it all!

I made it through that first night and then, without a second thought, through the next night as well. I survived! And I had a great time just... being.

Survivors adapt and keep going—just like the critters outside my tent.

Waves of emotion and loneliness sometimes hit me during my stay, but the rush of accomplishment from the solo adventure strengthened me. Awareness of all that I had overcome coupled with the fuel of independence kept me going.

As I packed the tent and shook the pine needles from the tarp, I wished I had booked a third night. That thought surprised me. I had gone from making one-day/one-night deals with myself to wishing for more nights. As I drove home, I planned. Could I get in one more trip before winter?

When I first arrived two days before, I had packed doubt and fear with my camping gear. It was okay to have them, but unpacking them and letting them run wild wouldn't have done me any good.

As I pulled up to my apartment, eager for a hot shower, the biggest awareness hit me harder than the gravel against my tent that first night: I had never felt more fearless than I did in my tent those two nights. And I did it solo.

— Lisa McManus —

# 54

# Trading Stuff for Opportunity

*Anything that you possess that does not add to your life*
*or your happiness eventually becomes a burden.*
~John Robbins, The New Good Life

I sat on the closet floor, cross-legged on the cool tile, and touched every piece of clothing I owned. Every scrap of fabric I had accumulated over seven years of living in that space, over thirteen years of marriage and even my college days, was up for examination. It was a tedious job, to be sure, but necessary. My closet in California was a gaping space inside an even larger primary bathroom where cabinets held a collection of enough make-up, lotions, and potions to stock a high-end cosmetic store. But my closet in Ireland would be... Well, I didn't know. I was stepping into uncertainty by moving to a country I had never seen. I only knew that I would not be dragging a mountain of unworn clothing with me into that unknown.

I sat there for the better part of the day, my muscles stiffening as I attempted to sort clothing into three piles: keep, donate and toss. I am honest enough to admit that the sorting and purging did not go well at first. Nearly two hours into the process, my husband stepped into the room, hoping to help me carry out bags of donations. Instead, he saw a tall pile of "keep" items and blank space where the other stacks should have grown. He was smart enough to exit with merely a raised eyebrow.

Eventually, I made hard choices about things I felt attached to. I said goodbye to the red and orange floral dress I wore on our Hawaiian honeymoon. I tossed the T-shirt from when my high school's football team went to the playoffs. But it wasn't just sentimental items I needed to purge. The black cashmere sweater was impossibly soft and lovely to look at, but it simply didn't suit my style, so it went unworn. The gray, one-shouldered evening gown with silver sequins was possibly my favorite thing I had ever worn, but it no longer fit, so it could not stay. My collection of steep stilettos made no sense in my work-from-home life, and the many pairs of flip-flops would never get worn in Ireland.

Letting go was hard, and not just on an emotional scale. There was also math at play since every item represented money. I could see price tags attached to everything, sometimes figuratively and sometimes literally, since the telltale bits of paper still dangled from several articles. Had I gotten the value for what I spent? Would I end up paying more to replace things down the road? I could see the way those price tags equaled time. How long had I worked to earn the money for that cashmere sweater?

My closet clutter was a security blanket. Even though I never wore them and rarely even looked at them, those forgotten pieces of clothing kept my memories and investments safe. If I ever needed a zebra-print handbag or a pair of polka-dotted rain boots, I would have them.

As morning turned to afternoon, I stopped focusing on the past, the memories made, and the money spent, and I started looking toward the future. My husband's company was transferring him to an office in Ireland. Moving to a new country was an enormous life change, and I wanted to connect to the moment and embrace new opportunities. But I couldn't open my arms to change if I was clutching what had come before.

When the project was finally, and painfully, done, my suddenly smaller wardrobe filled just three suitcases. On the other side of the Atlantic, the contents of those bags fit neatly into my new closet. But I never missed anything I had given away (except, occasionally, that silver dress).

Accumulating so much stuff took time and money, and all those things anchored me mentally and physically. Yet, I found new freedom without the weight of so much physical stuff. Evenings in pubs, chatting to my neighbors, and cheering on local teams in sports I hadn't previously heard of connected me to a new community. Hikes to waterfalls and drives down bumpy country roads connected me to nature and new ways of life. Quickly tossing a few items into a backpack before a weekend away made me feel adventurous and carefree.

The truth is, I was terrified of making a big move or even a small change because I hesitated to sacrifice what I already had. But was what I had worth keeping if it wasn't serving what I really wanted from life? I could only connect to new experiences, people, and places when I tossed off the anchors that weighted me in place. And, oh, what a trade that was… the experiences of a lifetime for just a pile of old shoes.

— Michelle Baker Sanders —

# Stubborn Love

*To care for those who once cared for us
is one of the highest honors.*
~Tia Walker

"Bye, Mom!" As I drove away, I burst into tears. I felt my heart ripping apart, like a new mom who had just dropped off her newborn at daycare. I hated leaving her there at the retirement home, but what could I do? I had no idea how to take care of an old person. Besides, I needed a house. My mother had money, but it was tied up in stocks. I wanted to care for my mom, so I started planning.

First, I called my cousin Evonne, a retired nurse who loved the elderly. When I asked her if she wanted to help me care for my mom, she said, "When do I start?"

Next, we needed a place to live, someplace affordable. Within three days, I found a manufactured home in a park with three bedrooms and two baths, for only $60,000. Perfect, but I still wasn't sure about my mother's finances. It was time to call my brother, Bill, who guarded my mother's money like a mother bear guards her cubs. I was worried about asking him, but I wouldn't stop. I took a deep breath and called.

"No!" he bellowed. "You don't have any experience, and Mom doesn't have that much cash."

"Can't you take some out of her stocks?"

"I could, but Evonne can't do this. She has a bad back," he retorted.

"Bill! Evonne has worked with a bad back her whole life. I need her."

The conflict continued for several days. I felt like a bull elephant charging through the jungle. I wasn't going to give up. He brought up every possible problem. I answered all his questions. Finally, he came out and looked at the manufactured home. With a heavy sigh, he finally relented.

The house had no furniture, pots and pans, towels, or food. I went shopping at the Salvation Army and garage sales, something I had learned from my mom. My brother was pleased that it didn't cost that much.

Because of my mom's dementia, I needed her bedroom to look exactly like the one she was in. I painted it pale blue with a flowered ruffle over her window. Then, I hung up her favorite Monet painting. Finally, I strategically positioned her Shirley Temple dolls and teapots around her room.

Within two months of buying the house, my persistence paid off. My impossible dream became a reality. Mom moved in. Her bedroom looked so much like her other one that she didn't even know she had moved. When Evonne moved in, I helped her unpack. We figured out a schedule; our journey began.

Every morning, when Mom woke up, I would plop my little Pomeranian, Sassy, on her bed. Sassy would cuddle while my mom cooed, "You're a good little girl," over and over.

After that, Mom and I would go into the bathroom. I would clean her up, do her hair, apply pink lipstick and rouge, and finish with a spritz of White Shoulders perfume. The feminine fragrance filled the room, bringing back memories of younger years. I made sure my mom's clothes and jewelry matched. She would look at her reflection and smile, something I hadn't seen in a long time.

Later, Mom and I would go for a walk. I would push her wheelchair with our little Sassy curled on her lap. Those afternoon strolls were the highlight of her day. She said the same thing every day. "This fresh air feels so good." She had always been social and enjoyed talking to the neighbors out doing their yard work.

I loved preparing my mom's favorite foods. The smell of home-made soup or pot roast wafted through the house. I served meals on her beloved vintage dishes. She never failed to thank me. I thought about the thousands of meals she had prepared for me. Now, it was my turn to bless her.

In the evenings, Mom and I watched *Annie Get Your Gun* or *Singing in the Rain* over and over. Thanks to the dementia, my mom never got tired of watching Gene Kelly dancing in mud puddles or Betty Hutton sharpshooting while riding on a galloping steed. I loved it, too.

On Sunday mornings, Mom and I attended church. We sang songs like "Be Thou My Vision" and "How Great Thou Art." At the end of the service, we would take communion and recite the Lord's Prayer in unison, something she still remembered. Afterward, we met in the fellowship hall, enjoying hot coffee and home-baked cookies with friendly church folks.

After church, we watched the Seahawks and ate hot, buttered popcorn. Actually, Mom watched me while I watched the game, yelling and hooting. Sometimes, my children and grandchildren would stop by, making it a family affair.

By the end of the first year, my mom's ER visits increased due to multiple bladder infections. Another time, there was a frightening drop in blood pressure. One time, after a nasty fall, her doctor said, "Your mom needs to be evaluated for hospice."

"No! Not yet! You're wrong," I argued.

The next day, a hospice nurse came out and did a complete evaluation. "Your mom's time is getting close." I was blindsided. I thought hospice was for people on their death bed. I was wrong. Hospice turned out to be a blessing. No more trips to the hospital or pharmacy. If Mom had a health problem, the hospice nurse took care of it, and they brought her medications directly to us.

They gave me and my cousin an end-of-life booklet. It explained how the patient would sleep more and eat less, something we had already noticed. The booklet also said she would probably have an "unexpected burst of energy" just before dying.

A few months later, Mom and I were absorbed in a nail-biting football game. The Seahawks had the ball. It was third down with twenty-three yards to go. Out of the blue, my mom shouted, "You better hurry up and do something! This is your last chance!" I couldn't believe it, but there it was: the burst of energy. The next morning, Mom fell into a coma. In twenty-four hours, she was gone.

I reflected on our time together. When I first decided to care for my mom, I had no idea what to expect. I wasn't a nurse and had never done anything like this, but I was determined. My only goal was to give her a home where she would be happy.

I wanted to bless her, but I was the one who was blessed. Caring for my mom gave me such an inexplicable sense of peace and joy. It was the most gratifying sixteen months of my life.

—Barbara McCourtney—

# In the Long Run

*I don't run to add days to my life,*
*I run to add life to my days.*
*~Ronald Rook*

'd been a runner for thirty years. The marathon was my game, and as the years went by, the race became a test to maintain a self-imposed time limit, which I kept increasing: 4:15 in my forties, 4:30, and then 4:45 in my fifties. After my fifteenth marathon and a 4:49 that took everything I had, I realized my next race would be more than five hours.

After a hard inner debate, I decided my marathon days were over. The sense of loss was deep. Having an endurance event to train for and a goal to work toward and achieve had kept me energized and focused for nearly two decades. Now, it was over. I could run forever; I just couldn't run fast anymore.

Wait. Was I crazy to even think what I was starting to think? Could I trade speed for distance? Could I trade the marathon for an ultra-marathon? Could I run farther than 26.2 miles? I researched and found that the 50K — thirty-one miles — was the shortest common ultra-marathon distance. The thought of it scared me, and that's what convinced me to try. I registered for a 50K six months away. I had a new game; now, I had to figure out how to play it.

When facing a challenge, it helps to have positive people in your corner. My husband and kids — ever my cheer squad — were happy I had something big to chew on. Their belief in me fueled my belief in myself, and their support would fuel every step I took. But I knew that to pull off an ultra, I'd need both positive thoughts and purposeful preparation.

I knew the additional five miles required an approach, mindset, and training different from the marathon. I'd reached every marathon finish line totally spent, so I had to learn what it would take to run five miles farther. I devoured articles and videos on ultra training. I'd honed my marathon prep and execution over the years, and I'd enjoyed the process, science, and psychology behind the endeavor. Now, I was having just as much fun figuring out how to squeeze out those five extra miles. I moved from grieving my loss of the marathon to being excited about experimenting with this zany new thing. I went from defeated to empowered.

I got used to two weekly long-run days in a row—called a block—instead of the one weekly long run the marathon required. I learned what and when to eat and drink to fuel myself and stave off gastric distress. Fig Newtons, Cheez-Its, and chocolate milk joined Gatorade, water, and energy gel in the bag of tricks I carried or stashed in the bushes on my training routes. I bought extra running shoes and alternated them so I didn't wear out my race pair. No battery would last long enough to see me through an ultra, so I went audible cold turkey, replacing music with word games I played in my head. Speed was a thing of the past. Now, it was "just keep going."

I finished my first ultra about an hour before I'd expected to. I cried at the finish line (and then drank Coke to quiet my stomach). In the years since, I've done 33- and 35-milers and twice won my age group, which, admittedly, has very few competitors. But the medals and plaques on the basement wall make me smile as I pass them on my way to the washing machine. I'm in my mid-sixties now but I feel like I can do anything, and I just started training for my next 50K.

— Lori Hein —

# Swim Every Day
# in the Sea

*When we are no longer able to change a
situation — we are challenged to change ourselves.*
~Viktor E. Frankl

When my marriage crumbled, I couldn't stand losing my dream house, my beautiful furniture, and my life as a wife. Worst of all was missing half of my children's lives, since now my ex and I had joint custody. When they went with their father for a weekend, I wandered around the house weeping.

I finally started thinking about the me I used to be and the dreams that came before my marriage. That meant learning French. I wanted to learn French so I could read the letters of my favorite sculptor, Camille Claudel, in their original language. My husband had hated the vacation we'd taken in Paris, but I had been in my element.

When the children were going to my ex's for a whole month in the summer, I didn't know how I would survive without them. I knew I had to get far away or I'd end up howling on my ex's doorstep, begging to see my children during his parenting time.

So I found a language-immersion program and went to Villefranche-sur-Mer on the French Riviera. In the airport, I was so scared that I got a nosebleed. As I leaned back and tried not to bleed on my new, cream silk blouse, a woman approached me with an Evian bottle and poured cold water on my forehead. She said with a lovely French accent, "You must swim every day in the sea." I felt immediately and completely better. But, before I could thank her, she rushed away, and it was time to board my flight. I never figured out how she knew I'd be near the Mediterranean Sea.

I arrived in Villefranche-sur-Mer and walked to the beach from my villa. I sat on a big rock and felt the sun rise, and then I dragged my jet-lagged self back to my room and slept all day. I wanted to feel exotic and exciting, but I missed my children.

At the little bakery later that day, I stumbled around trying to ask for a baguette, spouting my bad French. The cashier rolled her eyes. A song called "Time to Say Goodbye" played as I was choosing vegetables at the market stand, and I burst into tears. Even though I was in a magical place, my heart hurt so much from missing my family and the me I used to be.

After class the first day, I walked to the beach. I wore my swimsuit underneath my sundress and carried a beach bag filled with sunscreen, a book, a towel, lip gloss, water, a snack, and strappy sandals. I wore a big sunhat and chic sunglasses. I put my toes in the water, leaped in and out of the sea, and then settled down with a book. The second day, I waded into the water and splashed around a while, staying close to shore to keep an eye on my bag and beach towel.

I got flustered and shy in class, and my French teacher patiently said, "*Pas de panique, pas de panique.*" No panic, no panic. I gave a long explanation of how a song was about stage fright, and the teacher laughed gently and told me that it was about a bullfight.

At first, I missed my children and felt like a scared, little housewife by the Mediterranean Sea. Bit by bit, I started feeling better. I noticed that on the part of the beach for "Les Naturistes," people were swimming utterly nude — instead of studying birds with binoculars like naturalists.

The words of the French woman who had helped me in the airport became my comfort and encouragement: "You must swim every day in the sea." And I did.

I befriended two classmates. When we visited Nice, I bought so many flowers for my villa that a tourist mistook me for a flower seller and tried to buy some from me. Another day, I got bold and went alone to Nice. I got turned around while sightseeing, and it got darker and darker. I asked a tall, scantily clad woman for directions. She wore very tall, thigh-high boots and a bra top with teeny, tiny shorts. My French had improved, and she understood my confusion but chastised me for being in the streets after dark.

"Go into that hotel, call a taxi and go home right now," she said sternly.

So, I did. I turned to thank her as I walked into the hotel, but she wasn't there. A few months later, I realized she'd been a lady of the evening, plying her trade.

When I went to get a baguette at the patisserie the next morning, the cashier smiled at me as she gave me my change. "Your French, it is getting much better," she said.

Everyone in class understood my presentation about the French sculptor Camille Claudel, based on her letters. My teacher told me that I had talent.

And, every day, I walked to the sea and went swimming after French class. I began to carry less and less. At first, I left the book behind, and then the sunscreen and the snacks. Soon, I realized that if I left my bag and beach towel at the villa, when I got to the beach, I could swim far out into the Mediterranean Sea without worrying about anything being taken from me.

By the end of the month, I would leave class, change into my sundress, swimsuit, and sandals, and rush to the beach. I'd tear off that dress, leap into the Mediterranean Sea, and swim like a seal until sunset. The last night before going back home, I ran to the beach after dark, stripped, and swam.

Yes, I learned French by the Mediterranean Sea — and so much more. I learned that all the things I had lost in my divorce — husband, house, furniture, identity as wife — had nothing to do with the very core and substance of me. I had to go all the way to France to realize that once I let go of all the things I carried, I could be truly free.

— Kiesa Kay —

# Hallelujah

*If you look confident you can pull off anything—*
*even if you have no clue what you're doing.*
~Jessica Alba

T he graduate student who ran my audition looked about fifteen years old. As an experienced but amateur choir singer, Junior didn't scare me. I wasn't intimidated by sight-singing from the hymnal or doing the vocal exercises. There is always anxiety when singing without people around me, but I accepted it as a necessary part of the audition.

I had to find a new choir because of a move. My criteria included performing challenging music, hence the audition, but not so demanding that my lack of training would hamper me. As I moved through this process, the fit felt right.

"Okay, you're a second soprano," Junior said, standing up from the keyboard.

"Wait, what? I've sung alto for years."

He didn't blink. "You've got the range of a second soprano."

While it's true I wanted to sing more high notes than alto allowed, I hadn't considered myself a soprano for a long time.

"But —"

"Try it. You'll like it."

I might have if the first piece wasn't "Messiah." This chorus performed it every year with the local symphony, and I'd just signed on to sing soprano. Even experienced sopranos drop down to alto because

"Messiah" is scary high.

What had I gotten myself into?

Maybe I made too much out of the whole thing. I'd started out as a soprano. At some point, I'd been assigned alto because I could handle the harmony, I was a quick learner, and the choir needed altos. After a break from singing, I rejoined choir at a time when I was insecure and felt more comfortable as an alto. It stuck.

Temperamentally speaking, altos are the choir's dependable work-horses, always on time and ready to support the other parts. Sopranos, on the other hand, are divas — flighty, talkative, and prone to making the choir wait on them.

"Just get some scarves," my daughter advised.

Being a soprano meant a lot of attention. And those super high notes? The "Hallelujah Chorus" alone gave me nightmares.

Week in and week out, I rehearsed soprano as if Junior had issued me a personal challenge, but I still felt like an imposter. Eventually I relaxed, finding an ease that surprised me. I was less vocally fatigued after two hours of singing soprano than singing alto. I was even accepted into the soprano section.

After weeks of rehearsals, I was on stage behind shiny horns and exquisite strings. All my doubts came back. I looked longingly at the altos at the other end, wanting to blend in with them as they huddled over last-minute tweaks.

I looked around at the sopranos. There was an excited gleam in many an eye, ready to take on each and every high note. This was their moment, and they owned it. And, by golly, I was one of them.

When I got to the "Hallelujah Chorus" (and maybe a few others as well), I went for it. I opened my mouth and told myself, "Just sing that sucker."

And I nailed it.

— Risa Brown —

# 59

# Discovering Home in a Small Space

*The most important work you and I will ever do
will be within the walls of our own homes.*
~Harold B. Lee

Five years ago, my husband and I started thinking about living in a forty-foot fifth wheel with plans to pay off our debts and save up to buy a house. We started following some YouTube channels of people who were already "Full-Time Living," as they called it. One Friday night, my husband found a listing for a fifth wheel that jumped out at him. Within a week, it was ours.

We had to downsize to fit our family of four into 400 square feet. I cleaned out our closets, garage, and forgotten corners of our bedrooms. I sold my KitchenAid mixer to a close friend. We got rid of dishes, books, clothes, and toys. We took load after load to thrift stores to donate. I carefully organized Little People, Magna-Tiles, and LEGOs into mini containers that would fit in our tiny shelf space. I found an idea for organizing board games like *Monopoly* and *Sorry* in long pencil boxes with labels, and I worked painstakingly to make everything fit.

The day we moved out of our rental and into the RV, I felt like we were jumping off a cliff. Did we know where we would land? Were we making a mistake? Our kids were five and eight years old, and giddy with excitement. We were closing a chapter of our lives to start this new adventure, but I never expected it to last long. We went grocery shopping and had to find a way to fit berries, milk, yogurt, ground beef, long stalks of celery, and a bag of potatoes in a tiny fridge with three little shelves and narrow door trays. I realized after placing the cereal boxes and RITZ crackers on the end of the counter that I would be left with just two feet of space to do any cooking or prep work. We also quickly learned that we could do about fourteen minutes on the hot-water tank, and then it took an hour for the hot water to come back.

Shortly after we moved into our RV, we realized that the furnace had a problem. It would rumble and rattle like a loud generator all night. A few months later, the air conditioner was leaking. When my husband took it out to repair it, he discovered some black mold inside the ceiling. I wondered what we had gotten ourselves into by buying this RV.

When a pipe was leaking under the shower, my husband had to take out a section of the wall in our bedroom. We had to move our bed to the floor of the front living room between our kids for a few weeks. Our son thought it was great that he could snuggle with us so easily in the middle of the night. When we could finally put our bed back in our room, I was grateful for a little bit of personal space again, even if it was tiny.

Recently, my husband and I had a weekend away without the kids. We had been saving and feeling hopeful that we were close to being able to buy a house. We decided to look at manufactured houses together on our way back home and immediately fell in love with a floor plan called the Mount Rainier. I loved the feeling of peace in my heart as we walked in awe through the master bedroom, the expansive bathroom with a sunken tub, and the walk-in closet that felt as big as our bedroom in the RV.

I stood in the little office with double doors and a built-in desk just off the living room, imagining the joy of having my very own space to write. We took in the kitchen with an island in the middle, gliding our hands over the smooth countertops and opening the fridge. I hovered in the mud room, thinking about how nice it would be to have a space for all the wet winter coats and boots. We wandered through two more bedrooms, talking about how amazing it would feel to have this space to spread out in.

While driving back home to pick up the kids, we fantasized together about buying land and ordering a home, as if we could do it tomorrow. However, over the past few years, the prices of real estate skyrocketed and competition was steep. Despite all our efforts, we were priced out of the market. When we looked at listings on Zillow, we got depressed and decided to watch a movie with the kids. We sat in the cramped living room of our RV, huddled close together for a family movie night.

Our kids have grown up in this tiny RV. We have many memories of watching movies together while munching on Red Vines and M&M's. The kids and I spent many weekdays around our tiny table as I was homeschooling them, reading about the fifty states or *Little House on the Prairie* books. I made a YouTube list of all my favorite hymns so my kids could learn the words.

It is still our dream to live in a house soon. Nevertheless, while this place may be tiny, our life together has not been small. I want to always remember, as someone told me once, "Family is what makes a home, not the house."

—JoAnne Michelle Bowles—

# Chapter
## 7

# Connect with Someone

# 60

# Christmas Renewed

*Forgiving isn't something you do for someone else.*
*It's something you do for yourself.*
*~Maria Edgeworth*

"Letting you know, Mom. We have had it with celebrating separate Christmases, and if you don't invite Dad for the day to your house, you won't see either of us or your grandkids."

I was taken aback at this ultimatum made by my adult daughter and son. There was a long silence on the phone. I had not seen my ex-husband for years, knew nothing of his current life, and didn't care.

"But, Lisa, I — "

"You've been playing victim now for how many years? Ten? Eleven? It's time you took the higher road. I know you can do it, Mom."

"You're probably right, but — "

"Think about it. Got to run. Love you."

I stood with the phone in my hand and the dialogue continuing in my head.

I couldn't invite Allen to my house for Christmas. I was still angry at him and vowed to never forgive. He was the man who didn't pay child support for years. The man who caused me to go to therapy. Him? Invite that man to this house for Christmas? She had to be kidding.

But she wasn't.

My daughter and I were good friends, and I'd come to at least listen to her advice. "Think about it," she had said, and so I did.

With that, memories swirled in my head. They were uncomfortable, almost forgotten memories, such as the times when I'd been humiliated in front of others, emotionally abused, and fled the room in tears of frustration. How could I possibly open myself up and chance it all happening again?

I mentioned it to Ken, my wonderful second husband, the next morning at breakfast. He had never met Allen but thought inviting him was a fine idea.

"Are you serious?"

"Of course, Cheryl. It obviously means a lot to your kids, and one more at our table would only make the day more celebratory. After all, what happened between the two of you was a long time ago. You're much stronger now, mature. You've come into your own. I'm here, and together we can get through anything, don't you think?"

"But I —"

"Think about it. Late for work. Talk to you when I get home."

Again, advised to think about it, I did.

Ken was right. I had come a long way since the divorce. I had a wonderful husband, good job, lovely house, well-used gym membership, good friends, and dedication to meaningful volunteer work.

Slowly, the prospect of inviting Allen became intriguing.

I had a choice to make. I could give into the fear and perhaps bypass Christmas altogether or face the holiday with the enthusiasm of Elf, Alcott's March sisters and my Uncle Raymond, who made sure that no neighbor ever put up one more outdoor Christmas light than he did.

*Okay, higher road, here I come!*

The decorating began. Menus were planned, and shopping lists were made. The house was cleaned and polished. Cookies, candies, nut breads and truffles prepared.

The scent of our pine tree, standing just inches below our tall ceiling, filled the house. Its branches gleamed with white and gold lights, outdoing the mantle adorned with candles and the angel collection left to me by my grandmother. Handmade wreaths decorated doors, each with a holiday theme. Intricate, glistening snowflakes enhanced our windowpanes. Garlands, holly and poinsettias filled nooks and crannies I didn't even know I had.

I decided I would not buy eggnog but would make it from scratch. And that incredible dessert I found online, an Italian cream cake? One practice run-through should be all I'd need.

I bought Allen a gift — a sweater — and a fine sweater it was. Dark, earthy green and made of cashmere. Size medium. I felt immensely satisfied purchasing such a fine gift for the man who had hurt my feelings so many times.

I remembered how much Allen had raved about my grandmother's spiced nuts and made a note to make sure there would be bowl of them on the snack table.

I wrapped all our gifts in lovely, muted-colored paper and ribbons, staying away from the cluttered, childish look of Santa, candy canes, sleds, and puppy dogs.

It all looked, smelled, and felt perfect.

But could I welcome what still felt like a dark shadow from my past into my home? I could only wait and see.

On Christmas Eve, the house began to fill with family. By Christmas morning, the house was bulging with kids, grandkids, aunts, uncles, siblings, presents, and foods to be set out and shamelessly gorged on throughout the day.

I was in the kitchen when Allen arrived just in time for Christmas breakfast. I could feel myself wanting to run out the back door and disappear, but I took a deep breath, then another, and walked with feigned confidence into the living room. There he stood, burdened down with an overabundance of beautifully wrapped gifts, two bottles of fine wine, and a lovely woman by his side whom he introduced as Roberta, his fiancée. His smile was broad and genuine as he was greeted with hugs and gleeful shouts of "Grandpa's here!"

"Hi, Cheryl. Good to see you. You look great."

Wow! What a nice compliment coming from the man who could never find one positive thing to say. I could not help but wonder how many times he'd rehearsed his entry line.

The day went surprisingly well, all except my being on edge, waiting for the subtle punch to the ego, a sarcastic remark, the surfacing of an old, embarrassing memory. Soon, without even realizing it, I found myself relaxing, truly enjoying the day. Instead of conflict, there was laughter, smiles, food, singing, giving and receiving, Fears of past trauma seemed to dissolve in the glow of the tree's lights. Memories of hurt evaporated in the merriment. Lingering old pains dissolved in toasts for a happy new year.

Later that evening, as Ken and I walked Roberta and Allen, wearing his new cashmere sweater, out to his car, a sense of healing surrounded us, although no one spoke of it.

The bride-to-be and I hugged as she said, "You two are coming to the wedding, aren't you?"

"We would not miss it for the world," I answered, knowing I meant it.

When all the company had left and Ken had gone to bed, I sat down in an easy chair to enjoy the serenity of the lighted tree, the comfort of the crackling fire, and the peace of the now messy, empty house. I had been impressed, surprised that Allen had grown, matured and become a fine human being, good father and terrific grandfather. I scolded myself for thinking I was the only one capable of such change.

But, most of all, I was filled with gratitude to my daughter for forcing me to go beyond fears, doubts and old suspicions. Not only did I know I was capable of taking the higher road, but now I had a new, beautiful definition of what a family could be.

— Cheryl Potts —

# 61

# Book Club for Strangers

*The great thing about new friends is that*
*they bring new energy to your soul.*
*~Shanna Rodriguez*

I'd been mulling over the idea for weeks. But it wouldn't work, would it? Actually, I used to do similar things all the time. But with four small children, how could I make it happen? I knew it would fail, and that would be awful.

So, I tabled the idea, and as summer drew to a close, I prepared my two oldest to go to first and third grade. With twin toddlers at home, I was not very involved at school, more of a ghost who breezed in for conferences and performances.

That's why the idea felt so preposterous. A book club for moms at school? I didn't know any moms at school. Sure, a few acquaintances from my ghost appearances. A few friends from other arenas whose children happened to attend the same school. But I could count them on one hand, and most of them had other obligations during the day. Where would I even start? Who would ever want to come?

A book club for moms at school had "no way" written all over it.

I'd been doing the stay-at-home mom thing for a while, and it felt familiar. I embraced it all — the bubbles, the play dough, the constant cleaning up, the helping with homework, the packing of lunches, the wiping of tears and wiping of bums. My life felt small and contained but not unimportant. I was content.

Before becoming a mom, though, my life was different. Work and play kept me busy, and I often hosted guests in our home.

The idea of a book club felt like a weird crossover of my former life with my current reality — a strange meshing of two distinct but equally happy versions of myself.

In my former life, running a book club would have been a piece of cake. I'd probably have made a delicious cake and offered it to the book club. It would be perfect — candles lit, soft music playing, and well-prepared discussion questions. A thoughtful haven for my friends to discuss deep thoughts.

In my current life, book club meant letting strangers see my messy house. Things wouldn't be perfect. There would be store-bought snacks and no candles because, hello, safety hazard. There would be *Mickey Mouse Clubhouse* in the background. There would be distractions.

But the idea would not go away. Before I could think better of it, I grabbed all the class rosters from past school years and started texting down the lists.

"I'm starting a book club for school moms…" SEND.

"…We'll meet Wednesday mornings after drop-off…." SEND.

"…In my house, just a few miles from school. Are you interested?" SEND.

I invited *everyone* on the rosters. Thankfully, it's a small school. My stomach was in knots. I was certain I would never be able to show my face at school again.

Then, my phone started to buzz.

"Sure! I'd love to come!"

"Sorry, I work then, but let me know if you do it another time."

"YES! That sounds awesome!"

"Absolutely! What can I bring?"

What? I had to scroll through them a couple of times. This was actually happening.

The first Wednesday arrived, and I welcomed about a dozen strangers into my far-from-perfect home. As we sat down with our coffee, it was as if something subtly shifted. No longer were we just fellow school moms. Suddenly, we felt safe discussing everything. We were vulnerable. We laughed and cried as if we had known each other for a lifetime, when in reality it had been less than a half-hour for most of us.

Something was happening here... something I didn't expect... something simple yet profound... something beautiful. Something real.

As the months went on, we saw some of our book club ladies through tough times. Marriage issues. Job changes. A broken engagement. Infertility. Cancer diagnosis and treatment. Through it all, we were there for each other, offering words, meals, prayers, and encouragement. We were a group of former strangers turned supporters — no, sisters.

It was a small, risky idea. But when I gave in, it changed my life. Because it was never supposed to be about books. It was about living unafraid and perfectly imperfect... together.

— Melissa Richeson —

# 62

# The Building Brunch

*Each friend represents a world in us, a world possibly
not born until they arrive, and it is only by this
meeting that a new world is born.*
~Anaïs Nin

When I noticed the piece of paper under my apartment door, I was sure it was another announcement of water shutoff for pipe repairs. I picked up the paper, glanced at it, and groaned. It was an invitation for all condominium residents to a "Welcome Brunch" for the new "season."

Aloud, I said to myself, "Absolutely not!" My husband had passed a year and a half earlier, and I stayed in most of the time, not wanting to see anyone. I buried myself in work — my editing and coaching business for graduate students and my personal writing. I spoke to very few people — an occasional call with a relative and a weekly call with Anna, my friend in the building, but that was it.

It was an ordeal just to go out for groceries. I couldn't face the bittersweet memories of my husband joking with me in the supermarket aisles. Very kind neighbors had been getting groceries for me, and the most I was able to do was to meet them at the door, thank them, haul in the bags, and give them the money. Six minutes every two weeks.

Anna asked on the phone if I was going. "No!" I said. She didn't pursue it.

But it kept me up at night. One dawn a few days before the event, despite the panic in my gut, I thought about the clothes I would wear, what I would say, how I would greet people from the past when I'd been securely part of a couple, and how I would respond when they offered condolences.

Just as fiercely, my mind kept shouting, *No, no, I can't go.*

Frightened as I was, something kept telling me to go. Not to go would be cowardice, and I knew I'd regret not meeting the challenge.

As the day approached, I made sure my clothes (casual, with tasteful earrings) were clean. Obsessively, I even wrote out a schedule to appear not too early, not too late.

Beforehand, all I could manage was a glass of water; I had no appetite. My hands shook when I applied my make-up, but I followed my schedule. Ready, I took a deep breath, opened the apartment door, and went to the elevator.

The room was buzzing. People milled around, carrying plates and filling them from the huge buffet. With my stomach in knots, I was tempted by nothing. I smoothed my hair and looked around. I didn't see a single familiar face, and I almost ran back to the elevator.

Suddenly, a man with arms outstretched rushed toward me. "How good to see you! It's been so long!" He hugged me. Gabe had known my husband, and we'd all had some great visits at the pool.

He turned to two other men nearby. "She's one of my favorite people."

Gabe helped me to the buffet to fill my plate and poured me a coffee. Then, he shepherded me to an empty table at the far end. Setting down the cup, he said, "Enjoy your brunch-lunch. See you soon!" I thanked him, and he left.

I nibbled at my egg salad, tore my croissant into bite-size pieces, sipped the coffee, and regretted coming.

"Hi. May I sit here?" I looked up. A woman smiled. She had long, dark-brown hair, dangling silver earrings, a peasant blouse, and a flared skirt. Her plate was piled high.

"Okay," I said and moved over, pretending to concentrate on my coffee cup.

"I know you," she said between bites. "I'm Dorothy. We met in the gym a long time ago. I was so sorry to hear about your husband. A great man, and fun."

"Thank you." I looked up and recognized her. "Aren't you a writer, too?"

"Yes! We should get together." She wrote her phone number and e-mail on a napkin.

Shortly, two other women came over and greeted us. They sat down at the table.

One said to me, "Where have you been?"

The other added, "Haven't seen you for so long!"

They also remembered my husband, empathized and shared reminiscences. Both offered to go out to lunch, to the park or to the mall. I nodded uneasily. They kept talking, exchanging bits of news, gossip, and confidences.

I admired their ease and ventured a few sentences. And then a few more, and after a while, a joke or two. They listened and appreciated.

To my surprise, I was enjoying myself!

I spied Anna at another table and waved. She came over with her plate. "I was sure you wouldn't be here," she said. "That's why I didn't offer to come together." She sat down, and I introduced her to Dorothy and the other two women.

After Anna ate her eggs, she left. I stayed through two more cups of coffee, went back for seconds and thirds until the buffet was decimated, and kept talking with the other women. Finally, having collected three new phone numbers and e-mails, I wished them warm goodbyes and went to the elevator.

Still somewhat stunned, I reflected on the events. The women had been so friendly and accepting! What had I been afraid of? What had I been depriving myself of?

Over my protestations, my Better Self had known what I needed to do and kept at me until I relented. For the first time, I felt able to face people without my husband. I could hear him saying he was proud of me. I thanked him silently and knew that somehow it would get easier.

I transferred the three numbers and e-mails into my contacts and told myself—or my Better Self did—that I'd call Dorothy the next week.

—Noelle Sterne—

# 63

Chicken Soup for the Soul

# Diversity Dinner

*Since there is nothing so well worth having as friends,*
*never lose a chance to make them.*
*~Francesco Guicciardini*

W e were a military family stationed at Quantico, Virginia, when we welcomed our first child, Kaitlyn, into the world in 2002. Forming new relationships can be tricky for military families, given the frequency of moves and deployments for the service member. We'd been stationed at Quantico about two years during a very challenging time for our nation. The world changed for us all on September 11, as we experienced a loss of lives, trust, safety, and confidence.

We were fortunate to have a close friendship with our neighbors since we were ten hours away from our Georgia home and family. When Kaitlyn was about two years old, we were devastated to learn those neighbors would be moving to care for their aging parents. As we helped them pack and load their lives into the U-Haul, we were sad for the changes we'd face and the loss of a family we had grown to love.

A few weeks later, the moving vans arrived, indicating the arrival of our new neighbors. We went out to introduce ourselves and offer our help. We learned they were a multigenerational family from the Philippines with a teenage son. We began the initial steps of getting to know one another as we unloaded their belongings into their new home and agreed to have dinner once they were settled.

The following week, another moving van arrived with more new neighbors for the townhome to our left. As we'd done the previous week, we introduced ourselves and offered to help them unload. This was an African American family from New Jersey, who had a daughter close in age to Kaitlyn. They had family with them to assist with unloading, so we said our goodbyes and left them to get settled into their new home.

In the evenings, we'd often go into our small front yard. We had been outside about ten minutes when both sets of new neighbors came outside, too. We gathered to share where we were from and the typical pleasantries. Kaitlyn shared her swing with her new neighbor, Zhaunie. The girls hit it off immediately. They shared their outside toys and took turns on the swing.

A short while later, a car pulled into the end of our row of townhomes. A young man got out of the car and waved as he went inside. Just a few minutes later, he returned with his wife and two daughters. As they joined the growing gathering in the front yard, he shared they had also just recently moved into their home from New York. They were of Puerto Rican descent, and their youngest daughter, Brianna, was the same age as Kaitlyn and Zhaunie.

From that night forward, our four families gathered outdoors after dinner, watching our children play as we began forming new friendships. We had everyone over one night. We grilled burgers and hot dogs, with baked beans, potato salad and brownies. We played with the children in the back yard and learned more about one another and the journeys that led each family to our neighborhood.

Somewhere over the course of the evening, we realized what an opportunity we had to learn more about one another's cultures and help our children learn about diversity. The families decided to take turns hosting monthly dinners with foods from our ethnic backgrounds. We were excited as we worked out the details and decided where we'd be for the next Diversity Dinner.

Over the next six months, we learned about cultures and traditions while enjoying amazing foods. In such a short time, these families had become our support system. We babysat for one other, prayed for and with one another, assisted each other with projects, celebrated birthdays, and spent many wonderful hours together. We learned that while we may have differing traditions, practices, beliefs, and food preferences, our commonalities far exceeded our differences.

The next U-Haul parked in front of our row of townhomes was for our family. This time, our neighbors were the ones offering to help us pack up our life as a military family as we prepared to transition back to the civilian world and return to Georgia. After a final evening outdoors together after dinner, we said our final goodbyes, knowing these families had given us so much more than food, friendship, and fun. They had restored our faith in people and given us the confidence to step out of our comfort zone into a diverse world filled with new potential friends.

— Laura Vertin —

# 64

# All Things New

*I have found that among its other benefits,*
*giving liberates the soul of the giver.*
*~Maya Angelou*

I sat next to the open fire, watching her stir the cast-iron pot of *nsima*. Her dark skin shone with the warmth of the sun, and her shaved head showed evidence of past starvation, with patches of light, reddish hair. She looked up at me and smiled. The square, mud-brick hut behind her had a messy straw roof where termites rained down droppings. A handmade chicken coop and a pit latrine could be seen behind the hut.

Seven years earlier, I brought together a group of seven Canadian women and Malawian teachers, and we started a high school for girls in rural Malawi, the eleventh poorest country in the world. Girls there were marrying in their early teens, staying in school until only Grade 5 or so, and had little knowledge of how to keep their future babies healthy. An opportunity to go to high school would delay the marriage age, and it would give them opportunities to have a greater quality of life and more knowledge to better provide for their families.

The woman who was stirring her meal sat on her haunches, using a handcrafted, large wooden spoon to stir the mixture of finely ground maize and water. It would thicken and be made into a patty with the consistency of firm grits. It was not my favorite, but I ate it when I had to. The smaller pot held a mixture of onions and tomatoes, a "relish" to eat with the *nsima*.

She, named Beauty, spoke a dialect that I did not understand, although I greeted her in the national language of Chichewa, and she responded in kind, her knowledge of that language as limited as mine. Yet we were able to communicate with hand signals and eye movements, even eyebrow lifts. She had seven children, but two had died. I had two healthy children. She had a sister who lived in the hut next to her; I had a sister whom I loved but lived far from me. She believed God would take care of her needs; so did I. We had that in common, making the desire to communicate all the stronger, even if words were unavailable.

Another woman walked past and called out some words in their dialect, making my hostess jump up with joy, clapping her hands. She grabbed my hand, motioning me to come with her, leaving the *nsima* in the care of her oldest daughter. I ran laughing after her until we came to another hut about a quarter mile away. Still holding hands, we entered the hut to find a woman with a ten-minute-old baby resting on her chest. The two women talked quickly and excitedly in their language, both sharing joy over the safe delivery of this baby boy. Then the doula handed the baby to me; amazingly, he was already cooing with dark eyes wide open.

What a joy to share this moment. The child I held in my arms had no idea of the cultural differences between me and his mother. He looked into my eyes, and while seemingly not possible at that early age, he smiled. It felt like a blessing for me and the work in which I was involved. It didn't matter that I was sleeping in a mud hut, peeing in a pit latrine with cockroaches, eating strange meals, and trying to communicate in a part of the world where the culture was so different from mine. My eyes locked with the new mother, and she and I shared a wonderful sisterly smile. What a lovely connection. Communication again beyond words.

In more recent years, I have found that the early classes of students at that school, in the heart of Malawi, have created a WhatsApp group where they communicate regularly. They invited me in for a discussion of what the school had meant to them and how their lives had been affected. All expressed gratitude and simple thankfulness for women from across the ocean who cared enough to come and start a high school just for them in their remote community. They spoke of new jobs, healthy children, and good marriages. The sacrifices we had made to create the school in their rural village were all worth it.

Before taking the steps to create this school, stepping out of my comfort zone in such a dramatic way had not crossed my mind. I did my job, raised my kids, and loved my husband. Sure, I loved to travel, had gone back to university for my degree while raising teenagers, and rode my own motorcycle, but this was beyond all that. Yet, while riding in the back of a truck in the middle of rural Africa, I felt the most alive I had ever been. I was living on the edge of my comfort zone and crossing over that line to make a visible difference in the lives of girls who would go on to make a difference in their community. I was using all my inner resources to not only survive but thrive. And it felt great.

The day the baby smiled at me was joyous, but there were days when I even thought I was crazy, when nothing worked right, and things didn't move forward. Yet I would not trade that experience for anything.

— Reno Ruth Doell Anderson —

## 65

# Leaping into Silence

*A ship in harbor is safe, but that is not*
*what ships are built for.*
*~John A. Shedd*

A light flashed in sync with each shake of my upper bunk. I rolled over, reached down, and tapped my roommate. She grumbled and hit her alarm clock, climbed out of bed, and flipped on the overhead light.

When she turned back my way, I asked her, "Why alarm much early? My bed shake! Not time wake up!"

"Work early. Must ready go," she signed.

What had I gotten myself into? We could barely communicate!

One year earlier, I sat in my dorm hallway with a deaf interpreter who attempted to teach me sign language. I was, at best, a slow learner and thus far hadn't been adept at languages. But my tutor accepted the challenge by repeating the signs until they stuck in my memory.

Grasping how much I wanted to sign well, she shared, "You'll learn quicker and better if you move in with deaf students and saturate your day with their culture and language. Would you consider that?"

Our college had a program specifically for the deaf. I watched them from a comfortable distance during on-campus services. But move in with them?

"No, I don't think so. I can barely handle the signs. I'm so slow and not a fan of anything new."

"If you genuinely care about the deaf, they'll be patient with you and help tremendously."

I was an introverted, learning-disabled, awkward girl who had left home for a college five states away — already a huge step for this seventeen-year-old who never even wanted to go to a friend's sleepover. Move into a silent world? The idea terrified me. It equally thrilled me because I'd long been fascinated by this beautiful language.

When I was a child, my family attended World Vision Korean Orphan Choir concerts where a deaf orphan "sang" along with the other children. I couldn't take my eyes off her! A handful of years later, I was in awe when hearing-impaired Nanette Fabray signed "Somewhere over the Rainbow" on TV. Then actress Jane Wyman portrayed deaf Johnny Belinda in the movie bearing that name, which captivated me.

Eventually, I decided to take the leap.

Now, here I was with willing hands that not-so-willingly formed rudimentary signs. But it was a start. And my tutor was right. Day in and day out with a deaf roommate had taught me what I couldn't have learned elsewhere. Oh, we had our strange moments, like when we argued, and she closed her eyes to avoid my opinion. But mostly it was one of the richest experiences of my life.

I finally gained some confidence and was asked to interpret in the church. I shied away from the offer, but one of the teachers who worked with the deaf encouraged me to go for it!

As I signed what the pastor was saying, the deaf students' eyes widened, and their jaws dropped. What had I done? I finished my portion of the service, and the next interpreter took it from there. Afterward, I learned of my blunder.

"Sarah, when they said, 'Welcome, visitors. We're glad you've joined our fellowship today,'" another interpreter whispered, "instead of 'fellowship,' you signed 'adultery.' They're very similar, but... um... of course, way different in meaning."

I slapped my cheeks in disbelief and cried, "How embarrassing! I'll never interpret again as long as I live!" But I need not have worried. They didn't ask me to.

I wasn't a totally lost cause, though. The day arrived when the deaf teacher approached me again. "We received a call from a family with a mentally and physically disabled young-adult daughter who is also deaf. They're looking for someone to live in their home with Susan while they travel for her father's job. I think you'd be perfect."

"Me?" I was stunned. "I don't know enough yet. And remember my mega-mistake in church?"

"The mother says Susan only knows simple signs. How about we go meet her and talk with the parents?"

We made an appointment, I met Susan, and we bonded on the spot. This led to me staying with Susan multiple times during my remaining college years and forming a life-long friendship with the family.

After college, I occasionally used signs at a camp for the disabled. And then many years later we went to a new church that worked with the deaf. I was asked to speak to the class and did, seeking a little help with my rusty signs along the way. They were only too glad to help.

When the current teacher moved away, the deaf pastor came to me. "Will you consider teaching the class?"

"Teach? Seriously? Oh, I'm not sure I could handle that. That's way outside my comfort zone! I'm not an advanced signer and barely ever taught much of anything."

"You know enough, and you have a heart for the deaf. They'll love you."

I prayed and agreed to try. That began five years of teaching the deaf weekly.

Over the next couple of decades, we moved often. The last time, we landed in a town where we attended a small church with a pastor whose own hearing was challenged. When he learned I knew sign language, he shared his desire to reach the deaf and asked for my help.

This time, I agreed to try.

Over and over, I stepped outside my comfort zone — from rooming with the deaf, staying with Susan, teaching that class, then interpreting for our pastor. I wasn't convinced I'd survive or even succeed in these efforts, let alone love being there. If I hadn't taken those leaps, though, I'd have missed not only learning to communicate with sign language but the many warm friendships I made that have lasted a lifetime.

— Sarah B. Hampshire —

# 66

# Love You Didn't See Coming

*Nobody has ever measured, even poets,*
*how much a heart can hold.*
~Zelda Fitzgerald

O
n my sixty-fifth birthday, I decided love was no longer an option after losing two men whom I dearly loved: one to pancreatic cancer and the other to a younger, prettier woman. To say I was heartbroken was an understatement. From then on, I was staying close to home so I wouldn't be hurt again.

What I hadn't counted on was meeting an eleven-year-old boy named Lenny.

I like to go out for coffee early in the morning when the place first opens. By the time people start coming in, I'm already out the door. But I wasn't alone; Lenny did this, too. We'd often meet up on our way out like two ships leaving port.

One day, I noticed a minor commotion at his table. He was short paying his bill. I quietly said to Beth, the waitress, that I'd take care of it, figuring that was that, but Lenny had a fit. He marched over to say that he didn't need any help, that they knew him and should know he'd pay tomorrow. Though his reaction seemed extreme, I simply said, "Well, you can pay me tomorrow. How's that?"

After thinking it over, he said, "Okay," before storming out the door.

On the following day, while I read at my usual table, I noticed

Lenny wasn't at his. Nor was he there the next day, or the next.

Oh, well.

I finally asked Beth about him. She said she wasn't totally sure, but his mother had been sick, so she guessed his absence was about her.

My heart, which was under wraps, suddenly made an unexpected appearance. I asked if she knew where he lived. She didn't but said she would ask one of the other kids who came in after school.

It turns out that Lenny's mother had been in the hospital with breast cancer that she'd been fighting for three years, taking what would be a last fatal turn.

Alas, now it all made sense.

Finding out where the wake was, I went, not knowing what I'd find. His dad was there, although his parents were long divorced. His father had remarried with a new family, while Lenny sat by himself in the back of the funeral home, just like at the coffee shop.

When he saw me, he said, "Why are you here? Is it to get the money I owe you?"

Despite the circumstances, I had to laugh. "Don't be silly," I said. "I asked after you and was told what happened. I came to say I was sorry."

He stared at me like I had two heads before bursting into tears, something I wasn't prepared for. I put my arms around him and let him cry. It was quite a moment for both of us.

"You know, Lenny," I said, once he pulled himself together, "I wasn't lucky enough to have a boy like you, or any kids for that matter. And, believe me, I'm not trying to move in on your mom, but maybe, when things settle down, we can have coffee together one morning. What do ya say?"

He blew his nose on his sleeve and said, "Okay. And I'll still pay you for the eggs." He seemed better after that, especially after I handed him a Kleenex.

I'm humbled to say that Lenny and I see each other most mornings. But instead of him glued to his phone and me rereading Jane Austen, we talk. He wants to be a scientist so he can help find a cure for breast cancer. He doesn't want other kids to lose their mother the way he did.

We've added ice cream cones after school and strolls in Central

Park. His dad, with whom he now lives, totally supports the relation-ship, often thanking me with notes and an occasional bouquet by way of Lenny.

To say I'm humbled by this boy opening my heart, which I thought was shut forever, can't be truly expressed.

Just when you think it's over, God throws you a curve.

It's going on two years since I met Lenny, and every once in a while he slips and calls me Mom.

— Susannah Bianchi —

# Teachable Moments

*Poverty can teach lessons that privilege cannot.*
*~Jack Klugman*

During my annual check-up with my optometrist a few years ago, I noticed a shoe-collection box placed next to the used-eyeglasses collection box in the waiting area. I asked the receptionist why they were collecting shoes. The receptionist told me that one of their optometrists participated in an annual eye-care mission in Africa. For a few weeks every year, the mission serviced people who didn't have access to eye care or glasses. During the optometrist's previous trip, he observed that many of the children who lined up for eye care had bare feet. He planned to take the donated shoes and offer them to his patients on his next eye-care mission.

The woman sitting next to me snorted and mumbled a derogatory comment about the impoverished. I was shocked and disturbed by her offensive remark. Although it's not my nature to be provoked into addressing insolent remarks from a stranger, I felt compelled to honor my own boundaries and clarify that her remark was not acceptable to me. I told the woman there were many other countries in the world that had similar issues. She challenged me to provide a personal example of how I was aware of this.

I described our first trip to Cuba years ago when our family spent Christmas at what was advertised as a luxury resort in Holguín, a city in eastern Cuba. The resort was pleasant, although definitely not the high level of luxury found in deluxe hotels in Canada or the USA. The good-natured hotel staff and beautiful beach made up for the lack of personalized services and amenities at the hotel.

My husband is a tennis enthusiast and decided to take some tennis lessons, while I sat on the sidelines observing his performance. During his first lesson, we both noticed the instructor's tennis shoes were in poor condition. My husband enjoyed his instructor's company and, after each lesson, we would have a chat with the instructor about the social and economic challenges of everyday life in Cuba. One day, the instructor commented on how much he admired my husband's tennis shoes. He talked about how expensive it was to obtain good tennis gear in Cuba. During their conversation, my husband learned they had the same shoe size.

When he finished his last lesson, my husband gave his instructor the customary monetary tip. Then he took off his tennis shoes and, rather than putting them in his sports bag after changing into his sandals, my husband offered the shoes to his instructor. The instructor became very emotional as he thanked my husband and accepted the shoes.

After telling this story to the woman, I commented that, like many other families, we regularly discarded shoes that were still useable. After our trip to Cuba, we became more conscious of donating our gently used clothing and shoes to organizations that redirected these items to people in need.

The woman sat in silence until she was called for her appointment. As she got up, she turned toward me and mentioned that she wasn't much of a traveler. "I've learned a lesson today. We should be thankful for what we have and never take things for granted," she said.

When the woman walked by the receptionist, I overheard her ask how late the office would be open that day. I was delighted to hear the woman tell the receptionist she planned to return later in the afternoon with a bag of gently used shoes for the donation box.

I had also learned a lesson that day. Respectfully speaking up in the face of offensive comments can actually work!

— Kathy Dickie —

# You're the Minister

*Act as if what you do makes a difference. It does.*
~William James

I t was another long night at the hospital. Thankfully, my pager didn't go off, so I got some sleep, but it's difficult to sleep in a room the size of a pea with walls so thin you hear the nurses' and doctors' pagers beep all night long.

This was my first overnight shift in my training as a hospital chaplain. I had enjoyed volunteering as a chaplain in a small country nursing home for many years. When my minister suggested I pursue professional chaplaincy, I applied for the program, I was not prepared for the intensity of the training. Instead of joyfully visiting the residents in the nursing home, listening to their stories, laughing with them, or quietly sitting with those who could no longer speak, this training required years of internships in a large medical center. As an introvert I was not comfortable constantly meeting new people, not to mention finding my way around the gigantic hospital. I hadn't realized I would have to do overnight shifts, nor did I understand the enormity of emotion I would feel on those evenings as I made my rounds in the intensive care unit.

On this night, I did my best to offer comfort to the patients, grateful when I came to the final room where an intubated elderly woman slept soundly. I sat by her side for a while, praying silently, and appreciating the peaceful energy that surrounded her. It was late by the time my shift ended, and I was exhausted. All I wanted was that little bed in the on-call room.

The ICU in this old hospital had many corridors and doorways, and I managed to get myself turned around, so I asked a nurse where the exit was. She smiled and said, "Sure thing. This is the way to the family waiting room." Confused, I followed her. I didn't know what the family waiting room was. She was practically sprinting, and it was hard to keep up as we whipped down a hall and through two doors.

She opened a third door and said, "Here you are." I had been delivered to a small waiting area where four people stood, looking even more dazed and exhausted than I felt. I turned to the nurse for guidance, but she was long gone. I turned to the family and introduced myself as a hospital chaplain. "Is there anything I can do for you?" I asked.

They looked at each other, shrugged their shoulders, and finally one of them said, "I think we are fine for now. But thank you." I left the room and was glad to notice an exit sign nearby. Finding my way back to my tiny sleep room, I realized that they must have been family members of the woman in the ICU who was on life support. *Bless them all,* I silently prayed. I found my bed and tucked myself in, letting go of the evening and looking forward to going home bright and early in the morning.

The morning may have been bright, but I was exhausted. It took all I had to gather my little overnight bag and find my way to the long corridor toward the parking garage. Up ahead, I noticed a woman walking in my direction. She looked as tired as I felt. With a puffy face and hesitant gait, she walked slowly, as if she had no desire to reach her destination. Suddenly, she looked right at me, and her face lit up. Did I know her? I didn't, but she sure seemed to know me. Her pace picked up as she walked straight toward me and stopped in front of me. She looked straight in my eyes and declared, "You're the minister."

Now, I was positive she'd mistaken me for someone else. I was not a minister; I was just a chaplain intern. I hadn't even decided if I wanted to go to seminary. After the previous night's discomfort, I wasn't sure I even wanted to continue this internship. All I could think was that I just wanted to go home. *Please, no more awkward interactions,* I prayed. Suddenly, I realized who she was. Last night, in the family waiting room, she was one of the four people. Pulling myself together, I remembered my chaplain role and looked back at her with love. With tears filling her eyes, she said to me, "I can't believe I'm seeing you right now. This is amazing. I'm on my way to say goodbye to my mother. We're taking her off life support this morning. I didn't think I could do this, but seeing you right here, right now, I realize I can. Do you have any idea how important your work is?"

"I think I do," I said as I realized that this sacred work was not about me but about my willingness to be an empty vessel, to be filled again and again with love, not for my sake but for others. For her. For her family. For her mom. I watched her walk away, now with strength and steadfast purpose in her stride on her way to one last love-filled morning with her mother. I noticed that a similar strength and purpose were also building up inside me as I knew, in that moment, that no matter the discomfort, my journey as a professional chaplain was just beginning.

— Lava Mueller —

# Romance in Bloom at 92

*Love is like swallowing hot chocolate before it has
cooled off. It takes you by surprise at first,
but keeps you warm for a long time.*
~Author Unknown

Who would have thought that two people in their nineties, strangers from different backgrounds, would fall in love? My past was mostly that of a wife and mother, and his was farming and heavy equipment operator. We both had been married, raised a family and widowed late in life. It was after being single for over fourteen years, that I thought I might be interested in dating.

While grocery shopping one day, I happened to meet up with a friend who asked me what I was up to these days. I told him that I was doing just fine, taking care of myself and my dog. My grown kids were busy and I was living in an apartment north of the college. He invited me to join a group of seniors on Thursdays at the American Legion for a social gathering. He said I would probably know everybody, and they just visited over a beverage or two and then either went home or went out to dinner as a group. I thanked my friend and gave it some thought.

I had become satisfied with my life. I was able to get around independently, driving my Kia for errands and appointments during the day. It had been a long time since I had relaxed with friends. I knew I should do it.

When I got there, I found the women were sitting at one end of the table, the men at the other. It reminded me of high school.

I recognized almost everyone. I was welcomed and given a membership chart to add my birthday. The women would bring desserts for celebrating those months. As I added my birthday to the list, I looked at the only man I didn't know. I had noticed him right away when I arrived.

He sat taller in his chair than the other guys, despite the fact that he and I were the oldest people there. We were sitting at opposite ends of the table, but we had introduced ourselves when I first came in. When it was time to leave, he asked me for my number! I was so surprised that I didn't actually give it to him. And then I was embarrassed by my behavior and decided to join the group for dinner after all so that I could apologize to him.

When I got to the restaurant, there was Stan, opening my car door and escorting me inside. Still embarrassed, I only had a piece of pie at the restaurant, and I escaped to my car early.

The next day, I shared my experience with my family. I decided I would give Stan my phone number at our next meeting. Well, he asked me out to dinner after that meeting! I was a nervous wreck but I went. And then at dinner he asked me if I would go with him to visit his mother in Arizona. It was happening so fast! I had my grandson check him out, and Stan even gave me a test ride in his motor home so that I would see that he was a safe driver.

I had not been anywhere in years and decided to jump aboard with my new friend and have an adventure. I felt secure and safe; and at my age, it's best not to wait!

The first thing on my agenda was to update my wardrobe. I wanted to look as young and sexy as was possible. Even though I am old, I am not dead.

We set off on our big trip. The plan was to stay a few days with Stan's brother. While we were there, we caught the flu.

When I thought I was better enough, I took a shower. But as I was washing my hair, I passed out. My head hit the door, and my knee hit the wall with a loud bang. When I came to, Stan was there taking care of me. In the shower. Naked.

Stan couldn't lift me so I crawled on all fours to the bedroom. We were getting to know each other even faster than I expected!

The rest of my adventure was enjoyable. We grew to appreciate, love and care for each other. We plan to laugh our way through life together for as long as we've got! Stan and I are blessed.

— Myrna L. Garvey —

# Chapter 8

# Do It Afraid

# Touch the Horizon

*You gain strength, courage and confidence*
*by every experience in which you*
*really stop to look fear in the face.*
~Eleanor Roosevelt

Kevin and I had been dating a few weeks when he asked if I would meet his parents. They were excited to meet me, so they invited us for a summer barbecue on the family farm.

We packed up his car and headed east. As we approached the property, I could see a beautiful house surrounded by two graying barns and a large outbuilding. Being a city girl, I assumed the barns were filled with happy cows, chickens, and tractors.

Bob and Janice greeted me with open arms. Homemade lemonade was served over ice, and I was offered a tour of the property. As we entered the first barn, an unexpected sound greeted me: barking. Lots and lots of barking. Bob and Janice weren't farmers; they were dog breeders! The barns were filled with large Irish Wolfhounds!

I was immediately confused. "If you're not housing livestock, why do you need that other huge building?"

"That's where we keep the plane."

"Um, the what?"

My mind did a 180. This wasn't the farm life I was expecting! What kind of person owns a plane and keeps it in his back yard?

Of course, I immediately wanted to see it. Bob proudly opened the rustic hangar door to reveal a small four-seater with shiny, red

**Do It Afraid** | 227

paint. It looked like a child's toy come to life.

He gently polished the propeller with his sleeve. "Owning a plane was my lifelong dream, and once we moved out to the country, I finally had the space to park it! Janice and I use it a bit for travel, but mostly we just fly around the neighbourhood, take in the sights, enjoy the view…"

He turned to me with a little wink in his eye. "Want to go for a ride?"

My stomach lurched a bit. I'd never been in such a tiny plane, but I suddenly realized the rarity of this offer. This wasn't the day I was expecting, but how could I say no to such an opportunity?

We put on headsets so we could communicate over the roar of the engine. Kevin climbed into the back, and I sat in the copilot seat next to Bob. It was then that I noticed the grass in front of us wasn't a field; it was a runway. The plane rumbled to a start, and we slowly rolled forward. As we picked up speed, I noticed the grass at the end lifted upward into a ramp.

If you've never flown in a four-seater, let me be very clear: You can feel everything! You know exactly when you've left the security of the ground and are suspended in the air. Your body knows every turn, every lift, every little air pocket. It's a very exposed sensation, and yet you really do feel like you're flying! It is just you and the sky.

And that view — floating above the landscape but not so far that you lose the details. You can see every branch and animal in the field below. And still, you can stretch your eyes out over the horizon. Everything looks familiar, yet strangely new. It's like seeing the world for the first time.

As we swept through the air, Bob waxed poetic about his love of flying. He explained the various knobs and dials spread out in front of us. He had me place my hands on the copilot controls, so I could feel the rumble of the engine.

"How's it feel?"

I smiled my little I'm-pretending-I'm-flying smile. "Awesome," I proclaimed, "like I'm a real pilot!"

"Good," he said, "because you're flying now." He smiled and lifted his hands off his controls.

I immediately started us into a nosedive.

"Pull up. Pull up. It's okay. Just a little dip!"

I did as I was told. Bob and Kevin laughed. Clearly, I wasn't the first person to make that mistake in this plane.

"Hold it steady, just like we talked about. Take a breath and loosen your grip a bit."

I realized my knuckles were white as I clung to the controls for dear life. I loosened my grip, took a breath, and looked ahead at the horizon. I held the controls as Bob talked me through steadying the plane.

"Okay, you're doing great. Now, take us around a bit."

"Where?" I asked.

"Look around, see what you want to look at, and take us there."

For the next few minutes, I flew us around the countryside. We saw fields, cattle and a shimmery brook. I didn't nosedive once. I took deep breaths and kept us steady. Before long, I started to understand why Bob was so passionate about having this little plane. I was flying, and it was glorious!

Before long, it was time to head back. Bob took control again and brought us in for a landing. Just like takeoff, I could feel every shake and bump, but I was ready for it this time. As we climbed out of the plane and back on to solid ground, my legs were shaking, and my head was swimming. I'd never experienced anything like this. I'd flown a plane!

The rest of the night was a blur. While glasses clinked and courses were served, I prattled endlessly about the shock of the nosedive and the thrill of leveling the plane. The next morning, I called my parents to tell them, "I touched the horizon...." For weeks, I recounted my aviation adventure to friends and strangers alike.

Summer turned into fall. Kevin and I amicably parted ways, and we both moved on to our next chapters.

But when my life feels threadbare and ordinary, and I feel intimidated by the challenges ahead, that country day comes back to me, and I remember...

I once flew a plane.

—Allison Lynn—

# 71

# Ten Feet of Fear

*The future belongs to those who believe*
*in the beauty of their dreams.*
~Eleanor Roosevelt

alfway between the ground and the trapeze, I clung to the ladder for dear life. With tears flowing down my face, I thought, *Happy birthday to me.*

Hesitantly, I lifted my foot to the next rung of the ladder. Looking up at the instructor, I wasn't sure if I could keep going. Peering out over the ocean for comfort didn't help. This was risky after undergoing a spinal fusion fifteen years prior. The surgeon would not approve of this activity!

In a personal-development conference I'd attended, we designed our dream lives in terms of love, career, health, time and money. I discovered a common theme: I didn't feel worthy, and my self-esteem would need some TLC if I was going to live the life I was longing for.

At the conference, a woman took the stage and shared about her transformative experience while taking trapeze lessons. Her story made me squirm and my palms sweat. Yet, I envied her. I'm terrified of heights and had no desire to fly through the air on a trapeze with the greatest of ease. But, more than anything, I wanted to be the type of woman who could do it if she wanted to.

Each year, I mark my birthday with a theme for the upcoming year. This was my forty-fourth year, and I shared with my then boyfriend my dream to spend my birthday with him in Paris. He didn't share my enthusiasm for Paris, romance, or a romantic getaway. Disappointed but not surprised, I realized that nothing changes if I don't change. If I wanted a better, more adventurous life, then I needed to do something to move the needle forward. Suddenly, the trapeze popped into my mind.

One of the tools I learned at the conference was the practice of "trying on" what it feels like to be the person who (fill in the dream). I imagined it like putting on an adult onesie. Every evening, I would walk a mile imagining I was the person who did the trapeze. As I walked, I felt happy, accomplished, and proud of myself. And then I would walk a mile imagining that I didn't do the trapeze. As I walked, I felt disappointed, defeated, stuck, and, worst of all, bored.

I had to do the trapeze for my birthday if I was going to swing into a new year as a new me.

My first step was to check out the trapeze at the Santa Monica Pier, but my back spasmed before I could leave my shoebox apartment. On my second attempt to look at the trapeze, I was halfway there when anxiety gripped me, and I had to pull over to throw up. Then, I promptly turned around and drove home. On my third attempt, I made it to the parking lot and then broke down sobbing. After wiping my tears and blowing my nose, I walked to the pier to watch a class in progress. I watched people delight in their adventures, and I shakily registered for a class on my birthday, knowing I could cancel and forfeit the deposit. Getting there was a win. Signing up was a win. One baby step at a time.

I didn't tell anyone about my birthday plan. It felt like a private conquest, and I didn't want anyone's fears spilling onto me. I had enough of my own. And then the day came, and there I was crying as I climbed the ladder, scared and alone on my birthday.

With the encouragement of the instructor and the gracefulness of a hippopotamus, I launched myself onto the plank and slowly stood up. I looked out at the ocean while the roller coaster filled with screaming passengers whizzed by behind me. I began to tremble. The instructor handed me the left side of the bar. It was heavy, and the right side flew out over the net. As I stood on a plank barely as wide as my feet, she expected me to reach out and grab the bar.

I remembered an affirmation from the workshop and silently repeated: *An ocean of abundance, a sea of possibility; an ocean of abundance, a sea of possibility.*

The instructor was becoming impatient. I had on a safety belt, which didn't increase my sense of safety at all. She sharply said, "Lean forward and grab the bar with your other hand."

"I can't reach it!" I said in a disembodied voice.

"Of course, you can. Your arms are the same length."

Valid.

I don't know how I did it, but I grabbed the bar.

*An ocean of abundance, a sea of possibility.*

I jumped.

It was ecstasy.

I flew through the air, wrapping my knees around the trapeze bar, letting my arms dangle and my hair blow in the wind. When the instructor yelled that my time was up, without hesitation, I let go of the bar and free-fell into the net thirty feet below.

Elated, I ran to get in line to do it again.

This time, I easily climbed the ladder right up until I was ten feet from the scaffold, where I froze. But the freedom of flying through the air motivated me to continue.

In hindsight, it came down to "ten feet of fear" between where my fear of heights kicked in to the time I could hold on with both hands and jump. That was my real birthday present. I was only afraid for ten feet. If I could get myself past the ten feet of fear, I was golden.

The real test of my aha moment would come when I decided to move out of my shoebox apartment and into one I loved. In Los Angeles, that was more daunting than the trapeze. The first apartment on my list didn't have any showings available until the weekend. The second place didn't have units available.

Driving around without a destination, feeling frustrated, I declared, "An ocean of abundance, a sea of possibility."

Turning the corner, Park La Brea, an iconic L.A. landmark, beckoned. The combination of high-rise buildings and cottages with lush landscaping took my breath away. The apartments with their old-world charm felt out of reach. All the reasons why it wouldn't work immediately flooded my mind. The lease was year-to-year, and the rent was a lot more than I was currently paying.

The next ten feet of fear was from my desk to my boss's desk to request a raise.

*An ocean of abundance, a sea of possibility.*

Once I was brave enough to walk those ten feet, the rest unfolded as quickly as a swinging trapeze. A unit became available on Saturday. On Sunday, I picked up the keys. On Wednesday, I moved in. I landed in a whole new life, and it was ecstasy.

—Jenni Murphy—

# 72

# I Am Not a Wimp

*Sometimes we have to step out of our comfort zones.*
*We have to break the rules. And we have to discover*
*the sensuality of fear. We need to face it,*
*challenge it, dance with it.*
*~Kyra Davis*

Several years ago, my husband Paul, three of our four girls and I flew to Hawaii. On our first day in Maui, I had a genuine dilemma. My family wanted to go snorkeling. It would be the first time for all of us, but while Paul and our three girls were accomplished swimmers, I had only passed Beginner One. And I hated getting my face wet.

I had always encouraged our children to try new things. Paul told me that if I went snorkeling, he would be right next to me. I didn't want any of them to think I was a wimp, so I agreed to give snorkeling a try.

We boarded a catamaran for whale-watching and snorkeling at Molokini Island. Clare, Erin, and Colleen stood by the railing, searching for humpback whales. I stationed myself next to my girls, looking out at the sky and the bay. The sky was beautiful in its unclouded blueness, and the water was never-ending. That was the problem. Water was everywhere.

I once read that a person could drown in a tablespoon of water. As I clutched the rail of the catamaran, I believed it hook, line, and sinker.

It was hard to get excited about the whales' tails slicing through the water after the captain announced that we were approaching Molokini

Island. My family had gone to get our snorkeling gear. I knew it was my only chance to find out some information.

"Sir, can I ask you something?" I asked the first crewmember I could corner.

"Of course," the crewmember replied.

"How deep is the water at Molokini Island?" I looked around and, thankfully, none of my family was nearby.

"About sixty feet," he said casually.

I clutched the railing as panic filled my chest. "Thank you," I squeaked.

"We are now approaching Molokini Island," the intercom intoned. "The rim that you see is the edge of a submerged volcano. When you get into the water, do not touch or step on the coral. The coral is living, and the reef is a protected area."

A different crewmember came close enough for me to question him.

"Do you provide life vests?" I asked.

"Of course. They're required."

"Good." My relief was pitiful.

The man peered at me closer and said, "You won't need it. The salt holds you up."

"Oh, I'll need it. I sink like a rock." I laughed one short, lonely snort.

The crewmembers instructed people on how to put on the life vests, masks, and flippers, and how to use the snorkel. They assured everyone they would be in the water with life rings. "Just yell if you need help or wave your arms," a crewmember said. That would be hard to do if I were at the bottom of the lagoon.

"We are anchored," the captain said. "Have fun."

As I stood on the platform of the catamaran, I imagined jumping into the *sixty feet* of water. Paul and our three girls were already snorkeling, enjoying the coral and the sea life.

Paul swam over to the catamaran. He had his hand outstretched and said, "C'mon. It's great."

My mask, mouthpiece, life vest, and flippers were all on. I had been standing on the ledge so long that my mask clouded up. I wasn't worried about people waiting behind me because I was the last one. I felt my life vest around my waist for snugness. I blew in a little more air. I felt it again. It seemed okay. I watched ten-year-old Colleen for a couple of seconds. I wanted to see if her life vest was holding her up. It was. Now, I was ready.

"C'mon," Paul said.

As I inched forward, my flippers snagged on the ladder. They released from the step with a jerk. I bellyflopped into the water. My mask filled with salty water as my face and entire body went under. I almost howled because the water was so cold, but I was terrified of swallowing the water. I bobbed quickly to the surface, however.

Paul cleared my mask, helped me make a tight seal on my face, fixed my mouthpiece, and took my hand. He showed me how to move my flippers up and down. I paddled while breathing out of the mouthpiece. The life vest kept me at the surface with my face out of the water. I was actually treading water!

"Relax," Paul said. "I told you I'd be right next to you. Now, put your face in the water and look."

"Okay." I stretched out my arms and legs and moved my flippers up and down. I checked the tightness of my mask again. As I gingerly placed my face underwater, I stared through the mask. It was incredible!

I opened my mouth to exclaim in wonder, but then I remembered about the tablespoon of water. I snapped my lips shut. With lips pursed, I gawked at the purples, yellows, oranges, reds, and blues of the exquisite fish darting throughout the reef.

My splashy entrance lured the three girls over to watch me. Soon, we were swimming together as we looked below the surface. There was so much to see. Erin pointed out a long, skinny eel whose nose stuck out of his hiding place in the coral. It disappeared in an instant. I didn't want to miss anything, so I kept my face in the water. Paul and Clare dove down, pointing at anemones.

After what seemed to be a few minutes but was actually almost an hour, the crew motioned for people to come back. I paddled around for one last look.

I was the last person to get back on the catamaran.

Snorkeling has become a passion for me.

Every winter, Paul and I book a cruise so we can snorkel. I never tire of seeing stingrays, nurse sharks, sea turtles, parrotfish, angelfish, squid, eels, clownfish, sea urchins, sea cucumbers, lionfish, porcupine puffers, filefish, trumpetfish, octopuses, and many others. I never tire of seeing fan coral, brain coral, and anemones. The stunning, living-coral formations remind me of an underwater garden.

Paul is still at my side, holding my arm. And I always feel like I did at Molokini Island. It is incredible!

— Mary Clare Lockman —

# 73

# Reclaiming My Voice Post Pandemic

*Don't limit yourself. Many people limit themselves to
what they think they can do. You can go as far as your
mind lets you. What you believe you can achieve.*
~Mary Kay Ash

Two years of the pandemic, during which I spoke to no one but my partner and the checkout lady at the local market, had taken a toll on my ability to function outside of our own living room. I was never comfortable talking to strangers, but my awkwardness had devolved into social ineptitude. "Do you take Visa?" and "I brought my own bags" were the only phrases I could say without practicing an hour beforehand. Phone calls had to be carefully planned, and if either party deviated from my carefully composed script, I feigned technical issues before hanging up and hyperventilating in the bathroom for an hour.

I was at a loss for words. Literally.

When I heard about the Story Slam, the concept sounded as foreign to me as hosting a tea party on Mars. Amateur storytellers were invited to a month-long workshop where they developed stories taken from their lives, culminating in a stage show performed in front of an audience.

Although I love stories — writing them, listening to them, reading them — the thought of performing one onstage, in front of strangers, caused my stomach to churn. I told my partner how impossible it would be to actually say words under a bright light before hundreds of unfriendly eyes, expecting to share a laugh, but he just looked at me thoughtfully.

Then, he reminded me of my last few Zoom job interviews.

Talk about disasters. By e-mail, I was the ideal candidate — well-spoken, interesting, knowledgeable, friendly. Potential employers couldn't wait to schedule an interview. That's when their great new candidate evaporated, replaced by a bumbling dolt with only a passing competency in her native language. Sometimes, I mispronounced words I'd mastered in third grade. One interviewer asked me if I spoke a language besides English, thinking that my vocal fumbles were a result of an unfamiliar tongue. And then there was the time I reverted to weird hand gestures when the words just wouldn't travel from my brain to my mouth. Unsurprisingly, I was never called back for a second interview.

If Story Slam could restore my ability to speak to unfamiliar people, maybe it wasn't such a bad idea.

The captain of our storytelling journey was a woman with the unusual name of Vogue. Ample of body and voice, she demanded attention with an absolute confidence in her ability to transform five ordinary people into accomplished storytellers. After her workshop, she assured us that we'd be capable of holding an audience's attention for eight to ten minutes. She guaranteed it, or we'd get our money back!

The workshop was free, by the way.

Four strangers and I met with Vogue every week to practice the story we'd perform onstage at the end of the workshop. Mine was about the time my friends rescued me from a difficult situation. We learned how to invoke our senses to draw our audience into the story, and how to craft a beginning that would spike curiosity, an end that would leave people satisfied, and a middle to tie them together. We practiced gestures, vocal inflections, and thoughtful pauses in order to get the best story possible. Were we clear? Could outsiders understand the flow of events, our motivations, the cast of characters?

I was always the last to volunteer during the weekly workshops.

Speaking to people other than family and friends was never easy for me, but talking about my friends' support during difficult times was important and close to my heart. I wanted this story told, and I was the only one who could do it.

Little by little, I finessed the characters, juggled the timeline, and explored my motivations and the feelings of other people. By living the story again and again, I became more comfortable with the words each time and, in turn, more comfortable with myself.

I could share my experience and not worry about feeling judged or that my words were boring. People who didn't know me might find comfort in my story. My story had value, and I had value, too.

Once onstage, blinded by stage light but knowing a hundred other people watched from the seats below, the story I had practiced glided from my lips naturally. I paused in the right places. My gestures added to the story. My words came from the heart.

The applause washed over me in waves.

After the Story Slam, people greeted me in the hallways. One woman even followed me to the restroom to tell me how my story had resonated with her. Her friends had helped her through a difficult time, too. We shared a smile across the bathroom mirror.

This unfamiliar woman appreciated me for the story I shared on stage that day.

I was accepted.

Maybe strangers weren't so scary after all.

— Brandi Hoffman —

# 74

# Recycling

*Your bike is a discovery; your bike is freedom.*
*It doesn't matter where you are when you're*
*on the saddle, you're taken away.*
*~Doug Donaldson,*
Bicycling Magazine's Guide To Bike Touring

"I'm not getting any younger," I told my daughter during a weekend visit to her home. "I've been thinking about getting a bicycle. I miss that feeling of freedom I experienced as a kid."

"Great," Kristen said. "Tomorrow morning, you can take mine out to get the feel of it."

"No, no, really. I'm good." I got up to brew a cup of chamomile tea to calm my nerves.

Kristen had no idea what she was asking. Take her bike out for a ride? Her modern hybrid hardly resembled my '60s-era girls' pedal-brakes Schwinn.

"Why the hesitation?" she said.

I took a sip of my soothing beverage. "All those gears and hand-brakes are intimidating. I don't even know how to stop the thing."

I didn't tell her the main reason. Nowadays, if I fall, which is a likely scenario, considering the last time I mounted a banana seat was sometime mid-last century, I could break a hip and be laid up for weeks.

"Besides," I said, "do they make one these days that I know how to ride?"

"Absolutely," she said, glancing down at her cellphone. She tapped the screen a couple of times and then held it up. "Here, look."

I slipped on my reading glasses and squinted at the mini screen.

"It's called a Townie," she said. "It's similar to the one you had when you were a kid."

The upright handlebars and low, curved center bar reminded me of my childhood bike.

Kristen leaned in. "This one does have gears and handbrakes."

I stopped her. "Gears? I can't —"

"You don't have to use them if you don't want to. And you'll get used to the brakes."

"It *is* cute. Maybe I'll check it out."

As soon as I got home, I headed downtown. Standing motionless inside the doors of the enormous sporting-goods store, I stared at all manner of sports and outdoor equipment.

"Need some help?"

"Um, I'm interested in an Electra Townie," I said.

The saleswoman steered me to the back of the store where the bikes stood lined up.

"I like that one," I said, pointing to a pretty, teal one.

She reached for the tag. "Okay, this one's a 21D. So, twenty-one gear combinations, and…"

I stopped her mid-sales pitch.

"Oh, uh, no. I want the one with seven gears."

She read a few more tags. "Looks like we only have that model in off-white or raspberry. We could order it in teal and have it for you in about three weeks."

No way was I going to allow myself a twenty-one-day waiting period. I needed to pull the trigger on this buy before I talked myself out of it.

"Off-white's fine."

She rolled it toward me. "You can take it for a test ride in the employee parking lot."

I hoped the sheer terror didn't show on my face.

I forced a weak smile. "Can't I just ride it up and down this aisle?"

I waved my fingers back and forth in front of me.

Spunky shook her head. "No, sorry. Insurance won't let us. Don't worry, there's plenty of room in the lot."

I followed her to a nearby counter where she plucked a helmet from a wall hook.

"Let's get this secured," she said, nearly choking me with the chin strap. "And you'll need to sign the waiver."

Of course. The waiver: "...not held responsible should aging Boomer babe, in pathetic attempt to recapture her glory days, requires life-saving measures on the premises."

I signed on the dotted line and then steered Townie outside. Once in the privacy of the employee lot, I hoisted myself onto the seat, gripped the handlebars, squeezed the brake levers a couple of times, and then pushed off.

After a wobbly start, I steadied myself and then took a moment to savor the rush of wind on my face for the first time in this millennium. I pedaled a couple of loops around the lot and then lurched to a stop. No broken bones or scuffed tires. Not bad for a something-genarian.

I led my new friend back through the store to finalize the purchase. With my precious cargo secured on the bike rack, I took off for the trail, anxious to try her out on my own turf. The time had finally come for me to wheel out of my comfort zone. Could I survive without wiping out on my first ride of the twenty-first century?

When I reached the end of my maiden trek, a sense of pride washed over me. A new chapter in my life had begun. I dismounted, grabbed one ankle and then the other to stretch out my now-aching quadriceps, loaded Townie back onto the rack and drove home.

With my confidence renewed, I decided to bring my new best buddy with me on my next visit to Kristen's home. I couldn't wait to show off my expert handbraking skills. I'll tackle those gears one day, too. Baby steps.

— Camille DeFer Thompson —

# 75

# Soaring Out of My Comfort Zone

*I learned that courage was not the absence of fear, but
the triumph over it. The brave man is not he who does
not feel afraid, but he who conquers that fear.*
~Nelson Mandela

A s far as I was concerned, skydiving was a sport for risk-takers. I wasn't one of them. I hate to admit it, but I wouldn't even attach a worm to my son's fishing pole. It's called being squeamish.

One morning, a colleague at work told me he had gone skydiving, and it was incredible and exhilarating. "You haven't felt freedom until you've made one of these jumps and floated in the sky."

"That's fine for you, but that's not my cup of tea. I feel a lot safer with my feet on the ground."

He smiled confidently. "You drive a car, don't you? I'd say that is pretty risky. As a matter of fact, statistically, you are safer skydiving than driving an automobile. What do you think of that? You can't argue with statistics, can you?"

He returned to his desk, opened a drawer, and pulled out a brochure for the skydiving school he had used. "Look it over. It might convince you to give it a try."

At first glance, I was startled by the picture on the cover. It was a guy harnessed to an instructor, suspended in space. The words on the cover read, "Flying in Tandem."

"What does that mean?" I asked.

"That's for novices like yourself who have never gone skydiving. A professional instructor harnesses himself to you, and you jump together."

I shrugged, smiled and smugly said, "Well, anyone can do that." I thought for a moment. "Hell, that's no different from flying in an airplane and trusting the pilot to get you wherever you want to go."

"Now, you've got the idea."

At that point, I realized I had stuck my foot in my mouth.

For the next couple of weeks, my colleague told me it really didn't take any knowledge or courage to jump in tandem with a professional skydiver.

"The instructor," he said, "is licensed and has logged many hours of skydiving. He also knows his parachute is in good condition and packed properly. How much safer is that?"

Reluctantly, I decided I would jump on my fifty-eighth birthday. This gave me three months to get ready. I conditioned myself by doing self-hypnosis every day, so I would have the courage to achieve this incredible feat.

After my wife refused to drive me to the skydiving school in Perris, California, my son Marc volunteered.

His only question was, "Dad, is your life insurance paid up to date?"

After signing in and writing a check, I was asked to sign several legal documents releasing the school from liability for any injuries or death. That alone scared the daylights out of me. I was one step away from changing my mind.

Then, a group of us who were going to jump were asked to sit in the bleachers to hear what was expected of us once we were inside the plane and after we were in skydive mode. Those instructions said that we were to participate by pulling the ripcord when instructed to do so at 5,000 feet.

"Wait a minute," I said. "I didn't sign up to pull anything."

"We do this," he said, "so you can have the experience of participating."

"I have no desire to participate," I said.

"Don't worry," he said. "If you don't pull the ripcord, the instructor will."

That didn't give me any reassurance.

Then, he added, "Make sure you don't drop the ripcord because it will cost you another twenty dollars."

An hour later, the instructor and I crawled into the small, twin-engine airplane along with a Canadian team of skydivers. Our team also included a photographer, who would videotape and photograph the two of us skydiving.

Inside the airplane, it was no more than five feet from floor to ceiling. I'm six feet tall. As we all sat down, we spread our legs so the person in front of us was sitting inside our legs. Then, the instructor attached his harness to me.

Finally, we took off. While still climbing, my instructor yelled out, "It's Benny's birthday today. Let's wish him a happy birthday." They all sang "Happy birthday, Benny." I sat there with a nervous smile. After thanking them, my instructor put a cloth-covered headpiece over the top of my head and a pair of goggles over my eyes. Not another word was said between us. Sensing my anxiety, he kept patting my shoulders.

Twenty minutes later, we were at 12,500 feet. I felt extremely apprehensive. I knew I could still change my mind. After everyone else jumped out of the plane, our photographer, with two cameras strapped to his head, climbed out of the plane to hang onto the door so he could get a picture of us standing at the doorway waiting to jump.

After duck-walking to the edge of the open door, I looked down at the awesome white clouds.

At that moment, the photographer gave us a thumbs-up. My instructor loudly yelled into my ear, "Now, start rocking back and forth a couple of times."

I looked down and saw nothing but beautiful, white clouds.

Seeing my head tilted downward, the instructor grabbed my chin and yelled again.

"Keep your head up so we won't go into a tumble and lose control." That was the scariest thing I'd heard yet.

He then gave me a slight shove, and we began our descent. We were in freefall for the next 7,000 feet. Almost immediately, I started to have trouble breathing. I began to panic. With the wind blowing up my nose at 120 mph, I yelled as loud as I could, "HOW AM I SUPPOSED TO BREATHE — WITH MY NOSE OR MY MOUTH?"

With the wind howling, he leaned over my shoulder and yelled back, "ANY WAY YOU CAN!" I still had a hard time catching my breath. I thought I was going to pass out. This was not the happiest moment of my life.

One goal was for me to participate by releasing the ripcord at approximately 5,000 feet. I looked down at the altimeter, which was on my chest, but I couldn't make out what it read. He then tapped me on the shoulder a couple of times, yelling, "PULL THE CORD!" I used my left hand to grab the cord but could find nothing. By now, we were at 3,000 feet.

At this point, the instructor pulled the ripcord. With one huge jerk, the chute opened. We were now gliding gently down toward the good old Earth. The incredible noise level we had when we were in freefall went to zero. It was peaceful and beautiful the rest of the way down. I had survived the freefall.

After making an almost perfect landing, I felt fearless, indestructible and invincible. It was hard to believe I had done something I thought I would never do in my lifetime.

The following day, I did something else I thought I would never do because of my fear of needles: I donated blood.

I had left my comfort zone and felt damn good about it.

— Benny Wasserman —

# 76

# Ripple Effect

*The water is your friend... you don't have to fight with
water, just share the same spirit as the water,
and it will help you move.*
~Aleksandr Vladimirovich Popov

"Y ou got this! You can do it! Come on!" I heard his encouraging words, but I just couldn't do it. I couldn't let go. I tried to nod and muster a smile, but I was completely terrified.

My swim instructor tried once more to calm me. "I am right here. No worries. I got you." I was fifty years old, and there I was white-knuckled, tightly clinging to the pool's edge. At the far end of the same pool, children were splashing, diving, bellyflopping, and tucking their knees as they jumped into the pool's deep end and boisterously yelled, "Cannonball!" Meanwhile, I was reciting prayers under my breath.

I was beyond mortified. There were multiple layers to my embarrassment, and akin to an onion's skin, each one was peeling off, causing me to become teary-eyed. For starters, my new bathing suit: a one-piece, blue tank, which was a bit too form-fitting except for the shoulder-strap fasteners, which were extremely loose. I was in desperate need of a safety pin, maybe two. Despite the fact I was physically fit, ran daily and had acquired an impressive collection of racing bibs from various marathons, it still seemed that no matter how much asphalt I kicked, my thighs had an uncanny resemblance to cottage cheese. Of course, the nude-colored bathing cap plastered to my head wasn't exactly a confidence-booster either.

Why was I taking private swimming lessons at my age? I had always wanted to compete in a triathlon but needed to learn how to swim. I was in awe of triathletes — their determination and stamina. Sure, I had run my share of marathons throughout the years and had even completed a few biathlons. I could run and bike, but I could not swim.

I had procrastinated long enough. I had promised myself that, by the age of fifty, I would have completed a triathlon, perhaps even two. Well, age fifty-one would arrive in six months.

Once more, my swimming instructor tried his best to reassure me. "You are ready. This is a defining moment for you." In the weeks prior, my instructor and I had practiced floating and kicking together. I had finally mastered both and was actually pretty good at flutter kicks. Of course, my proven abilities to float and kick required that I hold onto the edge of the pool for dear life. I cringed as my instructor tried for the fourth time. "Come on. Today, no more holding on. Let go of the edge. You can do it."

I couldn't. I was too frightened. I screamed, "Noooooo!" I sounded like a child whose favorite toy had just been thrown away.

A lifeguard approached and asked my instructor, "You need help?"

My instructor answered, "Thanks. She's fine. She's ready."

The pressure was on. The lifeguard stood at poolside with my instructor next to me. I took a deep breath, exhaled, and let go of the pool's edge. I was floating. My instructor let out a deafening "Woo-hoo!" The lifeguard smiled and gave me a thumbs-up.

In the weeks to follow, my swimming lessons gradually became easier. I was far less apprehensive. Dare I say, I was practically relaxed. I no longer felt compelled at any point to grab my towel and flip-flops and run to the nearest exit. I was learning to swim. I made measurable progress, for sure. My confidence in swimming gained momentum, as did my training regimen. I designated certain days of the week to run, bike, or swim. With each breaststroke I swam, pedal I pushed, and calf muscle I pumped, I was getting closer to achieving my goal. There was a triathlon finisher's medal out there with my name on it.

I was beyond excited.

And, so, the big day arrived. It was a beautiful day, perfect weather for a triathlon. I was nervous but determined. I sweated. I persevered. I finished. As I ran through the final chute, I victoriously raised my arms high above my head and screamed, "Yes, I did it!" I wept when a finisher's medal, dangling from a red, white and blue ribbon, was placed around my neck.

Almost two years have come and gone since I completed my triathlon. I had faced a lifelong fear, earned a medal, and checked off a box on my bucket list, all at the age of fifty. I realized just how liberating it is to let go of trepidation and worry.

I often think back to that day in the pool when my instructor gently coaxed me to let go of the pool's edge. His words still echo: "This is a defining moment for you." It was a defining moment in a far greater way than I could have imagined. These days, whenever I am immobilized by fear and uncertainty, I take a deep breath and close my eyes. I visualize myself back in that swimming pool clinging to the side. I exhale and remember what it felt like to finally just let go and float.

— Patricia Rossi —

# 77

# Breaking Free

*If it scares you, it might be a good thing to try.*
~Seth Godin

A wave rolled in, up to my chest, and sucked me completely under. Even with my head submerged under the swirling water, I could hear my oldest child's booming laugh. Apparently, he had found it funny when the wave took me out.

As hard as this trip had been for me, that laugh brought me so much joy.

A week prior, I had been curled up in the corner of my couch having a full-blown panic attack. It was nothing new, but every time I had one, it felt just as new and terrifying as the previous one.

I had grown accustomed to rarely leaving my home. I had suffered from anxiety attacks and agoraphobia since I was eleven years old. At their most extreme, I couldn't walk out onto my porch or get my own mail.

Curled in the corner of the couch that Tuesday, I decided that I was not going to let agoraphobia diminish my life anymore. My husband of sixteen years and I had three teenage kids. Because of my anxiety problems, we never went on vacations or traveled anywhere. When my panic attack subsided, I made the decision that we were going to make the ten-hour drive from our home in central New York to see Stephen King's house in Bangor, Maine.

I called my husband on Tuesday while he was at a hotel in the

Adirondacks. He works on the railroad and stays out of town during the week. I told him what I wanted to do that Friday. He was caught off-guard for sure but was one hundred percent on board. It was such a last-minute decision that we weren't able to rent a vehicle, so we drove our old, beat-up van and prayed that it would hold up. It did.

Our kids were so excited. I was, too. Stephen King had been a huge part of my life since I was eleven. His novels helped me get through so many stressful times in my life.

My excitement quickly turned into anxiety as we hit the road, though. It was very scary, especially for the first three hours. Even with my anti-anxiety medication, I still had to have my husband pull over thirty minutes into the trip at a rest stop. I got out, breathed in the fresh air, and calmed myself.

We stopped two more times on the way. Multiple times, when we became trapped in traffic that was not moving, I felt the need to get out of the vehicle and run. Several times, I thought I was going to chicken out and make my husband turn around and head back home.

By the grace of God, I made it to our hotel in Bangor after what turned out to be a twelve-hour drive. Walking into the hotel room, I breathed a sigh of relief. I had made it without a full-blown attack.

Over the next two days, I watched how happy my children were. I was so glad that we had made the trip. Was the rest of the trip easy for me? Absolutely not. I had a panic attack in Walmart. I cried as we left the old cemetery because I was starting to have an attack, and I felt like I was cheating my kids out of being able to enjoy the trip. They assured me that it was not the case. Besides those couple of bumps, the rest of the trip went well. We saw Mr. King's house. We found a bookstore near the hotel that we loved so much that we went three times before leaving for home.

Sunday morning, we left. Little did I know that my husband had planned a side trip on our way home. My anxiety went through the roof. I can't handle surprises or not being in control. We drove for two hours back toward our home. My husband got off on an exit that took us to Portland, Maine. None of us had ever been to the ocean. We had always wanted to go but hadn't been able to because of my agoraphobia.

We ended up at Cape Elizabeth. It had a beautiful lighthouse and a small slope that led right down to a cove where the ocean came splashing in. It was September, so the water was quite chilly. We were all so excited that we didn't care. All five of us walked into the ocean to some extent. We've already established that I went too far, but that's okay. My son got a good laugh out of it.

That trip showed me that I could do anything I wanted to, especially if I knew that it was going to make my children happy and give them good memories. If I hadn't taken that trip, I would have missed my daughter's ear-to-ear smile as she tried to stay standing when the waves rolled in. If I hadn't taken that trip, I wouldn't have the memory of my older son's laughter as I floundered in the water. If I hadn't stepped out of my comfort zone, I wouldn't have seen my younger son run up a ninety-degree incline to see headstones from the 1700s. If I hadn't stepped out of my comfort zone, I wouldn't have the memories of my husband smiling for nearly three days straight. If you know my husband, you know what a miracle that is.

For as long as I can remember, anxiety had controlled my life and dictated what I could and couldn't do. But for those three days in September 2021, I took one scared, shaky step out of my comfort zone. When I did, my anxiety and panic didn't magically go away, but I did learn that I could let those bad moments roll over me. I could enjoy all the amazing moments with my family that I had been missing out on.

My comfort zone had grown smaller and smaller over the years, essentially imprisoning me. Those first scary steps I took broke some of those chains. Now, I know that I am free to go in and out of my comfort zone whenever I choose. I might be scared and shaking when I do it, but I know there are amazing experiences to be had if I just keep pressing forward. After all, you can only have a *comfort* zone if you know what being *uncomfortable* feels like.

— Danielle Stauber —

# 78

# The Ride of a Lifetime

*Attitude is the difference between*
*an ordeal and an adventure.*
~Bob Bitchin

For as long as I could remember, I was *that* child — the one who screamed so loud on a kiddie amusement-park ride that the attendant had to stop it. If I was pushed more than a foot high on a park swing, I yelled for my parents to "Stop!" I was always worried something might happen, and it inhibited me from trying fun activities that my friends enjoyed.

That worry followed me into adulthood. Although I'd overcome many of my fears, it had been difficult for me to try new endeavors. I'd always looked at the big picture of "what ifs." What if I break my leg while skiing? What if the kayak tips over? What if the roller coaster gets stuck at the top? The list went on and on.

It wasn't that I didn't want to try new experiences. It was just that my fear of a mishap kept me from trying. I sat on the sidelines as a child watching everyone have fun. As an adult, I was still a spectator.

That was until one Saturday afternoon when my friend Marge popped in and exclaimed with excitement, "You have to come." She had just received free tickets to Six Flags Great Adventure. She knew how I felt about going on rides, so she assured me that we would only see a few shows, enjoy the drive-through safari, and eat a huge amount of junk food. No rides.

Since the amusement park is local, I had had season passes before.

I loved going when my kids were small. Back then, they enjoyed the carousel, entertainment and arcade games. It was a "safe zone" for me until my children got older and begged me to go on a roller coaster with them. Visions of me screaming on that ride came flooding back to me.

After about five minutes of Marge begging and pleading, I agreed to join her at the amusement park. "Remember, I am not going on scary rides," I repeated, just to make sure she kept her promise and didn't try to persuade me once we got there.

We had a nice, leisurely day at the park. As promised, Marge kept her word. Not once did she suggest going on a ride other than the carousel. After seeing a few shows, playing arcade games and eating a ridiculous amount of food, we were making our way to leave and head home when Marge stopped abruptly.

"Look!" she shouted, clapping her hands as she jumped up and down, pointing off to the side. I slowly turned my head, thinking she had seen a Looney Tunes character stroll by. But, to my horror, she was pointing at the Skull Mountain roller coaster.

"No, don't even think about it," I warned her. "You promised!"

When I saw the enthusiasm drain from Marge's face, I felt awful. I didn't want to disappoint her. As we walked toward the exit to leave the park, I blurted out, "Let's go on Skull Mountain!" The words escaped my mouth without thinking. I don't know what came over me. Marge was just as surprised as I was.

As we walked back to the ride, I secretly hoped the line would be too long and Marge would change her mind. No luck. There were only about a dozen people waiting. We could get on with the next group. I felt a bit better when I saw several parents waiting in line with their young children. The kids were chatting and giggling. I tried to convince myself that if the kids weren't scared, there was no reason why I should be.

The time came for us to board. To say I felt like my heart was about to beat out of my chest is an understatement. Marge must have sensed how nervous I was. "Hey, are you alright?" she asked with concern. "We can forget about it," she assured me. Although nervous, I had gotten this far and was determined to see it through.

Buckled into our seats, I took a deep breath and closed my eyes. Marge reminded me that the ride was an enclosed roller coaster, in almost total darkness. "You can open your eyes," she snickered. Now, I worried if it was better to see the upcoming twists, turns and descents or to unexpectedly drop down a hill.

My thoughts were running wild but were interrupted when we started to move along the track. There was no turning back now. Marge took my hand for support.

With every twist and turn, ascent and drop-down, I screamed along with all the others on the ride, including Marge. The giggling of the little boy who sat in front of us was comforting.

It seemed to be the longest few minutes I'd ever experienced, but I survived and wasn't as terrified as I thought I would be. Best of all, I felt exhilarated from my accomplishment.

Will I ever ride another roller coaster? I'm not sure. But, because of that one attempt to put aside my apprehension, I've gained the courage to experience many new adventures that I was afraid to try in the past. I finally went skiing and kayaking without breaking a leg or flipping over a boat. I still get nervous before I try something new, but I replace my negative "what ifs" by making myself remember the proud feeling of accomplishment I get afterward.

— Dorann Weber —

# 79

# Acting on a Whim

*Everyone has talent. What's rare is the courage to
follow it to the dark places where it leads.*
~Erica Jong

In elementary school, my mom took me to the local high school
production of *Hello, Dolly!* I sat awestruck at the talent on stage as
the students sang and danced in their colorful outfits beneath the
bright lights. Mom leaned over to me and whispered, "Maybe one
day you'll be on that stage!"

My breath caught in my throat at the thought of performing with
an auditorium full of eyes staring at me. I wasn't sure I could ever do
that, but I loved the thought of holding people spellbound the way
these students captivated me.

Fast forward to my freshman year in high school. As a recovering
anorexic, I was as skinny as a rail, with a terrible bob haircut to boot.
Looking in the mirror, my self-esteem was at an all-time low. When
audition sheets were posted for the fall musical, a pit formed in my
stomach as I read the list of students who were trying out. Every one
of them was gorgeous, popular, and uber talented. Sure, I had taken
some dance lessons and participated in choir all through middle school,
but compared to these star students, I felt worthless.

"You should at least try!" my friend told me.

"And risk humiliating myself?" I said. "No, thanks!"

"But what if you make it? Just audition and see if you get a callback."

Honestly, at that point in my life, I had a knack for taking any situation and finding a reason why my presence would make it worse. Maybe my low confidence was still residual self-loathing from anorexia. All I knew was that I could talk myself out of anything.

My first three years of high school, I never tried anything new. My knee-jerk response to any suggestion was always "No." My senior year, I finally worked up the nerve to enroll in a theater class.

At first, I feared I had made a terrible mistake. The drama teacher, Mrs. Forester, scared the living daylights out of me. She had a gruff, gravelly voice that she used to bark at any student who didn't immediately snap to attention the moment she called their name. Her face, wrinkled and pruned from decades of smoking, rarely displayed a smile. But when it did, it was devilish like the Grinch.

Despite Mrs. Forester's scary appearance and demeanor, she was an amazing theater teacher who taught me not only how to emote on the stage but also the importance of growing self-confidence. By year's end, much of my fear had melted away.

Freshman year of college, I was on my way to lunch when I came across the public library. I decided to go inside and meander a bit. Wandering through the lobby, I came across a message board with a flyer that said, "Auditions today for one-act plays, noon–2:00 P.M. Room 121."

I glanced at the clock on the wall. It was 1:30 P.M. I had no idea what this audition entailed or if actors were supposed to have prepared a monologue. But, for whatever reason, I found myself headed for the basement of the library. Slowly, I pushed open the heavy auditorium door and peeked inside. Someone had just exited the stage, and an older man with a beard and bifocals, sitting in the front row, called out to me, "You here to audition?"

I stuttered, "Uh-uh, um," and then found myself saying, "Yes!"

Perhaps he read my awkward body language or heard the croak in my voice and assumed, rightfully so, that I was exceedingly nervous, not to mention unprepared.

"No worries if you don't have a monologue," the man said. "Just come grab a script. I'll have you read a couple of scenes."

I made my way toward the stage and reached out my quivering

hand for the script. It was wrinkled with a big coffee stain in the center, but I could still make out the lines.

"Your name?"

"I'm Christy," I said.

"Well, thanks for coming in, Christy. My name is Hal," said the bearded man. "I'm the writer and director for this one-act play, which is about a husband and wife, David and Liz, who are experiencing marital conflict. The wife's sister comes to visit, and the husband makes a pass at her, which obviously doesn't help improve the marital discord. I'm going to have you read the part of Greta, the sister."

I read two different scenes: one with the husband character and one with the wife.

"Okay," Hal said. "I think that's all we need. Just leave your name and contact info at the desk, and I'll let you know by Monday if you got the part."

I stumbled out of the library in a daze, shocked that I had done something so brave on a whim.

The following day, Hal called to tell me I'd gotten the part of Greta. All the blood rushed to my face as I squealed. I'd never been so excited to get something that I didn't know I wanted or even existed.

When I read the full script, however, my mouth went dry. One scene called for the husband character, David, to physically force himself on his sister-in-law. My character fights back and knees him in the groin. I didn't know if I could pull off such a scene. My first instinct was to ask Hal to change the scene, but this was clearly a pivotal moment that was integral to the show because it helped propel Liz to make a tough decision regarding the future of her marriage.

I thought back to how petrified I was of Mrs. Forester initially. As I absorbed what she was teaching, however, I gained both practice and confidence. It was time to employ those same methods here.

I'll admit that rehearsals were awkward. One time when Mark, the actor playing the husband, went in for the kiss, I kicked him with extra *oompf,* and he fell hard to the ground. I thought he was going to be hopping mad, but he said instead, "That was awesome, Christy! You've been holding back in this scene, and that was the first time you really went for it. Promise me you'll do that on opening night."

It was the first and last time I would ever be praised by a man for kneeing him in the goods, but Mark was right about my having been holding back. No more of that.

When opening night came, I was energized. This was no big musical production with six-part-harmony songs, flashy costumes, and cool props. This was community theater with a small stage, intimate audience setting, and actors wearing our own clothes. But I didn't care. It felt good to embody the part of Greta and take the audience on a journey through David and Liz's relationship.

I thought back to elementary school when my mom had encouraged me at that *Hello, Dolly!* show to one day take the stage. I peeked out from the wings prior to the start of the show and saw my mom in the audience, waving and blowing me a kiss. I smiled and took a deep breath, ready to take the stage.

—Christy Heitger-Ewing—

# 80

# Don't Look Down

*Do one thing every day that scares you.*
~Eleanor Roosevelt

ome people create bucket lists — things to do before they die. Although I didn't plan on dying anytime soon, an impending fiftieth birthday stirred up enough unrest to prompt me to take an accounting of my life.

Did I have a good life? Absolutely. I loved my husband and enjoyed teaching and writing. Our two Boxers kept us busy with their antics. We had been blessed with relatively good health.

But unwanted baggage had wormed its way into my life, too. A practice of sitting in front of a computer, writing about life instead of experiencing it. A childhood fear of heights that carried into adulthood. A habit of focusing on tasks to be accomplished rather than on people to love and enjoy.

In honor of the approaching milestone birthday, I decided to stop talking about change and start doing something about it. First up: tackling my fear of heights. And I knew the perfect location for my challenge: the Jupiter Inlet Lighthouse, 150 years old, 105 steps to the top, and a mere twenty-five miles from my home. We set a date, and I mentally checked this item off my list as practically done.

But when we pulled into the parking lot, I second-guessed my plan as I gazed up at the lighthouse. What was I thinking? This was a bad idea. Not just bad, it had all the ingredients for an unmitigated disaster. Thankfully, my husband accompanied me or I would have never exited the car. He helped me out, and with an arm around my waist, alternately walked and propelled me to the entrance.

We paid the entry fee, proceeded through the displays of local history, and made our way to the base of the lighthouse. Once inside, I came face-to-step with my nemesis: a narrow, spiral stairway that appeared to end in the heavens.

Did I really want to follow through with this crazy plan? Living with a fear of heights wasn't so bad. After all, I had managed to survive with it for fifty years. Besides, wouldn't I have been wiser to start with an eight-foot ladder instead of a 108-foot staircase?

I squared my shoulders and dismissed my doubts with a surprising boost of courage.

The first step was easy. But with each succeeding rung, my bravado dissipated. I began to chant under my breath, "I can do this. Don't look down. I can do this. Don't look down."

I did do it. All the way up 105 steps. Slowly. Deliberately. Eyes straight ahead. Never looking down, but never looking up, either. Until we reached the outer platform at the top of the lighthouse.

The panoramic view was amazing. Of course, I hugged the wall, refusing to venture to the outer edge of the platform. My breaths came quick and shallow. But there I was, despite my fears. Yes! I even took pictures to document the event. The photos were a bit blurry thanks to my shaking hands, but I didn't care. Those imperfect pictures documented a breakthrough for me — proof that I did not have to allow fear to control my life.

Unfortunately, my celebration was short-lived, stifled by a steady parade of people who continued to spill out onto the platform. What goes up must also come down.

I stepped back into the doorway and clung to the railing. Frozen with fright, I couldn't decide which was worse: being stuck 108 feet off the ground or attempting a descent on a narrow spiral staircase with open-weave, metal grates for treads.

As a growing crowd jostled for space, individuals flowed around me and down the stairs. I gripped the railing and willed myself to take the first step despite the panic that squeezed my heart and paralyzed my feet. "Don't look down!" I reminded myself. Easier to accomplish when I climbed *up* the stairs. Now that I needed to descend? Next to impossible.

Fear coursed through my veins and oozed out of my pores. My heartbeat pounded like a bass drum in my ears. I was too old for this. What did I think I was proving, anyway? It was not as if climbing a lighthouse was something I would ever need to do again.

Then, I noticed him just ahead of me: a tall, sturdy, young man. He was probably in high school because he appeared to be part of a student group. His body language was all too familiar to me. Fear drove him to sit on the step in front of him. As he sat, he turned his head to reveal an ashen face. He scooted down on the seat of his pants, one agonizing step at a time, oblivious to the chattering crowd streaming past him.

At that moment, the realization hit me. Age had nothing to do with my problem. And fear was not my real issue, either. My problem was in how I responded to the dread that assailed me. I had a choice. I could push through my fear, or I could spend the rest of my life a prisoner in a cell of my own construction.

I made my decision, one step at a time, descending the same way I had climbed those 105 rungs. Slowly. Deliberately. Eyes straight ahead. Never looking down.

But while resolve was crucial in getting me to the bottom, it wasn't the only motivating factor. At my side, every inch of the way, my husband cheered me on. "You can do it, honey. I'm proud of you. Another step. Yes. That's it. Keep going. You can do it!"

I wish I could say I am free of my fear of heights. I'm not, and I don't know if I ever will be. Still, I have stopped allowing fear to control what I do. And perhaps that's the best freedom of all.

— Ava Pennington —

# 81

# Mud Girl

*It doesn't matter how fast or how far you're going.*
*If you're putting on your shoes and going out*
*for a run, you are a runner, you are in that club.*
*~Kara Goucher*

Sure, as a child I made mud patties and loved to play in the sandbox and build sandcastles at the beach, but at fifty-three years old I couldn't imagine myself playing in the dirt much less *mud*.

It started so casually. Six months earlier, while warming up for a workout, the trainer at my gym announced that she was signing up for the Mud Girl Run, a 5k obstacle race dedicated to women, with money going to breast cancer research. She asked if anyone wanted to join her team.

I really didn't know much about it. My first response was just to keep my head down, as clearly she wasn't directing the question at me. After all, I complained each time we were told to run a simple lap in the parking lot. Obviously, she didn't care that I was ignoring the conversation because suddenly she singled me out, directly asking if I was going to sign up.

My response was, "I'll have to check my calendar."

After being a member of her gym for over a year, she seemed to know me too well and replied with, "You don't have anything on your calendar *six* months from now." And… "Didn't you just tell me you were working on a book about getting out of your comfort zone and saying yes to new opportunities?"

She had a point, and I did envy those who were willing to commit to trying new things. Still, I spent the next few months coming up with every excuse I could to cancel. It was around the same time that we had scheduled the *Chicken Soup for the Soul: Get Out of Your Comfort Zone* Zoom party during which story contributors would meet each other online. During the Zoom, my colleague Amy asked each of us to share how we were trying something new or stepping outside our comfort zones. It was at that moment that I knew I had to go through with it. I told everyone on my screen that I was going to participate in the Mud Girl run. I now had a couple dozen "accountability partners."

Although I was still extremely nervous, I have to admit I was also excited. I was going to push myself to try something new and honor the commitment I made to not only my friends at the gym but also the Chicken Soup for the Soul contributors.

I watched YouTube videos of the 5k run/obstacle challenge to prepare myself for what was to come. There would be seventeen obstacles consisting of a weight pulley system, mud pits, hills to climb, sandbags to carry, and even cargo nets to climb over, among others. Did I mention mud? All obstacles take place in mud. They did allow participants that did not complete an obstacle the option of taking an easier path around it. Knowing that there was an escape route put me a little more at ease.

The day of the race arrived and not only was I up and ready early, mostly because I really did not sleep the night before, but I found that my son, sister, and parents were also ready to go to cheer me on. I am sure I was the only fifty-three-year-old with her mom and dad on the sidelines. I know for sure I was the only one with a parent taking pictures with an actual camera, which some of my teammates could not help but comment on.

When I arrived at the race, while still nervous, I could not help but feel the excitement of being a part of a group of women in pink shirts, tutus, crazy wigs, and a number of other costumes representing their particular groups. People were so creative, and nothing was off limits.

I spotted my group in matching pink tank tops made especially for the day in honor of breast cancer awareness month. Hearing the music and announcements from the loudspeaker about start times created an excitement I had never felt — I was ready!

I told myself that I had to try to conquer each obstacle as I did not want to have any regrets when it was over. I also told myself this was a "one and done" bucket list item so this was my only chance to give it my all.

How wrong I was! Not only did I conquer each obstacle, I was smiling and having fun doing it despite the fact that I was a complete muddy mess. This wonderful group of women, some strangers before that day, pulled each other over mud walls and cheered each other on when someone needed a little encouragement. It was powerful to be a part of something so great.

The "one and done" idea has flown out the window! I had so much fun I have already started looking for other events in my area. After all, my shoes are already dirty.

— D'ette Corona —

# Stepping Up to a New Life, Gratefully

*The water is wide, I can't cross o'er*
*And neither do I have wings to fly*
*Give me a boat that can carry two*
*And both shall row*
*My love and I*
*~Scottish Folk Song*

It was almost impossible to say the words, but I dried my tears, picked up the phone, and called my closest friend, La Verne.

"After all this time, Tom was finally diagnosed — he has MS," I told her. "Even though it's a relief to finally know the truth, I'm really scared now."

LaVerne is a retired nurse and probably had already guessed what Tom's symptoms meant. But Tom and I had been in the dark for years while specialists put Tom through many exams, tests and scans.

"Your life is going to change now," said La Verne. She'd tended her life partner through his declining years with grace, and she knew from personal experience what it's like to be a caretaker. Although she's the kindest person I know, she also doesn't sugarcoat the truth.

"Your relationship is going to change now, too," she added. Was there no end to the good news? My friend sounded like a biblical prophet uttering dire predictions. I didn't want to hear it! And yet, she was right, in more ways than I'd imagined.

After twenty years of a loving second marriage, Tom and I had been approaching old age with very good health — until we were suddenly facing this huge challenge.

Would it surprise you that my life has changed for the good? Or that my relationship with Tom is better than ever? Or, even more astonishing, that I'm grateful for what life has given me? It certainly surprises me now. But not at first.

At the beginning I was terrified. How would I live my own life when I'd spend it taking care of my husband? I'm not a caretaker by nature, like La Verne. I'm a writer and a gardener, not a nurse. I don't have it in me!

I'm embarrassed to admit that I pictured abandoning my marriage, my home, even my beloved garden. I'd move to Israel where I'd spent a gap year during college, or return to New York City, where I grew up. Maybe I'd move in with my widowed sister. Fantasies abounded as I refused to face reality.

But despite daydreaming about escape, I worried about the present reality. What if Tom fell and broke a bone? What if he couldn't drive anymore? We'd married late in life and kept our two homes so that we could each "do our thing." A passionate musician, Tom sings and plays piano and trumpet most every day. As a gardener and writer, I tend my flower-filled acre and write in solitude. What if I'd have to give up my home and garden to move into Tom's house as his caretaker?

Meanwhile, life went on. I went with Tom to his medical appointments to learn more about managing his disability. Sadness and anger were early companions as we slogged through appointments with a neurologist, a physical therapist, and a psychiatrist. Together we shopped for a motorized wheelchair to relieve Tom's MS fatigue, for a foot brace to offset his foot drop. Each visit brought me closer to Tom as I joined him on his path. I'd loved him from the beginning, but a new kind of love was burgeoning inside me.

I watched in awe as Tom faced his situation with determination and courage. He pushed himself to exercise and strengthen his weak right leg. To compensate for his weak right hand, he used a Mixmaster to fix his favorite tuna salad and bake brownies. A passionate musician who played piano and trumpet, Tom taught himself to play left-handed by practicing ardently.

My admiration for Tom grew exponentially. If he could do all this, how could I not step up to help him navigate this unpredictable passage? What I'd considered a hardship slowly grew into an adventure. Driving him to medical appointments became an outing, especially during the pandemic when we rarely ventured out. Masked and distanced from others, we'd sit in the doctor's waiting room chatting, often laughing, thanks to Tom's unstoppable sense of humor.

Of course, it wasn't always fun. Sometimes Tom's spirits would plummet, and I found it tough not to share his dark mood. The house would feel like one big sigh. Sometimes worries about the future would overwhelm me, and when I couldn't control my fears I'd snap at Tom. What had been a loving evening could turn sour in a hurry.

After a few rounds this roller coaster began to feel like the film *Groundhog Day*. How many times would I step into the pit of sadness and anger? I was losing sleep and becoming exhausted. How could I find a way out of this pattern?

I thought about how I'd handled a similar situation more mindfully. When a friend lost her husband, she was often sad and fearful. I listened attentively, honoring her feelings as she expressed them. How could I become a better friend to Tom?

I sat on the sofa and asked this question, waiting quietly. My cat Webster jumped into my lap and we sat, with only the sound of Webster purring as I stroked his fur. From somewhere deep inside me, a mantra arose. *Don't react; have compassion.* A feeling of calm relief swept through me. Yes, that would be an antidote to fear and anger.

I thought about how hard Tom was working to do his best. He'd immerse himself in music to lift himself up. Singing and playing piano had always made him happy, and this continued to be his personal Prozac. He organized a singers' group on Zoom, hosting it every week with joy.

I decided to create my own joy. Gardening was my retreat. Writing was another safe haven. I promised myself to garden, even in the rain, and write, even when I was worried. Especially when I was worried.

Another piece of wisdom came back to me from the past. "Gratitude is the best antidote to fear." Oh! At one time I'd started a gratitude journal. I found it buried under a pile of books, pulled it out, and made my first entry in years.

Earlier I'd expressed gratitude for friends, family, a beautiful home, and garden. Now my gratitude expanded for unexpected blessings: for Tom's neurologist, for his physical therapist, for his psychotherapist. For Tom, who was working so hard to get stronger. For my own good health, which allows me to help Tom. As I listed these blessings, I felt fear and despair lifting.

There will be more tough times, but facing a challenging illness together, both of us rowing in the same direction, has made our marriage even stronger. In doing his very best to enjoy his life, even with its limitations, Tom is my role model for aging with courage, determination and grace. I never could have imagined how much my life would change for the better, how my relationship would grow deeper than ever.

— Barbara Blossom Ashmun —

# Don't "Act Your Age"

# 83

# Living on the Edge

*Passion is energy. Feel the power that comes*
*from focusing on what excites you.*
~Oprah Winfrey

I've discovered that my life really begins when I choose to leave my comfort zone. Wanting to experience life on the edge has driven me to trek in the Himalayas twice, to venture into the Sahara Desert on a weeklong odyssey, to climb the Torres del Paine in Patagonia, to ascend 14,000-foot Longs Peak's technical North Face, and, most recently, to tackle both the Second and Third Flatirons, two technical rock-climbing formations that rise over Boulder, Colorado. In doing so, I keep uncovering priceless knowledge about myself and the world in which I live.

So, what does it mean to live on the edge of life? It suggests that one undertakes a risk that most people would avoid — doing something physically, psychologically, economically, or politically dangerous. Alex Honnold, the rock climber who successfully soloed El Capitan, and Erik Weihenmayer, the first blind mountaineer to summit Mount Everest, epitomize this. For me, it means crossing a threshold of fear into a special dimension that exists apart from the day-to-day world in which I live. It is a dimension where I will find the answer to the existential question: *Can I?* And it is where I can explore the full complement of sensory experiences accompanying that revelation.

In my own life, I started out by taking the "safe" course. I remember thinking, when I was in my early twenties, that it would be "a cold day in hell before I ever got on skis." Yet, twenty years later, I was teaching downhill skiing to the handicapped and witnessing blind skiers barreling down black-diamond slopes. What I had previously thought was impossible was actually possible.

Trekking in the Himalayas was a challenge and could be very dangerous. Indeed, the adventure company sponsoring these wilderness trips emphasized the perils associated with them. On at least a couple of occasions, I experienced these risks up close and very intimately. On my first trek in Nepal, an uncontrollable wildfire engulfed the terrain just a short distance from a tiny mountain village and our encampment. Fortunately, on that night, the wind was our friend and blew the flames away from us. However, we all realized that a sudden shift in wind direction would mandate an immediate and terrifying evacuation in the middle of the night from this remote and rugged spot in the wilderness. Our group and the inhabitants of the threatened village were at the mercy of Mother Nature and all her whims.

What did I learn from the experience? As I faced this threat, I discovered unexpected reservoirs of strength, flexibility and resilience that lay deep inside me and the people with whom I shared this close encounter with death.

Before my recent climb of the Third Flatiron, a formation that rises to a height of 7,220 feet over Boulder and is 1,200 feet long, I knew that I had the skills to manage it. But, at eighty-seven years of age, did I have the stamina to endure hours of climbing? At the end of the day, the answer was clear. No problem! But in addition to realizing my ability to handle a long and grueling climb, I had the priceless opportunity to view the world below me from an incredible perspective. The magnificence of the surrounding landscape viewed from the top of this majestic rock was breathtaking... and very different from the view below.

Like American businessman and publisher John H. Johnson, I believe "that living on the edge, living in and through your fear, is the summit of life."

— Mary Ann Paliani —

# 84

# Staying in the Game

*There is something to say about believing in your dreams.*
*And having the support and courage to go after them.*
*You can do anything you put your mind to.*
*~Serena Williams*

The news predicted that Hurricane Nicole would be passing near Miami, with wind nearing seventy-five miles an hour and torrential rain. Florida had just begun to recover from Hurricane Ian. It was November, and I wanted the storm season to be over.

Since everyone was cancelling their appointments due to the storm, I decided to treat myself to a mani-pedi from my manicurist. There was nothing left to do but sit back and wait it out. At the salon, with my feet soaking in a warm, pink bubble bath, I heard my phone beep. I opened the text.

"Dear Joyce, you have been kindly requested by your Miami agent, Susan, to audition tomorrow at 1:20 P.M. at Universal Casting. Please go to your Casting Networks page and accept or decline immediately."

I felt a rush, and my adrenaline kicked in. If you're an actor, learning that you have a casting is a high. I had done a lot of commercials in my thirties: Levitz Furniture, Carnival Cruise Line and Popeyes Louisiana Kitchen. When I first started acting, I thought I would be doing it forever. I even pictured myself someday in a Depend commercial, providing it was a black-lace bikini. But, at age seventy, I had fallen into an undefined age group — not the gray-haired-grandma type but no longer the young-mom type. As much as it hurt, I had to accept that perhaps it was time to quit acting. But now here was a chance to reclaim my dream.

My heart skipped a beat as I opened my Casting Network page and read the breakdown. They were casting for a beer commercial. They wanted a stuffy, old-line, golf-club member with great facial expressions. *Wait. That could be me!* No, I didn't belong to a country club, but I knew lots of my husband's friends who did, and they were stuffy. I was sure I could pull this off, or I could fake it.

But then the "nasty doubt devil" popped up. *You haven't been on an in-person casting in a year. What if they don't like the way you look? Your headshots are really dated. And you have gained a few pounds. And what about Hurricane Nicole that's coming into Florida? Are you willing to drive through a raging storm?*

Then the "positive angel" nudged me. *The casting director requested to see you specifically. They wouldn't waste their time if they didn't like you. Give it a shot!*

As I slipped into my flip-flops with my freshly painted red toes, I Googled the address of the casting director. It was a two-hour drive on highways I didn't know. Admittedly, I have the worst sense of direction. I can get lost coming out of Bloomingdale's.

I called my husband, whom I consider to be the voice of logic and reason. "Honey, you're going to think I'm crazy."

I heard him sigh. "This can't be good."

"I want to go on an audition to North Miami tomorrow. They asked for me specifically."

I heard a long pause. "If you can, get up there early and get back on the road before 2:00 to beat the storm."

"I love you!" I shouted and clicked off. I raised my arms in the air and chanted the *Rocky* theme. My manicurist looked at me as if I'd lost my mind. I explained it was a quicker way to dry my nails and then raced out of the salon.

As soon as I got home, I ransacked my closet, trying on every possible golf-club outfit I could find. None of them fit. After seven pairs of pants, I finally found a pair of white jeans that were snug but doable and a pink-cotton, V-neck sweater. I checked myself out in the bathroom mirror. Yep. Upper-class and snooty.

The next morning, the sky was ominous, dark and threatening, but the rain hadn't started. I was on the road by 9:30 A.M. I followed my GPS's voice. What I didn't plan on was the detour that took me twenty minutes out of the way.

I was nervous as I walked into the casting director's office and signed in at the front desk. I was two hours early. Would they even see me? As I signed the paperwork, I heard a familiar voice. "Well, hello, lady. It's been a while."

I turned and saw the owner of the agency, Eva, a gorgeous blonde who could pass for a model. She hugged me. "Thank you for driving out in this weather. We've missed seeing you." Suddenly, I was floating on Cloud Nine. I walked into the waiting room and spotted three other older female actors whom I considered to be some of the best in Miami. They had all decided to brave the hurricane. At least I was in great company.

Someone handed me a script. I read it quickly. Next thing I knew, the casting director, Carlos, came out and motioned for me to come into the casting room. I took a deep breath and mustered as much confidence as I could. I kept repeating, "I can do this. I can do this. I can do this."

Carlos handed me a golf club and motioned for me to stand in front of the camera on the large X marked on the floor. On the first take, I acted as if I were horrified at what an imaginary golfer had done. I frowned and yelled at the camera, telling off the golfer. On the second take, I smiled and waved a thumbs-up to the camera and applauded the golfer. Carlos smiled, turned off the camera, and said, "That was perfect. Just what we wanted."

In the lobby, I was buzzing with adrenaline. I texted my husband and told him it was a success. By the time I left the CD's office, the clouds had opened. A crack of thunder made me shudder. My umbrella turned upside down with the force of the wind. I walked through six inches of water to get to my parked car. My shoes were drenched, and the legs of my pants were sopping wet. But I didn't feel a thing except pure joy. I drove home with my windshield wipers flying. By some miracle, I made it home doing about thirty miles an hour.

I felt like I had conquered the world.

I decided on my drive home that it didn't matter if I booked this commercial or not. I had done something I loved doing most in the world. This was a grand victory. At age seventy, I had conquered my fears and was back in the game.

—Joyce Newman Scott—

# The Penn Oak Tree

*The courage to soar to great heights is inside all of us.*
*~Kerri Strug*

At the park where my children play, beside the fishing pond, stands an oak tree. Like a grande dame, she has watched over me and my children for two decades as we play and dream beneath her canopy. She stands tall on a hillside of mown grass that sweeps down to a pond encircled by a walking path with a footbridge. Her lowest layer of branches hangs heavy on the ground like an old woman resting her elbows on the table to drink her tea. When I join hands with my children and circle around the thickly ridged trunk, our fingertips barely touch. Called a Penn Oak, the tree is said to have been standing when William Penn first came to Pennsylvania over three hundred years ago.

For a time, my family lived within walking distance of the park. On Sunday mornings, my husband would push the double stroller while I walked the dog on a five-mile circuit past the Penn Oak tree. For fourteen years, I had been a stay-at-home, baby-wearing, cloth-diapering, making-it-from-scratch, homeschooling mom. I didn't just use cloth diapers; I crocheted all my own wool diaper covers from my own pattern. I didn't just make our meals from scratch; I made our homeschool curriculum, too.

One morning while walking and talking, I said, "I just can't have one more conversation about cloth diapers and homeschool curriculum." Although our youngest was still wearing diapers, with hand-crocheted wool covers, our oldest was soon to graduate from high school. My husband pointed out that I had a long road ahead of me. If my life were like our walk, I had only begun the first mile. "Why don't you go to college and finish your degree?" he suggested.

For that comment, my husband received a five-mile-long earful of reasons I could not go back to school. Besides being too busy crocheting diaper covers, I was not comfortable with the idea of going to college as a middle-aged adult. As we walked along, I imagined myself sitting in a classroom next to students the same age as my oldest daughter. What kind of conversations could we have? I imagined receiving grades from professors who were younger than myself. What would they think of me — a stay-at-home mom?

Then, one day, with a child or two on my lap, I read Shel Silverstein's *The Giving Tree*. For my children, it was a story about a boy who makes friends with a tree. For me, it was a description of my life with a less-than-promising future. After the tree has given her apples, branches and trunk to the boy, all she has left to give is a seat on her stump to an old man. I understood that I was the tree giving tiny pieces of myself away to my children every time they asked. When my story ended, like the tree in the book, I would be nothing but a sagging stump. I realized I did not want to be the Giving Tree; I wanted to be the Penn Oak tree. I wanted to stand tall and strong, to stretch out my branches and invite my children to play and dream beneath my canopy.

A year later, with wooden train tracks and LEGOs at my feet, I began a course of study in literature and history from my kitchen table. Weekly, I sat in a virtual classroom taking copious notes, drinking up every word from my professors, and sending my roots down deep into the fertile soil of historical texts, literature and poetry. I began to question everything. One day, to introduce the Enlightenment, my professor showed a slide of a quotation by Kant, "Sapere aude! Have the courage to use your own mind!" I hastily scratched the quote into my notes with bold exclamation points. Although the Enlightenment had occurred as a movement over two hundred years earlier, I had never experienced it personally. I had been living in my own dark age. Over the next several years, as I walked through the history of religion, philosophy and literature, I experienced my own personal Enlightenment. I learned how to ask questions and explore answers. I learned how to use my voice.

This summer, I graduated with honors. My husband traded in the double stroller for a camera and followed me around as we walked through the shaded outdoor courtyard where the ceremony and luncheon were held. I stood beneath a tree and posed beside my school's banner while he took a picture. We ate a box lunch at white cloth–covered tables ornamented with bowls of spring flowers. Then, he sat in the audience while my name and degree were announced and displayed on a large movie screen. I walked across the stage, shook hands with the dean, and smiled.

Going back to school as a stay-at-home mom was not always comfortable. Sometimes, my classmates were the same age as my children. Sometimes, my professors were younger than me. However, what took greater courage than re-entering the classroom was daring to use my mind. I stepped out of the comfortable mental space I had lived in for decades and looked at life from a new perspective. I found a society of courageous thinkers in the lives of the historical figures, writers and poets who lived before me. I read Anne Hutchinson's defense when accused by the patriarchal leaders of the New England colony. I smiled at Anne Bradstreet's display of the female intellect at a time when serious academic study was considered too strenuous for a woman's mind. I delighted in Jane Austen's veiled critique of gendered cultural norms. I found the conversation of these women to be more enriching than another conversation about cloth diapers and homeschool curriculum.

On a warm day this summer, when the shade of the Penn Oak tree invited me to come, I sat beneath her cool canopy reading a book while my children stood around the pond fishing. As I read one of the foundational novels of the Gothic genre, written by a woman in the eighteenth century, I realized I had found another friend. No longer do I feel like the sagging stump of a stay-at-home mom — worn down and tired out. Now, I know where to find the enduring riches of conversations past to sustain me for a lifetime. Now, I have more than apples, branches and a trunk; I can give my children words and ideas that will abide. Now, I am standing tall — a woman whom my children can admire. If I could live to be three hundred years old, like the Penn Oak tree, I would live to see my children and grandchildren and their grandchildren playing and dreaming beside the banks of the sun-flecked water in the dappled shade of my canopy.

— Carrie Cannon —

# 86

# Who's the Old Guy on the Skateboard?

*Life begins at the end of your comfort zone.*
~Neale Donald Walsch

Against her better judgment, my wife bought me a skateboard for Christmas this year. It was not without some consternation and deliberation on her part, along with my repeated assurances that I wasn't going to break my neck.

"I used to skateboard all the time," I told her. "My freshman year in college, I didn't have a car. My skateboard was how I got around."

I'll admit that wasn't the most persuasive argument given that I was thirty-some years removed from college and hadn't been on a skateboard since. So, when I noticed that look in her eyes and could tell she was thinking the same thing, I hastily followed with, "Tony Hawk's in his fifties, and he skateboards."

Without missing a beat, my wife replied, "But you're not Tony Hawk!" Touché.

Nonetheless, I was unwavering in this request for a skateboard for Christmas. There was really nothing else I wanted. I was good on sweaters, ties and cologne. And sure, maybe there was a little (or a lot of) midlife crisis involved. But it had been a difficult couple of years for everyone, in lots of ways, and maybe I just wanted that feeling again of being youthful and reckless.

The kids—I mean, the young salespeople—at the skateboard shop were very kind and patient in demonstrating the various skateboard models for me. They didn't seem to be snickering behind my back as I feared might happen when I went up to one of them and asked to be shown something that a former skateboarder — "who hasn't skateboarded since the 1980s," my wife was certain to clarify — might be able to manage.

The salesperson directed me to a row of skateboards in the back that were longer than the others, with thick wheels and a lower center of gravity that I could possibly, as he stuttered to put it politely, "Um, cruise around the neighborhood on, ya' know — but not to really do any tricks."

"Oh, he's not doing any tricks," my wife was fast to confirm.

"I might do tricks," I mumbled meekly under my breath.

I was particularly taken with a low-rider skateboard that had a parquet design on the deck and a colorful, sort of South Pacific motif underneath. Aesthetics aside, there came the task of trying it out and stepping onto it, as I wasn't getting this just to decorate my office.

Cautiously and carefully, clutching my wife's shoulder with one hand and gripping the sales counter with the other, I, to my surprise and amazement, was actually able to stand on the skateboard without careening into the adjacent display of T-shirts. It helped that the store was carpeted. All the same, I gleefully proclaimed that it was "the board for me, dude!" (And I honestly would not have blamed anyone in the shop for snickering behind my back at that comment.)

I left the store, leaving the fate of my resurgent skateboarding career completely in the hands of my wife. And, lo and behold, come Christmas morning, there was that same skateboard under the tree. I instantly did what anyone my age who got a skateboard for Christmas would do: I texted pictures of it to my friends to show them how cool I still was (and really, how cool my wife was for getting it for me).

Since it was the middle of winter in Kentucky where we live, I had to be satisfied for the time being with just standing on the skateboard in our living room and imagining myself dropping into a half-pipe. Yet that did afford me ample opportunity to watch Tony Hawk's MasterClass on skateboarding so that I would learn everything

I needed to know — or, rather, simply refresh my memory (the former skateboarder that I was).

On the first decent day in mid-January, I began the first day of the rest of my life as a skateboarder by skating up and down our driveway, making sure to stay within arm's reach of the garbage cans, side fence and our cars in case I needed to grab onto something for support. I was certain that the neighbors thought I had lost my mind, but so be it. I felt like a kid again. I felt great. Maybe I did still have it, I thought.

I was so taken with my prowess on the skateboard that I filmed a few snippets of footage on my phone (before I went stumbling into the grass), which I posted to Instagram. My friends cautioned me to be careful ("...at your age"), but my college-sophomore niece replied simply with the word, "King." I was not entirely sure what that meant (and, truth be told, sometimes I can't tell if my niece is making fun of me or not), but I decided to take that as a positive.

As the days wore on, and I became more confident in my skateboarding ability, I aimed to take this show on the road — or, more accurately, down the street where there was a little park with a walking track and a basketball court. It was midday middle of the week, and the basketball court was empty, so I dropped in (so to speak) and skated back and forth the length of the court. I also incorporated some turns by slightly leaning my body in the direction I wanted to go (thanks to Tony Hawk for that pro tip).

I was having a blast. I even progressed to doing figure eights and loop-the-loops (although I doubt those are part of the skateboarding lexicon, but they should be). While folks passed by on their constitutionals, their anxious dogs yapping at me, I could only imagine them looking at this fifty-five-year-old man skating circles in an abandoned basketball court and wondering, "Who's the old guy on the skateboard?"

A few more outings like that followed, regardless of the weather — I just bundled up. The overachiever in me was determined to perfect my push-off (one of the fundamentals of skateboarding to get speed and gain momentum) as that was giving me the most difficulty. One afternoon, I spent a couple of hours pushing and pushing and pushing with my right foot. I had what was referred to in the parlance as a regular stance, with my left foot leading on the board.

As I kept on like this, I started to feel the stress and the strain in my right foot, until it became too painful to continue. I picked up my skateboard and limped the several blocks back to the house. Once I got home, my right foot really hurt, especially my heel. The pain was more intense the next morning as I stepped out of bed. My foot throbbed and ached throughout the day, with an unbearable stabbing sensation whenever I put any weight on it.

That was when I realized that, in my exuberance to master the fine art of pushing off on a skateboard, I had re-aggravated my plantar fasciitis (basically, inflammation of the ligament under the foot that connects the heel to the toes), brought on from years of running. Alas, my skateboard would become a decoration in my office after all, at least until I recovered from this lingering injury.

The next few weeks were spent hobbling around, popping ibuprofen, icing my foot and sleeping in a night splint. To my wife's credit, she refrained from saying, "I told you so" (although, in my defense, I didn't break my neck). To add insult to injury, winter promptly turned to spring, and it became ideal skateboarding weather. I couldn't even re-watch the Tony Hawk MasterClass lessons because that only made me further long to skateboard. I would just have to wait this out.

Eventually, with minimal pain, I was ready to return to my skateboard. Unfortunately, in that intervening period of skateboarding inactivity, I had forgotten most of what I had accomplished and had to resume skating up and down in the driveway under the judgmental eyes of my neighbors. But it came back to me quicker than I had expected, and before long I was skateboarding at the abandoned basketball court (which wasn't as abandoned as it was in the winter, so I had to go there at the crack of dawn to get my skateboarding sessions in uninterrupted).

I am pleased to report that I'm still blissfully skateboarding (albeit with a neoprene brace strapped around my foot with Velcro that I bought at the medical-supply store). Maybe next I'll venture to the skateboard park downtown and give that a try.... Or perhaps I'll just stick with our driveway and the abandoned basketball court. Either way, I'm happy. I skateboarded in the '80s (when my body was a tad more flexible and forgiving) and, with any (or a lot of) luck, I'll be skateboarding into my eighties because I just like how this makes me feel — the plantar fasciitis aside. Who cares if I'm the old guy on the skateboard?

—Peter J. Stavros—

87

# YOLO

*Life is not about living the safer option.*
*Life is about living a life worth living.*
~Robert Thier

There I was, a seventy-year-old widow, hanging by a steel wire, so high above the ground in Guatemala that terra firma was not visible to me. The canyon floor in the Sumpango hills was hidden from view by the trees specifically imported to filter both rain and sunlight, maximizing the yield of the coffee plants growing beneath them. Among all this, the Yalu coffee farm had carefully strung a series of ziplines and other tourist attractions.

My teammates, a small group of mostly young medical workers, and I, an old lady, had been on a weeklong mission trip, setting up medical clinics in rural Guatemalan villages. On our free day, before flying back to the States, the team decided to be adventurous. I could have declined, but I have always been a chicken about everything. I wanted to conquer some of my fears and phobias. A zipline seemed like something I could do while surrounded by wonderful, supportive women.

I thought the bus would drop us off at the platform, but we were picked up in Antigua and driven, for at least an hour, up into the mountains at an elevation higher than Antigua's 5,000 feet. We were immediately fitted with zipline harnesses, gloves and helmets. Then, we started to hike up the mountain on a trail I believe was carved out by wildlife. It wound around rocks and boulders, often not being wide enough for both feet. In places, it required holding on to a sapling to

288 | Don't "Act Your Age"

keep from falling off the trail's edge. It went up and up, higher into the mountain. My old-lady lungs began to pant for oxygen. The young gazelles I was with scampered up the side of that mountain like it was a mere speed bump. I do not like to be made to feel or look old. I continued upward, maybe not keeping pace but moving ever forward toward that first platform.

By the time I arrived at the jump-off point, my heart raced, my lungs burned, and my throat felt raw.

I watched as each of my teammates' harnesses was hooked to the zipline. They lifted their legs and whizzed across the canyon, skimming over the treetops and out of sight. As each one landed, shouts of congratulations and celebration roared back across the canyon.

Soon, only our team leader Linda and I remained on the platform. Being the responsible party, she had to go last. I stepped up and had the Yalu staffer hook me up to the zipline... and unhook me... three times. I just couldn't step off that platform and trust my life to that wire.

As time passed, and I did not appear on the other side of the canyon, calls of "YOLO! YOLO!" began to reach me from across the canyon. I knew what that meant. It had become sort of our team mantra during the week: You Only Live Once!

"It's okay, Linda," I told the team leader. "I will walk back down the mountain and meet you all at the bottom. You may only live once, but you only die once, too!" I just couldn't do it. Heights were one of my biggest all-time fears. What had I been thinking? I had a disabled son at home who would need me in his life until the day I died—of NATURAL CAUSES. No, I was going to continue being a wuss.

"Mason, you know I can't go if you don't go," Linda said.

Well, no, I didn't know, and guilt will get me every time. I let them hook me up. I stepped off that platform, and the steel wire took me over the treetops for the ride of my life. What an amazing experience. Fortunately, my YOLO teammates got it all on video, so I could watch it myself.

I faced the second zipline without fear. I zipped toward the landing platform, feeling a bit smug and sure of myself, and began gazing around at all the beautiful Guatemalan country. I caused myself to brake too soon and ended up at a dead stop, dangling somewhere high above the canyon floor.

At Yalu, they have a plan for this. They tell the young, fit zipliners how to rescue themselves by turning around and doing a hand-over-hand maneuver to pull themselves to the platform. However, if you are a seventy-year-old woman and find yourself stranded out on a wire, a handsome, young Guatemalan staffer calls out to you, "Wait there. I will be out to get you."

While I continued to relax and enjoy the view, he hooked himself to the cable, pulled himself to my location, wrapped his strong, muscular legs around my waist, and pulled me to safety with his powerful arms.

Some people think I intentionally braked too soon. Maybe next time.

— Mason K. Brown —

# 88

# A Love Story for the Ages and the Aged

*Life can be strange — a person who once was a*
*stranger across the room is now the love of your life.*
*~Andy Atticus*

Getting married at the tender age of seventy-two? How crazy is that? It wasn't even on my radar. But, after thirty-six years of marriage and four years of adjusting to the sudden death of my husband, I thought I might be ready to start dating.

"Go online," I was told, but I was intimidated by that whole process. Just getting started — selecting the dating sites, writing a profile and putting it up online with photos — was daunting. And then there was the hassle of reading and reviewing profiles, choosing and contacting men of interest or responding to those interested in my profile, or, even more distressing, facing rejection if no interest was shown at all. But I found a service that did all the grunt work and I made some contacts.

Surprisingly, my first few dates went well. No serial killers, psychos, stalkers, or con men showed up. They were nice guys. I couldn't believe it. I was happy to meet them, had a good time and enjoyed their company, but something was missing. I couldn't quite pin it down until it happened. It was the spark, an electric connection that passes between two people. I didn't think, at my age, that electricity was important. Being a mature, rational person, I figured that if the other qualities and attributes I considered significant were present, the spark wasn't necessary. I was wrong, and I recognized it when it happened.

On a beautiful, warm day, I met Terry. He was tall and slim and dressed nicely in khakis and a plaid shirt. Our conversation was easy from the start — just your basic getting-to-know-each-other stuff. Time passed, and we just kept talking and talking, way beyond having eaten our lunch, dessert, coffee, etc. About two hours in, I asked him what he had done for a living because I couldn't quite tell from his profile. He looked a bit sheepish and said he had purposely left his career information on the website ambiguous.

"Why?" I asked.

"Because it might put off some people," he replied.

Well, that sent up a big red flag.

"Um," I mumbled and hesitatingly asked, half-joking and half-serious, "are you on the sex-offender list? Because that would definitely put me off."

"No, no, nothing like that," he said, waving his hands back and forth and laughing. Whew.

"Do you have any kind of criminal background?" I inquired.

"No, no, no." Again, the hand waving and laughing.

"Well?"

He looked me in the eye and said, much to my surprise, "I'm a retired Presbyterian minister."

Who was laughing now and feeling a bit squeamish? But I could tell this guy had a sense of humor, so I said straight-faced, "That might be worse."

And the more I got to know him, the more I fell for him. Thank God, it was mutual. We dated and just clicked. Everything was easy and natural. The fears I had harbored about fitting into his life, and his fitting into mine, about religious differences and geographical distances, and the really scary intimacy thing, turned out to be no big deal. The ease with which we faced these potential stumbling blocks assured me that we had something special going on. And so we fell in love, easily and naturally.

On the anniversary of our first date, he asked if it was time for a real commitment. I replied that I was already committed. Wasn't he?

"Didn't we agree almost immediately after meeting to take our profiles off the dating sites?"

"Yes, of course," he said, "but I mean a deeper, richer, more serious commitment."

"Oh," I said and began to get where he was going with this. I took a moment and then asked, "Do you mean the 'M word'?"

Well, I loved this guy dearly, and it did seem like the next logical step. So, I put my arms around him and said, "Let's look each other in the eye and ask, 'Will you marry me?' at the exact same time." We did, and we did.

The wedding was planned for May of the following year. What a great time we were having. Family, friends and even total strangers got caught up in the idea of a marriage between a now seventy-two-year-old woman and a seventy-nine-year-old man. It was just so exciting and life-affirming.

But, around March, things changed. I started exhibiting some weird symptoms. I had been in excellent physical condition, taking exercise classes at the gym regularly, working at a demanding part-time job three days a week, and having the energy of a twenty-year-old. But I found myself almost debilitatingly fatigued at times. My left hand would start involuntarily shaking, and I experienced some strange balance and memory issues. Originally, I wrote these off as a normal part of the aging process, but they became more extreme. So, I went to the doctor — and then to doctors.

Finally, I went to a neurologist because I thought that maybe I had Parkinson's, which is not a good thing to have. Terry and I were relieved when the doctor said definitively that it was not Parkinson's but strongly suggested I get an MRI to see what might be going on in my brain. A week before the wedding, we found out I had a brain tumor that needed to be removed as soon as possible. As the reality of the diagnosis set in, I told Terry that I was calling off the wedding.

"What are you talking about?" he asked incredulously.

"Absolutely no wedding," I insisted. "I was healthy when we met, at least I thought so. I am not letting you marry a sick old lady with a brain tumor who you might be pushing around in a wheelchair for the next ten years!"

He gave me a funny, intense look and quietly said, "It would be my privilege." Chills started going up and down my spine, and I burst into tears. Who thinks like that? Who says things like that? How did a man like that love me that much? What could I do? Despite telling him multiple times to get in his car and drive as far away and as fast away from me as possible, he wouldn't do it. So, I had to marry him.

We kept my health situation a secret before the wedding so as not to cast a pall over this much-anticipated event, and we had the most wonderful, joyful, loving day ever. The following week, I had an eleven-hour surgery where a tumor the size of a fist was removed. Talk about relief. I survived it and had some rocky times, but, incredibly, I bounced back and am as close to normal as I get. Terry was with me every minute, literally, and every stumbling step of the way. We are looking forward to many more happy years together. It is truly a love story for the ages, but particularly for the aged.

— Sally Schofield —

# 89

# The First Step

*If you are afraid to take a chance, take one anyway.*
*What you don't do can create the same regrets*
*as the mistakes you make.*
*~Iyanla Vanzant*

The photo album tumbled to the floor from the upper shelf of the closet, landing face up. My late husband Jerry beamed from the photo on the cover beneath the words, "Heavenly Ski Resort." He looked so handsome in his red-and-white ski jacket and black stretch pants, poised on the snowy slope with poles in hand and skis pointed, ready for action.

It was 1980. Jerry was forty-six years old when coerced by business associates to join them on a ski trip even though he had never skied before. They promised, "You will love it! This is just the first step."

I had worried that entire weekend about possible accidents. True, Jerry excelled in golf, bowling, and archery, but taking up skiing at his age?

When Jerry returned, he was so black and blue that I immediately sent him for X-rays. No bones were broken, but he soon began to sound like a broken record. All he talked about was skiing! Then came outlandish claims. "I'm going back next ski season but as a non-smoker, twenty-five pounds lighter, and in shape."

*Yeah, right,* I thought. *Nothing I've ever said has convinced him to do that!*

I was surprised when Jerry began a weight-loss program, cut

back on his cigarettes, and joined an aerobics class. Amazingly, by the following ski season, he had accomplished each of his goals. I was impressed! And excited for him — until he suggested I go skiing with him.

"Not on your life!" I exclaimed. "You know I can't stand being cold." I didn't mention my fear of chairlifts and heights. "You go and have fun, sweetheart!"

So, Jerry went skiing with his nephew and his wife, also new skiers. More trips followed with increasing excitement that became irritating.

Yet, I couldn't ignore their genuine joy in skiing nor the positive changes in Jerry — now a lean, mean machine. I began to feel guilty. Didn't I owe something to this sport and to my husband? Shouldn't I at least try it?

"What?" my friends exclaimed when I said I was considering skiing. "You're forty-six years old! You're going to break a leg."

Though they echoed my own fears, I mustered enough courage to take my first step: I told Jerry I might try skiing. Ecstatic, he immediately planned a trip just for the two of us.

Though filled with fear, I feigned excitement as we drove to California's Big Bear Mountain Resort. After checking in, Jerry's blue eyes sparkled as he signed me up for the next day's beginner class.

The following morning, after fitting me with rental ski boots, leading me to the instructor, and kissing me quickly, Jerry rushed to the nearest ski lift.

I stood in a straight line with all the other beginners, like ducks in a row, and listened to the ski instructor. Now freezing and miserable in my too-tight boots, which I swore were made of lead, I peeked from my fur-lined parka cap at the other faces. So young! I felt like Grandma Moses! Last in line at the upper end, I tried to appear invisible until the unthinkable happened: I lost my balance and fell, resulting in a domino effect with all the other ducklings falling in slow motion. So much for invisibility!

I tried to follow instructions, but my feet, which I couldn't feel, refused to cooperate. I could only turn in one direction — left.

Worse, I couldn't remember what to do with my skis when I

needed to stop, so I just fell over. And I kept forgetting the rule: "Never point your skis downhill when trying to get up." One time, I just lay there, exhausted.

"I hate skiing!" I mumbled, finally getting upright. "I wish Jerry still smoked, and was fat and out of shape."

To say Jerry was disappointed when he met me after class was an understatement. I watched as my weary instructor led Jerry out of my earshot. With far-too-exaggerated hand gestures for my comfort, including running fingers through his hair that looked thinner than when the class began, the instructor exhibited a wide range of facial expressions. Jerry nodded occasionally with looks strangely resembling sympathy. Finally, they parted with the instructor refusing to shake hands.

Sensing this was my first and last ski trip, Jerry did the best thing he could: He plied me with food. I devoured my tuna melt and onion rings while Jerry carefully wove a plan between his burger and fries to make me a great skier. Wisely, he blamed my instructor and promised private lessons.

The next morning, I fell in love with my new instructor! He was infinitely patient and actually made me feel confident.

Things started clicking. I learned how to stop, get up easily, and make right turns. Finally, I said goodbye to my instructor, who released me to Jerry for further practice on the bunny slopes. I still had difficulty getting on and off chairlifts, but with practice I soon accomplished that.

The final battle, however, mine alone to fight, loomed ahead. My monster nemesis was a certain chairlift where the hill, without warning, suddenly disappeared, and all I saw was a deep canyon below. Closing my eyes hadn't helped.

"What if I jump off?" I worried silently. I later learned that is a common fear among acrophobiacs.

I recalled reading an article about a mental exercise involving thought substitution — a technique where you break an unwanted focus by deliberately thinking something else. I decided to try it out on that dreaded chairlift. When the old fear-of-jumping-off tape began to play, I would say, "What if I stand up and remove all my clothes?"

That thought mortified me and seemed so absurd that my focus broke. Then, I reasoned, "It's also absurd to think I'd jump off this chairlift. I wouldn't do that either!" After performing those mental gymnastics several times, my fear vanished.

By the end of the ski season, I had conquered all my fears.

And now, paging through this beautiful, old photo album, I continued to relive the rewards of skiing.

After introducing this amazing new world to our married son and wife, and our teenage daughter and her friends, our ski joys had multiplied. We loved racing downhill to the clubhouse for lunch, yelling, "Loser treats!" Relaxing in the Jacuzzi under the stars after a hard day's fun, sharing our slope successes and failures amidst uncontrollable laughter, provided a magic all its own—made possible when I took that first step outside my comfort zone.

Gently tucking the album back on the shelf, I shuddered. What if I had never taken that step?

— Kitty Chappell —

# 90

# The Late Bloomer

*The size of your dreams must always exceed your
current capacity to achieve them. If your dreams
do not scare you, they are not big enough.*
~Ellen Johnson Sirleaf

Growing up, I aspired to be a teacher. I liked little kids, enjoyed spending time with them, and had a cosmic connection with their joyful spirit. So, when I landed a job teaching first grade in inner-city Los Angeles, I couldn't have been happier.

Since many textbooks were not accessible in the inner city, I began to write my own units of study: science, ecology, social studies, and more. I immersed myself in modern children's literature. I marveled at the poetic genius of picture books. Three favorites were *Frederick,* by Leo Lionni; *Where the Wild Things Are,* by Maurice Sendak; and *Elmer,* by David McKee. I loved these little jewels of sparkling prose and began toying with the idea that I could write for kids. I penned poems to augment lessons, made up riddles and rhymes, told tales, and encouraged my students to write every day.

At recess one day, a teaching buddy pulled me aside on the playground. "Dianne, you are so creative," she said. "You should be doing something more than teaching in a classroom. Have you ever thought of writing for children and publishing your work?"

*Publish? Could I actually publish my writing?* I was astonished and then intrigued. I continued to scribble words, words, and more words. My students giggled and laughed at my stories, prompting more and more experiments with rhythm, rhyme, and word play. Soon, I was convinced I could succeed. I would be an artist, with words as my medium. Yes, I would do it and perhaps eventually sell my work.

In the summer of 1984, I visited my sister in Southampton, New York, two miles from the most beautiful beaches in the world. I found the area exhilarating, filled with artists and writers. I quit my teaching job and moved to the country to write full-time.

I wrote, wrote, and wrote some more, and then submitted pieces to publishers. I had a smattering of publications. I sold three essays to *The New York Times*, a few to local and regional newspapers, and scored with two personal essays to *Woman's World* at $300 apiece. Soon, I was selling poems and craft ideas to kids' magazines. I created a Country Kids' Crafts column for *The Waldo Tribune*, a newspaper for children, published in Southampton. I loved every minute until...

My savings ran out. Then, I started a cleaning service, tidying up after wealthy New York City folks, second homeowners in the Hamptons. I liked cleaning. It was profitable and offered plenty of time for writing.

In 2004, I sold a poem to Peter Pauper Press for $2,500. My holiday gift book, *Santa Lives*, came out that Christmas.

Six years later, in March 2010, I spotted a call for picture-book manuscripts in a newsletter about children's writing. I thumbed through my files, took out a promising story, spiffed it up one last time, and mailed it off. I was contacted by children's book publisher Kane Miller two weeks later. My first book deal! With a traditional publisher! After thirty years of writing, my first children's book, *Hush, Little Beachcomber*, sold. Beyond ecstatic, I quickly sent them another manuscript and signed a second contract several days later.

Today, I'm retired and doing what I was meant to do. I'm further behind than the young authors I've met on Facebook — those who have mastered the art of online promotion, marketing, and self-publishing — but I'm pursuing my passion.

I may not be rolling in riches, but my books receive good reviews, and kids like them.

Bank Street College selected my second book, *1, 2, 3 by the*

*Sea*, for its "Best Books List, 2014." It went on to be a bestseller for Kane Miller, with over 92,000 copies sold to date, something I never imagined, even in my wildest dreams.

After thirty-plus years, my patience, persistence, and hard work have paid off. I am a children's picture-book author.

I may be a late bloomer, but I'm in full flower now... enjoying myself no end!!

— Dianne Moritz —

# Accidental Achievement

> *When you put yourself on the line in a race and expose yourself to the unknown, you learn things about yourself that are very exciting.*
> ~Doris Brown Heritage

After nineteen years of marriage, I went through an unexpected divorce and a move across the country. Beaten down, I needed to restore my confidence and find my old self again.

My therapy was hiking and walking. Mountains, sunshine, and music from my earbuds were my escape. When no one could see me, I lifted my arms and looked up to the sky. I found happy moments amidst nagging thoughts.

But after being a wife and mother for so many years, I yearned to achieve something. The question was, what?

When the weather was bad, I went to the gym. One day, I picked up my pace on the treadmill and started to run. During the next visit, and the one after that, I repeated it. I didn't know why, exactly. I had always considered running to be… crazy. I had a questionable knee from an old surgery, among other aches and pains. *I'm too old for this!* I thought. But I kept it up.

It soon occurred to me why I was taking this on. It was a solitary competition. I could beat my own records a little at a time. This, I could do.

Grabbing a knee brace and better shoes, I started running through parks and along canals. I lengthened my running times by moving my goalposts between stoplights and signs. When I thought I couldn't run another step, I ran twenty more. It was tough, but I began to think I could call myself a runner.

About to turn sixty, I decided to give myself a birthday gift: to run a 10K in the upcoming Rock 'n' Roll Marathon. With about 25,000 participants, it was the largest race in the state. My now-fiancé Mark, a seasoned runner, would go with me. The farthest I could run by race time was five miles. For the 10K, being 6.2 miles, I would have to push through over a mile more to finish. "You got this," Mark said. "Runners push through the last miles all the time." I had my doubts.

The day came. We got up in what seemed like the middle of the night. My running belt was organized like a tiny duffle bag. In it were my phone, earbuds, water, painkillers, and tissues. Although I'd never used them, I also included two packets of energy gel to sip on in case I needed them. I wore a sweater I could tie around my waist after I warmed up.

So many roads were closed for the race that it took us twice as long to drive to the area. Upon arrival, we walked to our staging area, which contained about 10,000 participants. Then, we found our place in the designated corral and waited.

Looking around, I noticed the superior athletic level of some people in the crowd. Although it was chilly, they wore the barest of clothing. They had thin, fine-tuned physiques. They wore no jackets or running belts, not even a bottle of water. I felt like a pack mule by comparison.

The air horn blasted for our corral, and we walked to the starting line. My heart was already thumping. Finally, we took off at sunrise. Sleek runners whizzed past me, but the event was entertaining. Live bands popped up along the way. People cheered and held up signs. I read one that said, "Don't look so miserable. You paid for this!" That made me laugh. Some folks were in tutus or costumes. There were even barefoot runners!

At about Mile 2, I saw a road to one side with runners going in the other direction. I realized I had seen them earlier. They had already finished much of the race and were on their way back!

Approaching Mile 5, a hill snuck up on us. I began fighting to breathe, and my legs felt fragile on the never-ending incline. I wondered whose idea this route was. I sipped on energy gel, which was the stickiest stuff on Earth. After finally leveling out, I saw the bridge that led to the finish line from a distance. It was time to cue up the rock song that had a soaring buildup to help me finish the run.

I plodded along but could still call it a legitimate run. My loud music propelled me. Not caring who saw me, I lifted my arms and looked up to the sky like I had during my hikes and walks. Although I felt I could keel over at any moment, I was so overcome with joy that I wanted to take off flying above the crowd. I crossed the finish line!

I called my son, gasping, "I did it! I ran it all!" I've never had a moment of pride quite like it. I was crying! Mark and I got our medals from a volunteer and assorted snacks and drinks from tabletops. We plopped on the grass to listen to a semi-famous band. Recovering, I fought some nausea. Despite it, I was plotting how to tell everyone I'd ever known what I had accomplished.

That was to be my only 10K. For a few months, I continued to run shorter distances but had increasing knee problems. Doctors warned me that if I kept running, my knee would be in serious trouble. After arguing with them and shedding some tears, I accepted the fact that I needed to stop.

I fell in love with something I once thought of as crazy. If only I were much younger! I could've zipped across dozens of finish lines in record speed, wearing the barest of clothing. I could've won one.... Who knows?

Now, five years later, I look at the picture on the wall from that day. A huge grin is on my face. I'm holding a bottle of water over my head like a trophy. In my other hand is a juice box. My bib is askew, my earbud wires are tangled in my sweater, and I have energy gel stuck in my hair.

It was the greatest birthday gift I could ever imagine.

—A.J. Hughes—

Chapter

**10**

# Rise to the Challenge

# 92

# Braving the Wilderness

*The country does what the city cannot. It quietens the*
*mind and brings simplicity into one's life.*
*~Donna Goddard,* The Love of Devotion

My husband and I would haul home armfuls of milkshakes, tacos, and burgers from our nightly tours through fast-food joints after working jobs we hated. We would numb ourselves with these caloric concoctions while bingeing episodes of shows on Netflix, only to go to bed and do it all over again the next day, and the next. Somehow, we were living a responsible life, keeping our bosses and families happy and our bills paid, never taking a step out of the hamster wheel we were running in.

But it wasn't what we wanted. We had dreams of adventure, fresh air and life. But in the city where we lived, those things were scarce. Dreams felt far away, existing in distant universes that we didn't know how to reach for.

Sadly, the years of our early twenties slipped by without much to remember.

We knew the routine we were caught in was suffocating us and slowly snuffing out the flame that kept us dreaming. We knew that if we wanted change, we'd have to escape all the things that kept us comfortable. But breaking out of the tight machine we were caught in felt impossible.

I would fantasize about a meadow with a little house in it. I'd be wearing a blue dress and hanging clothing on a clothesline, with a child or two running around my feet, surrounded by gardens and chickens. I'd write novels in that little house while my husband built things with wood out in the shop. How could such a scene exist for us, two young people who had so little money and no knowledge of how to accomplish anything beyond going into a job for a paycheck?

Discovering I was pregnant at twenty-three finally sparked the change. We wanted our child to know our dream of flowing grass and a small house in nature, where their mother wrote novels and their father hammered in his shop. Where meals would cook on a wood stove, and rain would fall upon a growing garden.

We spent months looking at homes for sale across the country, all on wooded acreage, and all too expensive for us. Then, we thought of purchasing land alone and building on it, little by little. My husband who loved to build things, if even just chairs and tables at the time, wanted to try.

But what would we live in until the house was ready? We thought and researched. Our days of junk food and television became days of strategizing and saving money. Finally, we decided to buy a thirty-foot-long Airstream trailer from 1970, renovate it ourselves, and park it on some land that we'd buy.

I prepared for the baby while my husband tore out the old walls, insulation, flooring, and grime-filled plumbing in the nasty, old trailer we bought, transforming it into something shiny and clean. He installed fresh floors, built cabinets and beds, and designed our off-grid soon-to-be home, composting toilet and all. Together, we decorated it with quirky treasures and handmade décor. We even painted murals on the walls, making it our tiny dream house on wheels.

I was in my third trimester when we bought seven acres of forest. My husband held onto my arm as we hiked up the unruly dirt road to the place we'd one day bring our Airstream. It was so quiet and still, encircled by mountains. Fresh, pine-scented air filled our lungs. Deer scattered at our presence. Though there wasn't another house to be seen, not even a gas station for miles, I envisioned our daughter climbing and playing here. And, oh, the things I would write! The things my husband would build.

A year and a half later, we sold almost everything we owned and towed our completed Airstream to our forest — eight hours north of everyone and everything we were familiar with.

We would have to start anew, alone. We'd have nothing but each other. It would be heart-wrenching and more difficult than anything we'd ever done. But we weren't afraid. We'd spent too long being afraid to change.

My husband got a job an hour away, and since we had only one car at the time, he'd need to leave our daughter and me alone in the Airstream without phone service, electricity, or running water until he'd return home well into the night. There was nothing for me to do in those long, cold and dark hours of winter except roll a ball back and forth on the ground with my toddler and read the same Little Golden Books with her by flickering candlelight until I'd memorized every page. I kept the wood stove burning with logs that I'd go out into the snow to chop.

A large part of me felt despair when I'd step out of our trailer, look at the misty mountains, and know there was no one to hear me scream if I needed them to. What if I cut myself on the axe I was still learning to swing? What if a wild animal saw me alone and made a meal of me? But I was learning, growing, and strengthening every day. We all were.

Even in the deep snow of winter, when we could hardly walk outside to chop wood, with the faint hours of daylight fading so quickly and the increasing difficulty of keeping the stove burning throughout the freezing nights, we never gave up.

When the earth thawed in summer and wildflowers bloomed around our silver home, we found it difficult to recall a hard day. When we strung up a clothesline and hung our clothes to dry in the sunshine, I knew indeed our dream had come true. We were living it. And we did for years.

I became the very best version of myself within those seven wooded acres, with nowhere for me to run and hide from myself. I wrote three novels and discovered the woman and mother I'd always wanted to be. My self-clarity was as pure as the summer sunlight drying my hair after an outdoor bath. My love for my husband and child was deeper than I thought humanly possible. And my husband built more than just wood structures—he built a life for us. He became the man and father he'd never been tested enough to become before. And our daughter grew to be brilliant and empathetic from all the books, birds, and wildflowers. They're all she knew.

Over the years, our dream has transformed, as we have. We've embarked on many new adventures that have only challenged us more, and we have no intention of stopping anytime soon. When I look back at this precious time of taking our first daring leap into the wilderness, I realize it wasn't the wilderness itself we were desperate to run to. It was us taking a chance on who we could be and what we were capable of as a family.

We never knew our potential before; it was only a faraway dream. Now, we know that we're resilient and clever, and together we're capable of beautiful and wild things.

— Stephanie Escobar —

# 93

# Saying NO to Fear and YES to a Grand Adventure

*If happiness is the goal — and it should be, then
adventures should be top priority.*
~Richard Branson

I remember sitting on the tarmac, patiently waiting for my plane to take off. The butterflies in my stomach were at max capacity, so I took a few deep breaths to calm my nerves. I was about to embark on a new adventure, spending the next six weeks in Europe, visiting friends and family who were scattered across several countries. I would be traveling on my own half the time, encountering new languages and customs. Part of me wondered whether I was just plain crazy for doing this alone.

Never in my wildest dreams had I imagined that my first trip to Europe would be a solo journey at age twenty-five. But when my sister decided to spend six months teaching in Italy, I knew I couldn't pass up the chance to visit her and explore Europe. There was really nothing holding me back except my own fear, and I was determined not to let that stop me.

My itinerary included Germany, Austria, Sweden, Denmark, Italy, France, Switzerland, and Luxembourg. Each country provided new adventures. I stood in the same Roman Colosseum where gladiators had battled it out so many centuries ago. I visited the Louvre and smiled back at the Mona Lisa, and I stood under the twinkling lights of the Eiffel Tower in the pouring rain.

I gazed up at Michelangelo's famous ceiling in the Sistine Chapel and marveled at the fact that, only a few years prior, I had been studying this great masterpiece in my college art-history class. I sang at the top of my lungs like I was an original member of the von Trapp family during The Sound of Music Tour around Austria. I practiced my newly acquired Italian words with a friendly local in the town square in Florence.

I attended Easter Mass in Sorrento and couldn't understand most of what the priest said, but I still felt a beautiful connection to my Catholic-Italian heritage. And visiting Luxembourg and passing by a truck that had my great-grandfather's name on it was an unexpected but fun surprise. The postcards I sent to loved ones back home could not do justice to the beauty of the land I was traveling through. I felt so lucky!

Yet, there were certainly times when I experienced loneliness and longed for a travel companion. There was no one to share my excitement when I accidentally visited the Vatican on the same day the pope was giving an outdoor speech. I didn't have anyone to snuggle with as I admired the beautiful lights of Venice while floating slowly down the famous Grand Canal. I had to rely on many friendly tourists and locals to take my picture in front of all the beautiful places I was visiting.

And it may sound silly, but one of the hardest parts was eating meals by myself. Without someone to help occupy the time while waiting for my food, I mostly sat there trying not to feel awkward among the tables of couples and families.

There were other challenges, too, like navigating confusing subway and train systems on my own and figuring out how to communicate with my very limited foreign-language skills. Most Europeans knew at least some English, but that wasn't always the case.

However, with every obstacle I overcame, I grew more confident in my ability to handle whatever was headed my way next. Looking back, I can honestly say that I'm glad I had those challenging moments. Were they uncomfortable? Yes! But when my plane landed on American soil, I didn't just bring back a suitcase packed with souvenirs. I also brought back a renewed sense of self-confidence, something that I had been lacking before this trip.

So many amazing memories were made over the course of six weeks in Europe. But none of them would have been possible had I not stepped out of my comfort zone and chosen to be brave enough to take this trip in the first place. I had to face the fear of the unknown, and I had to believe that I was strong enough to overcome the inevitable difficulties of traveling alone. To this day, it is something I am extremely proud of. And, in times of self-doubt, I can look back at this trip and remember just how much I am capable of!

Someday, I hope to travel back to Europe with my husband. I would love to show him all those magical places and revisit those unforgettable six weeks I had in my twenties. But if, for some reason, I find myself with another opportunity to travel solo to Europe, I know that I would once again be able to say NO to fear and YES to another grand adventure.

— Mary Ann Blair —

# 94

# Fifty-five Things I Have Never Done

*When you're open to receiving them,*
*the possibilities just keep on coming.*
*~Oprah Winfrey*

"This upcoming year, I turn fifty-five. I'm ten years from Social Security, and my life is heading down a boring path," I lamented to my latte buddy one fall day.

"I know you don't really believe that about your life," said my friend. "But, honestly, only you can change that, in both attitude and actions."

The truth hurts, especially when delivered before the second cup of coffee.

Driving home, I realized that I'm not a daredevil. I don't want to eat super-spicy foods, like ghost peppers. I don't really want to break the bank account to prove I am cool by doing something like renting a yacht for a week. But there had to be something to look forward to. I didn't want to just coast into my fifty-fifth year of living. I needed something new to focus on and get excited about.

The focus started on Christmas Day 2019. My husband's family was trying a new tradition for Christmas: wearing Christmas pajamas to the family celebration. That day, we had to make an emergency stop at a convenience store to pick up some ice.

"Who wants to go inside and get the bags of ice?" I asked. All three of our sons hid behind electronic devices because no one wanted to be seen in public wearing the PJs I had selected for our family unit.

Not wanting to fight on Christmas, I shrugged and said, "Guess I'll go inside."

"Thanks, Mom," said the boys with sighs of relief.

I marched into the convenience store, quickly found and purchased the bags of ice, and waved at our sons from the top of the steps outside as they took my picture.

Then, it hit me... I'd never worn pajamas out in public! But I'd done it and survived.

On those steps, I was struck with an idea: What if I did one new thing a week over the course of the coming year? That was fifty-two, and if I was an overachiever, I could do one new thing for each year I had lived: #55thingsIhaveneverdone.

All excited about my idea, I sought input from my husband's family at the Christmas dinner for things I could do throughout the year.

"Aunt Anne, you could vape!" That idea went against everything that I advocate for as an associate at a medical safety-net clinic. It was a quick no.

"Why don't you get cornrows in your hair?" I have a very high forehead, so I tucked this idea away as a "maybe."

"How about fish gigging?" Although I had never heard of this, the idea was ultimately thrown out as I decided that my "fifty-five things I have never done" all had to be legal activities.

The game (or challenge) was on! I decided that I needed to incorporate both my focus word for the year and my fifty-five things on the same thing: NEW. Fifty-two weeks to do fifty-five *new* things.

Throughout the year, when people have read my "fifty-five things I have never done" on social media, many times they laughed. Some of my actions were understandably funny, like the time I hung from a billboard. However, sometimes they would laugh because they were shocked at things I had never done in my life, like making a snow angel. I did that in a unique setting: the courtyard of a local hospital while visiting a friend's son who was a patient there.

Having this focus throughout the year was an attitude changer for me. My attitude began to improve because of my actions. I was having fun looking for new experiences.

Global events impacted some of my new experiences. Because of the pandemic, I had to change how I handed out Halloween candy (shooting it from a cannon). I tried using toilet paper made from bamboo, attended a Zoom baby shower, and organized a Covid-testing event for over 400 community residents.

My final flourish of events was to memorialize my GOAT (Greatest of All Time) year by milking a goat for the first time, picking farm-fresh eggs directly from a chicken coop, and making custard using the ingredients.

By little actions throughout the year, my attitude greatly improved. Each week was a new adventure, and I had a much more positive outlook on life. I didn't realize until near the end of the year the impact of my fifty-five things on others. Several friends said they were going to do a similar challenge the next year.

— Anne Foley Rauth —

# 95

# Avoiding the Shadows

*There are none so blind as he who will not see.*
~Proverb

first started wearing glasses at age five. I wore thick, black-framed glasses and many of my friends commented that the character Ralphie, in Jean Shepherd's *A Christmas Story*, and I were almost twins. Sadly, they were right.

As I got older, my nearsightedness worsened, and my lenses became thicker and heavier. I have a permanent depression on the bridge of my nose from the weight of my spectacles. I always joked that if the sun shone over my shoulder and through my lenses at the right angle, I could start forest fires.

In my twenties, I was hired by a Fortune 500 company and was required to get a physical, including an eye exam. I was told to remove my glasses and read the smallest line on the chart. I squinted and said, "What line?" Several adjustments were made, but my response of "What line?" remained constant. Finally, the lady administering the test said, "I always wanted to meet you, Mr. Magoo!"

I won't share my reply.

I celebrated the day when I was told that thinner lenses were available. Wearing them, I felt as light as a feather — at least from the neck up. Then, my first pair of genuine polarized sunglasses reaffirmed my belief that there really is a God! Before that, I simply darkened the lenses on my old glasses and used them for sunglasses. But polarized lenses not only protected my eyes but also brought the world's colors into vastly better focus for me. It was amazing.

Then, Dad went blind.

He had been diagnosed with macular degeneration and had ignored the doctor's advice concerning treatment. Soon, he only had peripheral vision, and his life was restricted to sitting in his recliner. Once very active and busy, now his limitations made him a prisoner of his living room.

An annual eye examination revealed I also had macular degeneration but only a tiny spot in one eye. The next year, it was in both eyes. However, it was not progressing, and I was advised to "keep an eye on it."

Then, I required cataract surgery on both eyes.

Several years later, just before retirement, I was diagnosed with an autoimmune disease, myasthenia gravis. This disease causes weakness in muscles, including the eyes and eyelids. Now, I had blurred vision numerous times a day as my eyelids became too tired to stay open. Ptosis surgery to shorten the eyelids offered some help. But, before the surgery, I was sent to a neuro-ophthalmologist to have my eyes checked.

The new doctor began by examining my eyes and vision. I was told to cover my left eye and read the eye chart, and then to cover my right eye and read.

Previously, whenever my vision had blurred, I did this same exercise, trying to see if one eye was worse than the other. I had not noticed any difference. But this time when I was using only my left eye, a large, black shadow blocked out much of what I saw.

Literally overnight, I had lost most of the vision in my left eye. I was shocked and blurted out, "Oh, my gosh, what's happened to me?"

I was now legally blind in my left eye.

I was told that the only way to avoid following my father into blindness was through injections.

Into my eyes.

I am not a fan of needles. When I was young, the mere mention of a shot upset me tremendously. However, an unfortunate experience with a dog resulted in me having to have a series of eight anti-rabies injections. Today, this is a much more gentle treatment involving three injections into the upper arm over four weeks. But when I was five years old, the treatment was a series of eight to twelve daily injections. These injections involved eight-inch-long needles because the injection site was the navel. And I refused to cry or scream. I would shut my eyes as tightly as possible and grit my teeth. However, the two nurses who assisted cried plenty for me. Even the doctor begged me to express the pain, but I didn't.

My reward for such bravery was a cherry Life Saver and the empty medicine vial.

Since then, needles terrify me. I won't even watch a needle being used on a television show. I look away and cringe. I was a very active blood donor for years, but I avoided the sight of me being pierced.

The idea of having injections into my eyes made me nauseous. During the days before my first ones, I thought of little else.

But I had one fear greater than needles: going blind. I saw my father struggle to live in a world of near total darkness. I would do anything to avoid that.

I joined a low-vision support group attached to the local senior citizens community center. I wanted to prepare for whatever might happen, and I'm glad I did. I met many people who have less vision than I do and learned how they adapted and learned to survive and thrive with blindness. I was impressed by their courage and fortitude. One, an older woman, went blind at the age of twelve. However, she lives alone, does her own shopping, has traveled the world and even gone scuba diving. My hero!

The day for the injections arrived. I went to the doctor's office, and my eyes were tested again. The right eye was now also losing sight, so I would need injections in both eyes. I elected to have both eyes done on the same visit. No need to return more often than required.

My eyes were cleaned repeatedly. Then, the doctor stepped to my right side, and I was instructed to look to the left. Each eye would receive two injections. Great! The torture just doubled! The first injection was to numb the eye, and I felt nothing. The second injection was noticeable, but I endured it. Then, he stepped to my left side and repeated the process.

His assistant began rinsing both eyes repeatedly. This was actually less comfortable than the four injections. Then, patches were placed over both eyes, and I was led outside. My wife drove me home.

A burning sensation began in both eyes. It was like having a large grain of sand under the eyelids — not comfortable but endurable.

It's been five years. I receive the injections every three months. I still dread the experience, but I rejoice that neither eye has worsened in that time. My right eye is healthy enough that I can still drive. I read, play cards, and enjoy the world and its beauty.

— Chip Kirkpatrick —

# 96

# Meant to Be

*Travel is more than the seeing of sights. It is a change*
*that goes on, deep and permanent,*
*in the minds of the living.*
*~Miriam Beard*

I woke up in a sweat like I'd been wrestling someone all night. My
cinderblock dorm room was pitch-black, except for the sliver of
light from the streetlamp peeking through the institutional window blind. The clock said it was 2:30 A.M. I tossed and turned,
but I couldn't sleep after that episode. *Was God talking to me?*

It was 1986, and jobs for recent journalism graduates were scarce.
I was at my university for a temporary job. If I didn't find something
soon, I would have to move home and continue my job search from
there.

There was another option: a career alternative that would involve
living overseas for two years and working with missionaries — a far-
fetched idea for a Mississippi girl. I'm a writer. Missionary work was
not in my plan and definitely not in my comfort zone.

My temporary job ended and I did go back home. I decided to
request an application for the missionary program, even though I had
never been separated from my family before. My older sister lived in
Texas, and we thought that was far from home. And this would be for
two years and much farther away.

It was a roller coaster of a summer. I'd get a lead about a job
and send a resume. I even had some interviews. Then, nothing. After

working some odd jobs to make some money, I broke down and started filling out the voluminous application. What did I have to lose? The next deadline was September 15th. If I hadn't found a job by then, I'd mail it.

September 15th arrived, and I drove to our small post office, praying I didn't run into anyone I knew. I had told only a few people that I was applying. As I drove home, I thought, *I don't have to go. Lord, you can help me find a job and stay here.*

The weeks dragged by as I waited for a response. Would they reject me, too? Then, it came: an invitation to the candidate conference in Richmond, Virginia — all expenses paid. Included in the packet were additional questionnaires and forms. I was a bit more excited than I thought I would be. And nervous. I had flown in a small plane, piloted by my uncle, but never commercially.

When I arrived and started meeting other candidates, I felt like I was among my tribe. A hundred and twenty young people were all congregated in one place, many with similar stories to mine. We were from all walks of life with different degrees and interests. Yet we shared the desire to serve in whatever way we could. It was three days of group times, one-on-one interviews, mixer games, and worship. We also had time to speak with area directors about the most critical positions for their area. I spoke with the South American director about a position in Ecuador in the business office. It wasn't writing, but I did have a minor in business and had studied some Spanish in college. It could be one of my top three.

Our small group of fifteen agreed to send postcards to each other when we heard where we were going. I left the conference feeling like now was the time. Even if I didn't get a writing position, I felt as if God, for whatever reason, wanted me to go.

Three weeks later, I received my assignment: Assistant to the Treasurer of the Ecuador Baptist Mission. I was going to Quito, Ecuador.

I flew back to Virginia for six weeks of training. I was joined there by forty-nine other candidates, almost two feet of snow, and colder temperatures than I'd ever experienced. The first person I saw was a young man I'd met at the interviews.

Weekday mornings began with 6:00 A.M. exercise, breakfast and then classes. After lunch came afternoon games, classes and learning about our host country and jobs. Evenings were filled with lectures, activities, language learning, social events and hanging out with like-minded people. Of course, there were some strange rules, like "no leaning" or "pairing off." One night, we were told to pack up our belongings. We were given new rooms and roommate assignments. It was intended to prepare us for the life we had chosen.

Friendships developed during this time, and a shared desire to fulfill our calling brought us closer than any other friendships I'd had. One particular friendship blossomed with a young man I'd met at the interviews. We seemed like opposites, yet we were drawn to each other. We spent as much time getting to know each other as possible for the remainder of our training. He promised to write me from his assignment in Africa.

He kept that promise. After two years of letter writing, that young man decided to visit me in Ecuador — on his way home to North Carolina. A year later, we were married. We've had thirty-three years together, with nine moves, two children, a dog, multiple surgeries, travels, some losses, more friendships than we can count, and a lifetime of memories.

It's not a perfect life but one orchestrated by God — all by nudging me to step outside my comfort zone.

— Sandi Johnson Ruble —

# 97

# I Belong Here

*All progress takes place outside the comfort zone.*
~Michael John Bobak

Alone in my tent, somewhere deep in the Ouachita National Forest in Arkansas, I held my breath as I listened to the noises coming from outside my tent. Raccoons? Armadillos? A bear? Or worse, a two-legged male predator?

I was on my first-ever multi-day hiking/backpacking trip, something that had been a bucket-list item for me for many years. It had just taken me a while to work up the nerve to finally do it. As I lay awake in my tent, possibly miles away from the nearest human, and listened to the noises just outside, I couldn't help but think, *Maybe I don't belong out here.*

I'm not your typical backpacker. I'm a thirty-seven-year-old female, a wife and homeschooling mom of two. I work part-time for a non-profit ministry, serve in my church, and bake cookies with my kids. I'm healthy and active but not exactly skinny or muscular. I like camping, but I'd never done it without having access to a toilet and a shower.

But there I was, on my own in the woods for the first time. I had trained for months by carrying a heavy backpack on long, rugged hikes. I had learned to pitch my tent without help and hang my food bag in a tree. I had researched backpacking essentials and was equipped with all the necessities: first-aid supplies, water-filtration system, food, clothes, tick spray, and sleeping bag. I had prepared as best as I could, yet I couldn't shake the fear that the next morning's local headlines would say something along the lines of: Mom of Two — Totally Unprepared for Backpacking Excursion — Found Mauled to Death by Black Bear in the Ouachita National Forest.

Somehow, I managed to find sleep that night (although I never did find out what was prowling around my tent). The next morning, I celebrated twenty-four hours of survival by enjoying breakfast by a campfire that took me an embarrassingly long time to set ablaze. I watched the sunrise and then prepared for another long day of hiking. Whether I belonged or not, I was there, and it was up to me to keep going.

Over the next couple of days, my confidence grew. I hiked up steep hills and mountains, crossed wide, rushing creeks, navigated around snakes that were lying across the trail, and saw beautiful waterfalls and panoramic vistas that served as rewards for my hard work. One night, I fell asleep to the nearby howls of coyotes and didn't fear for my life. Progress!

Physically, it was one of the most challenging things I had ever done. Hiking all day while carrying a heavy backpack was tiring, but I felt strong and happy. Going to the bathroom outside was a challenge. The goal was to find a spot far off the trail where I'd have complete privacy just in case someone else hiked past but not so far off the trail that I'd get lost.

Somewhere along the way, I began to feel reassured that I had made the right decision to give backpacking a try. Although I had struggled initially to define myself as a backpacker (I felt more like a wannabe), the hours I spent on the trail showed me one simple, beautiful truth: A backpacker is someone who backpacks. I didn't have to be an expert wilderness survivalist or in my twenties or in perfect shape. I could be me: someone who loves nature and hiking but can't identify more than two or three types of trees. Someone who simultaneously wants to see snakes because they're interesting but is also terrified of seeing them. Someone who is pretty lousy at hanging a food bag high enough or starting a fire but is stubbornly persistent at both tasks. Someone who would likely starve to death if she were forced to hunt or forage for food. Someone who couldn't stand to be out in the woods for several days without something to read, even though it meant carrying extra, unnecessary weight. I may not be a typical backpacker, but I am a backpacker nonetheless.

Four days later, I emerged from the woods — tired, bug-bitten, blistered, dirty… and triumphant. I had done something unexpected and difficult. I had created my own adventure. And I had found an unlikely place to belong.

—Jayna Richardson—

# 98

# It's the Little Things

*Challenging situations can lead you to
transformational experiences.*
~Wesam Fawzi

W hen we're young, we always think we'll be strong and
healthy, energetic and able. And as the years go by, we
don't notice the little changes occurring in our bodies
until they become more and more apparent. We begin to
struggle with some things we could do so easily during our younger
years.

When I was in school, back in the days when we were taught
cursive writing in class, I won awards for my beautiful handwriting.
For years I kept journals and loved to write letters to people. I did a
lot of crafts, counted cross-stitch projects, one after the other. I painted
worship banners for the church, made puppets out of stuffed animals,
and wrote scripts for the church's puppet shows.

Now in my retirement years, "familial or essential tremor" has
afflicted my hands with uncontrollable shaking when I try to hold a
needle or fork or pen. If I have to fill out a form, my daughter does it
for me. I thought my writing and crafts were gone forever. I felt my
life was now more about what I could *not* do and not at all about what
I *could*. I felt limited and like I had been put on the shelf.

My friend Kathy was in a group that gathered at the library once
a week to color; she kept asking me to join the group. For a long time
I declined, stating that I could no longer write legibly, so how was I

going to color? She was persistent, though, saying "just come and sit with us." Finally, I gave in. The library even provided copies of pages from coloring books and colored pencils for those who didn't have their own. Kathy urged me to choose one of them and try. Just try.

I was reluctant. It was embarrassing to have trouble writing with a pen. But it turned out that I could color and stay in the lines! I could even artistically shade like I used to do when I painted. I really could not believe how it was possible! I kept that first picture and eventually framed and hung it by my front door to remind myself that what I thought was lost — my artistic expression — had just changed. I still can't write legibly, but I have belonged to that coloring group ever since. A little thing like an invitation to a coloring group really did bring about a big change in me. I felt more confident and encouraged.

Kathy is also an avid quilter and belongs to a stitchers group as well. Seeing how well I was doing with the coloring, she urged me to come to the group, again saying that I didn't have to stitch anything; I could just meet the other ladies and have fun. Once again, I gave in. There is always a "show and tell" time at the start of each meeting when everyone shows what they're working on. There were quilters, knitters, crocheters, cross-stitchers, all with beautiful projects to show off. A lot of them made things to donate to different charities like homeless shelters and veterans.

When it was my turn, I explained my inability to do cross-stitch anymore. The ladies were so kind and offered lots of ideas and encouragement. "We'll find you something you can do," they all said. One of them, Anita, said she had a circular knitting loom she thought I could use. She brought it to the next meeting and gave it to me, explaining that all you do is wind the yarn around the 36 pegs and use the hook to loop the lower layer of yarn over the upper layer on each peg.

Long story short, I did learn how to make caps using soft yarn. I made hundreds of them and donated them to a men's cancer ward in a local hospital. The men loved them! And once again, my confidence and feeling of accomplishment grew!

Just from a little thing like an invitation. I'm still making caps but from there have also learned how to make tee shirt quilts! I have made one for each of my seven grandchildren as they graduated from high school. I utilize various tools and tricks to accomplish the sewing, but I can do it!

Those two invitations from Kathy changed my life. I learned that age brought me obstacles, but I could still find a way to be me. I had always been creative and had thought that part of me was gone forever. Instead, I found new activities that are just as creative and fulfilling.

— Beth DiCola —

# Into the Deep

*How we handle our fears will determine where we go*
*with the rest of our lives. To experience adventure*
*or to be limited by the fear of it.*
*~Judy Blume*

I have always been terrified of water, especially deep water. Especially water that is the home to creatures who might find me appetizing, or tear me apart just for the fun of it.

When the opportunity to go on a Caribbean cruise with my husband, stepson, and some friends came up, I forced myself to focus on all the other appealing things that I had heard about cruises, such as amazing food and beautiful beaches. I convinced myself that I would be safe and would not have to actually go into the water.

I was super excited about going until the moment when my family and our friends told me they wanted us to go snorkeling in St. Thomas. I went along with it, all the while planning that I would simply refuse to jump in the water when the time came.

My plan worked at first. The boat stopped at a serene location that came straight off a postcard. The sky was an amazing blue, and the turquoise ocean was calm and inviting. As everyone began to put on their snorkeling gear, I firmly announced that I would be staying on the boat. Even though everyone gave me lots of positive encouragement I crossed my arms around my life vest and shook my head.

Eventually, they gave up and jumped in the water. Suddenly, my husband yelled my name and pointed down at the dark mass below.

"Sea turtles!" he shouted excitedly. "You need to see this!"

I love sea turtles. They are graceful, calm, and beautiful creatures. I wanted so badly to see them! The captain of the boat was a kind, gentle soul, who had probably witnessed the panic attacks of many others who had a fear of the ocean. He helped me doublecheck my life jacket, assuring me it was secure, and then gave me a floatation device along with two pool noodles to hold onto, just for the added confidence. I jumped into the water with my heart racing, convinced I would drown. To my relief, all my "life-saving equipment" did its job!

Although my family laughed hysterically and said I was definitely "shark bait," I felt my body relax, and put my face down into the water. There they were. A whole family of sea turtles, gently dancing through a completely different world than the one above the surface, filled with movement and vibrant colors. At that moment, all my anxiety floated away. I was hypnotized by the absolute beauty that was right there in front of me, beauty I would've missed had I given in to my fear. Did I look completely ridiculous? Yes. Was it worth it? Absolutely!

How did that one experience of stepping out of my comfort zone change my outlook on life? It taught me that fear can change what we see, and more importantly, what we don't see. If we let it, fear can paralyze us and distort what we know as truth. Sometimes, it's okay to hang out on the boat for a little while, assess the situation, focus on the goal rather than the barriers, get our support systems in place, and jump into the water.

— Terri Turner —

# That Crummy Hotel

*Expose yourself to your deepest fear; after that, fear
has no power, and the fear of freedom shrinks and
vanishes. You are free.*
~Jim Morrison

I closed my laptop. My stomach was in knots. In my e-mail, I was notified that the first novel in my new mystery series had been nominated for an award—a Big Deal of an award. So, why the knots? The awards ceremony was in New York. Good grief. New York? It might as well have been Mars.

Taking my coffee and my cat Bianca outside to the deck, I looked at the familiar Pacific Ocean just across the lane from my house. New York? I'd never had any desire to go to New York. It wasn't that I was a travel weenie. I'd lived overseas with my parents, lived in Toronto for about a decade after college, travelled in another life to the Caribbean every March for a scuba holiday, and drove wherever I wanted to go. But I felt like singer/songwriter Bruce Cockburn says in "All the Diamonds": I'd run aground in a harbor town. And I liked it. It felt safe.

"New York?" my friend Kathy squealed in excitement when she joined me for our Tuesday morning coffee get-together. "Really?"

"Yes, really," I said dispiritedly. "This is cruel. I finally managed to get my new mystery series started, and, to my surprise, the first one is nominated for an award! But the awards ceremony is in New York. It's not fair. Last year, it was held in Seattle. I could drive to Seattle. But New York?"

"Planes fly to New York, rumor has it," Kathy pointed out.

"Uh-huh," I said.

"So, when is this awards ceremony?" Kathy asked.

"Late June."

"Omigosh, that's only a month away!" She was quiet for a moment and then said, "What's really holding you back, girlfriend?"

"Well, for starters, I'm up against more than a thousand other books. Well, seven in the mystery category. It's a little intimidating."

"Ha! So you're having literary cold feet. Is that it?"

"Maybe," I said. "After all, I'm my own publisher. Maybe I feel a little like the poor relation."

"Oh, fiddle faddle," Kathy said. "No one thinks less of indie-published books these days. It's a good story. I loved it. Your book got great critical reviews. *Publishers Weekly* loved it. Our book group loved it."

"Yeah, yeah, yeah," I said.

"Look, here's my parting observation," she said. "I think you really do want to go, but traveling to big, scary New York has you frazzled. Could it be you're just scared?"

I decided to admit the truth. "Okay, yes, I am. World traveler though I was, the prospect of New York has my knees quaking. As well, I'm having logistics paralysis. How do I get to the shuttle? How long will it take for the shuttle to get to the airport? How long will I have to wait for the flight? Who will be my seatmates? How do I find another shuttle to take me from the airport to wherever it is I'm going to stay? And then, how do I get to the place for the awards ceremony?"

"Such fretting," Kathy said. "My sister lives in New York. I visit her every couple of months. I can text you the travel info: the shuttle service on this end, the airline I use, the shuttle service on the other end... Then, all you have to do is pick out a hotel and research where the awards ceremony is going to be held. Deal?"

"Deal," I said, relieved. Suddenly, the trip seemed possible. Maybe it was like the old joke about how to eat an elephant: bite by bite. And, suddenly, going to New York had become not about winning the award, but about... something else.

"Okay," Kathy said. "We'll divide and conquer. I'll get you the shuttle and plane information. You make the hotel reservations. Just start looking in your AAA book and find a hotel near the awards ceremony."

I blushed. "I've been having a fantasy about this, you see, and already picked out the hotel just in case I could persuade aliens to teleport me to New York. It's the Washington Square Hotel in Greenwich Village — the hotel Joan Baez sings about in her song 'Diamonds and Rust,' the song in which Bob Dylan phones her after years and years. I've always wanted to see it."

"Yeah? What did Joan say about the hotel?" Kathy asked.

"It's a memory of Dylan. She sang, 'You're smiling out the window of that crummy hotel over Washington Square.'"

"Well, I bet it's not crummy anymore," Kathy said. "But is it close to wherever the awards ceremony will take place?"

"Yup. It's right across Washington Square from the Skirball Center for the Performing Arts."

"Okay," Kathy said. "Let's get on this."

So, we did. Fast forward a month. Somehow, I got to big, scary New York. It was one car ride to the shuttle bus, one shuttle to the airport, one plane ride (direct, mercifully), and another shuttle to the hotel. Whew.

And then I was there, at the steps of the Washington Square Hotel in Greenwich Village. It was decidedly not crummy. Rather, it was quaint, with a friendly doorman and lots of wood paneling. The room was small but lovely. And it did overlook Washington Square, which, in a fit of courage, I ventured out to explore. Hmm. It was not too scary: a couple of old codgers playing checkers, plenty of pigeons, a girl playing a guitar, and two cops patrolling from whom I asked directions to the Skirball Center. "Right across the park, ma'am," they said, pointing. Great! Now I was all set for the awards ceremony the next night.

I went back to the hotel, ate a great vegan meal in their restaurant, and collapsed into bed, exhausted from a day of unaccustomed adventure.

The next day, I slept in, took a cab to Times Square, v

a world-famous bookstore I had only heard about (The Mysterious Bookshop), left postcards advertising my book, went back to the hotel, changed, and walked across the park to the Skirball Center and the awards ceremony — where my book did not win Best Mystery.

Later, as I sat in the hotel bar with my editor, Christi, she misread my thoughtful silence for disappointment.

"Are you bummed out?" she asked.

"Phooey," I said. "Who needs a piece of plastic for their bookcase anyhow? I'm not bummed, Christi, because, in a weird way, I did win. Not the award, but... something else. Something I thought I'd lost."

"Care to share?" she asked.

"My adventurous self," I told her. "I thought I'd lost it forever. Retired it. But thanks to my wanting to see that crummy hotel over-looking Washington Square, I got reacquainted with it. If that doesn't seem too corny..."

"Not at all," she said. "So, is the next stop 'The Hotel California'? You know, the Eagles' song?"

"You never know," I said, laughing. "You never know. Today, New York. Tomorrow?"

— Linda J. Wright —

# The Camino Irishman

*Some old-fashioned things like fresh air
and sunshine are hard to beat.*
~Laura Ingalls Wilder

The call came at precisely the right time. I had been drifting into a depression after my recent retirement when my friend Prema called.

"Hey, Carol. There is this 500-mile walk across Northern Spain. I'd like to do a seventy-mile section. Are you in?"

I didn't think I could do it. It seemed impossible to walk seventy miles. I not only wondered *if* I could do it, but *why* I would want to. I had no answers but felt compelled to try. My six-mile knee, named for the pain that started at the six-mile mark of any hike, worried me. But I needed something more in my life, and so I decided I was in. For better or worse.

The walk was the Camino de Santiago de Compostela, a popular and ancient pilgrimage to the great Cathedral in Santiago that is the purported final resting place of Saint James. Taking a bus toward the small town of Sarria, we watched curves of rolling hills hide small farms, expose dark, tilled earth, and reveal an abundance of trees. A collection of houses appeared in the distance and gave way to the small gathering of shops, hostels and homes that was our destination. I was surprised to see mostly rock structures: slate roofs, rock walls, and stone streets in a cornucopia of shades of gray.

Our first morning started at sunrise, as I was worried about ho long it would take me to walk nine miles. After a quick warm croissant and café con leche, we double-checked our packs to ensure our two-liter water bottles were full, CLIF bars were tucked in, and rain ponchos were on board. "I can't believe we're here!" I exclaimed, as I hoisted my twenty-pound pack onto my back. "We are really doing this!" We posed for a Day One pic: Prema curling both edges of her sun hat toward her face, beaming with glee; me with my hands tucked in the pockets of my purple rain jacket, graying hair tousled, and a huge grin eating up most of my face.

We had agreed that Prema, ten years younger and a stronger athlete, would burst ahead on the trail, and we would meet each night at our *albergue*, the hostel where we would dine and stay the night. On the first mile of the packed-dirt track, I was enticed by old-growth oak groves while birch and elm trees fanned the air above my path, creating a slight and welcome breeze. I recognized a symphony of song from robins, wrens, and geese, but there was also the foreign sound of the cuckoo bird, like a forest of grandfather clocks chiming.

Day One was easy enough: nine miles with no sore toes or painful six-mile knee. But I felt anxious about Day Two with sixteen miles to walk. Could I do it?

As I walked, the strong odor of pigs enveloped me. I looked for swine but saw only trees and small, open fields — nothing that could issue these animal aromas. It was not a scent I expected on my Camino. I focused on the beauty of the rich olive greens I found in the neighboring trees and the delightful and delicate wildflowers at my feet. Around the next corner, I saw a small dairy farm. Ah, it was the cows that issued the rich, earthy odor.

Midway through Day Three, a faint sound interrupted the birds: the distant sound of men singing. Listening intently, I realized their voices were behind me. I could not see them yet, but I could hear a joyous melody interrupted by volleys of laughter. If I slowed my pace so they would catch up to me, I could join the frivolity. After a few minutes, they came into view. They were three men of similar age: gray, wrinkly, and a bit paunchy. Their laughter and teasing manner posed a deep friendship, one that I imagined had endured many years. To my delight, they were singing Irish folk songs.

We casually converged on a path that took us through a mostly deserted village. I introduced myself saying I was from the Bay Area near San Francisco. The tallest replied, "Hi, Carol! I'm Michael from Belfast, and these sorry blokes are Daniel and James."

Michael's and my pace put us at the back of the pack as we all drifted toward the outskirts of the little hamlet. Conversation between Michael and me was easy with the normal comments about the weather, the beautiful country, and being retired. We compared notes on teaching chemistry to college students, as he had done, and counseling middle-school students, as I had. We wound through the details of the dwindling education system worldwide, dreary world politics, and the grace of old friends.

"How is your Camino going?" Michael asked.

"I'm really loving it. So far, I've been able to keep walking. But I worry about how many fifteen-mile days I can do in a row. Today is my second and then another tomorrow...." My voice trailed off.

We continued to talk easily until I slowly eased into my real question. "So, now that you are not working, what's the most fulfilling thing you do with your time?"

Clearly struck hard by this question, Michael stumbled for words. He cleared his throat. "Taking care of my wife at the end of her life." His voice choked, and he wiped the tears that spilled over onto his cheeks.

"I'm so sorry. Did you lose her recently?" I asked, holding back my own tears.

"Yes, the day we end our walk will be the one-year anniversary."

We walked for a time in silence. Finally, I said, "You clearly loved her very much."

"Yes, I did. And these guys have been with me every step. Daniel and James and I have been friends since college. Fifty years together. We still live within an hour's drive of each other. Daniel suggested this little adventure. I was down without my wife when he said, 'I found what you need. This walk across Spain. We'll all go together.' And so here we are, three old, fat Irishmen in Spain walking seventy miles in honor of my dead Annie."

Suddenly, he stopped walking and put his hands on his knees. In the middle of a dirt path somewhere outside of Melide, Spain, I put my arm around his shoulders. We were strangers, but when he stood, we embraced and held each other.

A question that accompanies those who walk the Camino de Santiago de Compostela is, "What brings you here to walk: What is your why?" After arriving at the Cathedral two days later, I realized that Michael had given me my why. By connecting with this stranger, I had connected with Spirit, with God, with others, and with myself. I found a lost part of myself and began filling the void of retirement there in that ancient, emerald-green part of Galicia. It was the last place I would have thought to look for it.

— Carol Perry —

# Meet Our Contributors

**DeVonna R. Allison** began writing during childhood, being published for the first time in 2009. She is a wife of over forty years, the proud mother of four children, and a doting grandmother. She is a Marine Corps veteran, and enjoys working in her flower gardens, knitting, crocheting, and traveling.

**Karen Anderson** is a retired third grade teacher, who lives with her husband Larry less than an hour from Sacramento, CA. Top on her bucket list is to one day publish the novel she began during the pandemic. Her ultimate dream would be to see it made into a film.

**Reno Ruth Doell Anderson** is a fierce everyday warrior, writing for truth and light. She has travelled the world, lived in Canada, the USA, and Africa, and visited over forty countries. She loves sitting in the sunshine at a sidewalk *café* writing. Her eight books fall into many genres, including novels, biographies, Bible studies and poetry.

**Shannon Anderson** is an award-winning author and educator from Indiana. She loves conducting author visits, keynoting at events, and writing children's books. Learn more at www.shannonisteaching.com.

**Barbara Blossom Ashmun** has written seven gardening books, most recently *Love Letters to My Garden*. Her enduring love for her husband, Tom Robinson, her passion for gardening, and delight in her naughty, entertaining cats, Dolly and Harry, make her life joyful.

**Kimberly Avery** is a writer and self-described underachieving wife and mother of four children and one perfect grandchild. Her writing includes tales of travel mayhem, hot flashes, friendships, parenting, and a hilarious take on everyday life.

**Lauren Barrett** is a teacher of the deaf in North Carolina. She earned a master's in Reading Education. She balances her love for writing and running with being a mom to her four-year-old son Henry. She has published two books, including a children's book, *Henry's Hiccups*. Learn more at laurenbarrettwrites.com.

**Susan Bartlett** is a Registered Nurse Specialist in peri-anesthesia care and enjoys writing and gardening in her spare time. She has a daughter in Manhattan who she loves visiting at least twice a year. Essays, short stories, and a blog she started almost ten years ago provide a place to share her many experiences.

**Susannah Bianchi**, a former fashion model, now writes full-time. She loves running in Central Park and reading. *Pride & Prejudice* is still her favorite novel. She plans to write a memoir about her years as a model. She lives in New York City.

**Mary Ann Blair** is a stay-at-home mom and freelance writer living in the Pacific Northwest with her two little gentlemen and her hubs. Besides chronicling her motherhood adventures, she loves the outdoors, reading, and all things crafty. Learn more at maryannblair.com.

**JoAnne Bowles** is a writer who lives in Central Oregon. She is a wife, a mom to two kids, and a teacher to young children. She and her family enjoy life back in a house at last. She loves traveling, scrapbooking, and reading. She can be reached at joannebow@aol.com.

**Cassandra Brandt** is an Arizona author who lives with a spinal cord injury. You can find her books, which include *Iron Girl: Tomboy, Tradeswoman, Tetraplegic: a memoir*, on Amazon. Cassandra enjoys spending time with her only daughter, nature, and philosophy.

**Mason K. Brown** is an author and storyteller. She draws on life experiences to write inspirational nonfiction and humor. Mason lives in Oregon but travels the world collecting water and stories. E-mail her at masonkbrown@frontier.com.

**Risa Brown** is a retired school librarian in Texas. Author of fourteen series of nonfiction books for children and two local history books about Texas Wesleyan University, she lives in the Fort Worth area to be able to be involved with her family including two grandsons. Risa enjoys singing and traveling, especially to book festivals.

**Alice Burnett** has always enjoyed travel and adventure; her family's time in Czechoslovakia was one of the highlights of their lives. After she and her husband retired from teaching, they still look for opportunities for adventure and helping others. Alice likes to read, play tennis, hike and interact with her grandchildren.

**Louise Butler** is a retired educator with advanced degrees in administration and economics. She was a speaker at the Global Summit on Science and Science Education. She now enjoys the life of a writer. Louise is active in her community where she enjoys good books, great friends and mediocre golf.

**Carrie Cannon** received her Bachelor of Liberal Arts in Literature, with honors, from Harvard University Extension School. She teaches literature courses for an online classical high school and enjoys home educating four of her seven children. She likes eating soup and salad because every bite is different and interesting.

At age eighty-nine, widow **Kitty Chappell** continues to speak, write, volunteer for her local police department and serve as a TSA canine decoy. One of her three nonfiction books, *Soaring Above the Ashes on the Wings of Forgiveness*, is in six languages with film possibilities. This is Kitty's sixth story published in the *Chicken Soup for the Soul* series. Learn more at www.kittychappell.com.

**Carol Chiodo-Fleischman** has written for *The Buffalo News*, *Guideposts* and is a previous contributor to the *Chicken Soup for the Soul* series. She has also published a children's book entitled *Nadine, My Funny and Trusty Guide Dog*.

**D'ette Corona** received her Bachelor of Science degree in business management and is the Associate Publisher of Chicken Soup for the Soul.

**Michele Ivy Davis** lives with her husband of fifty-plus years in Southern California where she spends her time as a freelance writer, photographer, and grandmother of four. Her young adult novel, *Evangeline Brown and the Cadillac Motel*, received national and international awards. Learn more at www.MicheleIvyDavis.com.

**Kathy Dickie** lives in Calgary, a western Canadian city nestled in the foothills of the majestic Rocky Mountains. She enjoys adventure with her remarkable granddaughters, traveling with her husband, fami events, quilting, ancestry research and writing. Kathy is a recurrent contributor to the *Chicken Soup for the Soul* series.

**Beth DiCola** is seventy-five years old. She is a longtime member of a coloring group and Stitchers group. She makes hats for cancer patients and donates stitched blankets to homeless shelters. She thanks God every day for the blessings in her life and how God has shown her new ways to use her talents.

**Stephanie Escobar** is the author of Gothic fiction and fantasy, including the ghost romance, *A Song Beyond Walls*. When she's not writing, she's baking experimental sweets, tending to her voracious chickens, or cozying up with a book. She resides in the Pacific Northwest with her husband and daughter.

**Alice Facente** was a community outreach nurse and nursing instructor in Connecticut for forty-three years before retiring and moving with her husband to the San Francisco Bay Area to be near her daughter and her family. E-mail Alice at Longcovealice@comcast.net.

A former dancer and choreographer, **Andrea L. Fisher** is a dealer of French period art and a garden designer whose passions are art history and storytelling. Her memoir-style narrative, *My Russian Roots*, was published in 2022. She is working on a forthcoming book, *Inspired By Beauty: A Journey Through Time*.

**Judith Fitzsimmons** is first and foremost the mother of the most amazing person she knows — her daughter. She is also an internationally certified aromatherapist (of thirty years), a yoga instructor (ten years), and the spoiler of her cat, Oona.

**Myrna L. Garvey** was born in San Diego, CA in 1929. She married a sailor in 1948, which was the same year she graduated from high school. At fifty, Myrna attended Central Washington University in Ellensburg, WA and graduated with a degree in Fashion Merchandising. After graduating she owned a successful business, Myrna's Everything Fashionable, and is currently a member of the writers' roundtable group of Ellensburg, WA.

**Dawn Smith Gondeck** travels the U.S. via motorhome with her usband, Mike, and Bullmastiff, Lexie. She enjoys writing, photography, d getting messy in mixed media art. She struggles with rheumatoid arthritis (RA) but lives the best life possible while being active in raising awareness of the autoimmune disorder.

**Nancy F. Goodfellow** is a writer and public speaker, as well as a parent of three teens, one of whom has Down syndrome. She speaks to students and teachers about the importance of understanding intellectual disabilities and differences in order to fully accept and include everyone. Learn more at www.nancyfgoodfellow.com.

**Joanne Guidoccio** retired from a thirty-one-year teaching career and launched a second act as a writer. Her articles and book reviews have appeared in newspapers, magazines, and online. The author of six novels, Joanne writes cozy mysteries, paranormal romances, and inspirational literature. Learn more at joanneguidoccio.com.

**Sarah B. Hampshire** and her husband raised five children and adore their thirteen grandkids. Sarah loves writing and recently helped her disabled son pen his memoir. She enjoys playing violin, needle tatting, sewing, drawing, and keeping current with sign language. She lives with her husband and son in southwestern Missouri.

**Karen Haueisen** has lived a life full of interesting characters, wonderful adventures, and some harrowing experiences. She funnels that into writing, including parenting humor picture books. Karen lives in Columbus, OH with her Dachshunds, Professor Wiggles and JoJo. E-mail her at khaueisen@att.net.

**Lori Hein** is a freelance writer and the author of *Ribbons of Highway: A Mother-Child Journey Across America*, the story of a 12,000-mile cross country road trip the author and her children took after 9/11. Lori has contributed to other titles in the *Chicken Soup for the Soul* series.

**Christy Heitger-Ewing** pens human interest stories for national, regional and local magazines. She has contributed to twenty-five anthologies. This is her fifteenth contribution to the *Chicken Soup for the Soul* series. She enjoys running, writing, practicing yoga, and spending time with her husband, two sons and four cats. Learn more at www. christyheitger-ewing.com.

**Jan Henrikson** writes, dances, and hikes in the mountains of Tucson, AZ. She is happy to say that since writing this essay, she has been approved as a living kidney donor. Thanks to her transplant team and love to the future recipient.

**Nancy Hesting** is a published writer and poet who lives with her husband in Michigan's Manistee National Forest where she can be found shoveling snow, picking up pinecones, or hunting for mushrooms. Her work has appeared in *Ad Hoc Fiction*, *The Pangolin Review*, and *Chicken Soup for the Soul: Lessons Learned from My Dog*.

**Brandi Hoffman** lives in Las Vegas with her two pet snakes and her emotional support boyfriend Mike. When not performing a story slam or standup in front of an audience, she writes screenplays, practices conversational Chinese or volunteers at the local nature center.

**Kayleen Kitty Holder** is the editor of a small newspaper and a children's book author. Check out her book *Hello from the Great Blue Sea*, a fundraiser for children battling A-T including her niece Audrey. Around 1 in 3 children with A-T develop cancer. See how you can help find a cure at www.atcp.org/AudreysLight.

**Toni Hoy** is a freelance writer and has a B.A. in Communications. She is a mother of four and has won multiple awards for children's mental health advocacy including Angels in Adoption, a congressional award. She enjoys writing, painting, sewing, hiking in Tennessee, and plans to start writing romance novels.

**A.J. Hughes**, a freelance author, copywriter and editor, has been previously published in the *Chicken Soup for the Soul* series. For nine years, she contributed a humorous column to a local newspaper. She loves to hike her favorite mountains in Phoenix, enjoys music, eccentric art, and her two cats.

**Kaitlyn Jain** wrote *Passports and Pacifiers: Traveling the World, One Tantrum at a Time* and many stories for the *Chicken Soup for the Soul* series. She earned her B.A. from Davidson College, her MBA from NYU, and she now consults and coaches high school volleyball. She enjoys traveling and spending time with her husband and four kids. Learn more at www.KaitlynJain.com.

**Trudy K.** worked for twenty-five years in higher education. She is the mother of five and the grandmother of three grandsons and one granddaughter. Now retired, Trudy spends her time serving on er local Council on Aging, writing stories, playing pickleball, line dancing, doing yoga, reading, attending Al-Anon meetings, or hanging with her grandkids.

**Kiesa Kay**, playwright and poet, writes to reinforce resilience. She loves to dance, swim, and play fiddle and psaltery. Kiesa and her wonder dog, Rosa, live in a cabin on an acre in the woods with a panoramic view of the Black Mountains.

**Chip Kirkpatrick** lives in Northeast Florida with his wife, Grace. Retired, he does historical metal detecting and writes articles for magazines and local publications. He is a docent for the Amelia Island Museum of History. He published *ROSCOE: My CARDINAL SIN* and *TWEEDLES and ELLIE*.

**Wendy Klopfenstein** likes sunshine, sweet tea, and a good book, preferably all together. She enjoys putting the stories in her head on paper for others to enjoy. To sign up for her newsletter visit www.wendyklopfenstein.com.

**Shannon Leach** lives in Tennessee and is the owner of A Repurposed Heart. Her inspirational stories and books about leadership, life, and loving people focus on encouraging others and reminding them they are not alone. She holds a bachelor's degree in social work and is the co-founder of the nonprofit The Fostered Gift.

**Mary Clare Lockman** is a retired Oncology RN and has a B.A. in Creative Writing. She has written six books: three children's picture books, two young adult/adult novels, and a humorous memoir. Her stories have appeared in various magazines and several titles in the *Chicken Soup for the Soul* series. E-mail her at mcl1492@gmail.com.

**Karen Lorentzen** was raised on a farm with nine boys. She is retired and lives in Arizona with her cat.

**Allison Lynn** is drawn to the power of story to grow hearts and communities. Singer, songwriter and worship leader, Allison and her husband, Gerald Flemming, form the award-winning duo, Infinitely More. She has been published in *Guideposts*, *The Upper Room* and four previous *Chicken Soup for the Soul* books. Learn more at www.InfinitelyMore.ca.

Inspired by her adventurous adult children, **Diane Lowe MacLachlan's** stories sprout from her engagement with the people and places energizing her life. A graduate of Hope College and currently loving life in Chicago, she is encouraged by her writers' group to pursue her next projects: writing a fiction novel and a children's book series.

**John Marcum** is a graduate of St. Louis University with a bachelor's degree in arts and science. He worked in sales and service in the steel industry until his retirement in 2008. John is currently a member of the Saturday Writers of St. Peters, a chapter of the Missouri Writer's Guild.

**Barbara McCourtney, M.S.** is an award-winning author. Her book, *Does This Diet Make My Butt Look Fat*, is a humorous look at her weight-loss journey. It has all five-star reviews on Amazon. She is passionate about blessing others through her books and blog at wwwBooksByBarb.net.

**Kim Johnson McGuire** received her Bachelor of Arts in Literature from the University of California Santa Barbara. She works as a Pilates instructor and enjoys traveling, reading, playing golf, and volunteering at the animal shelter as a cat socializer. She has two cute, quirky felines and lives on California's central coast.

**Trisha Ridinger McKee** is a multi-genre author with nine published novels and short stories featured in over 150 publications, including the *Chicken Soup for the Soul* series, *Crab Fat Literary*, *Travel Magazine*, *Deep Fried Horror*, and more.

**Lisa McManus** thanks Jen, Jaime, Sam and all the girls for all the things. For VSAC, VWTH and the Wednesday Group for never-ending support, her mom and dad, Teresa and Suzanne for always being there. And most importantly, for her children, Mitchell and Matthew, who keep her going. She will always be there for you — Be fearless; keep going.

**Beckie A. Miller** began writing after the murder of her son in 1991. Writing was a means of survival at first, with journals documenting a journey no parent should ever have to make. She has had numerous stories published since. Her hobbies include bowling and gardening. She has two daughters and two grandsons and is married to Don.

**Dianne Moritz** has a California teaching credential, valid for life, from Pepperdine University. She taught grades K-3 in Los Angeles, CA. She now writes poetry and picture books. Her third book, *1,2,3 by the Sea*, is a bestseller and was on Bank Street's "best books list, 2014."

Find her on Facebook.

**Lava Mueller** lives in central Vermont. She is the founder and minister of Love Church, a non-traditional worshiping community, and the author of *Don't Tell,* a novel of teen secrets and intrigue that has been optioned for a movie. To receive her weekly Love Letter photo blog visit lavamueller@gmail.com.

**Jenni Murphy** is currently living in Arizona. Her life adventures include backpacking through Africa alone, visiting an elephant sanctuary in Thailand, and traveling to see Kenny Rogers in concert. She is currently working on *The Swear Jar* and can be reached at bookjunkie.murphy@gmail.com.

**Florence Niven** lives in Kingston, Ontario with her husband Don. This is her third time being published in the *Chicken Soup for the Soul* series. Her recently published *Step Into This Day: Thoughts on Connection* is a compilation of seventy of her poems that explore gratitude, love and loss.

**Mary Ann Paliani** has published opinion essays in her local newspaper. In addition to her writing interests, she is an avid bicyclist, rock climber and world traveler. Her adventure destinations have ranged from the Himalayas to the Sahara Desert. At the age of eighty-eight she is training for a technical climb in the Rocky Mountains.

**Nancy Emmick Panko** is a frequent contributor to the *Chicken Soup for the Soul* series and the author of award-winning *Guiding Missal, Sheltering Angels, Blueberry Moose, Peachy Possums,* and *The Skunk Who Lost His Cents.* A retired pediatric nurse, Nancy enjoys reading, writing, and being near the water with her family. Learn more at www.nancypanko.com.

**Ava Pennington** is a writer, speaker, and Bible teacher. She writes for nationally circulated magazines and is published in thirty-eight anthologies, including thirty *Chicken Soup for the Soul* books. She authored *Reflections on the Names of God: 180 Devotions to Know God More Fully,* endorsed by Kay Arthur. Learn more at www.AvaPennington.com.

**Carol Perry** is a retired middle school counselor who loves to welcome the first wildflower of spring with a greeting and a dance. She prefers to be outside rather than in and has a soft spot for vulnerable populations. When not writing she can be found playing her ukulele or adventuring to new places.

**AJ Peterson** is a college student studying for her B.A in Psychology. She hopes to go on to earn a Ph.D. in Psychology to help people in the same way she was helped as a teenager. Her hobbies include reading, writing, tennis, and playing *Dungeons & Dragons* with her friends.

**Cheryl Potts**, a native Californian, loves writing, gardening, and RVing with her dog, Katie, and husband, Richard. She is a retired social worker, a mother of two, stepmother of two, and grandmother of seventeen. She writes historical fiction through the eyes of women who lived American history.

**Art Prennace** is a licensed professional counselor living in a small town of approximately 250 year-round residents in Alaska. He conducts his counseling through telehealth via the Internet when the electronic gods allow. His hobbies include snoring, hibernation and keeping warm during cold and dark Alaskan winter nights.

**Connie Kaseweter Pullen** lives in rural Sandy, OR, near her five children and several grandchildren. She earned a B.A. degree, with honors, at the University of Portland in 2006, with a double major in Psychology and Sociology. Connie enjoys writing, photography and exploring nature. E-mail her at MyGrandmaPullen@aol.com.

**Judy Quan** is a retired registered nurse, who spent much of her career caring for cancer patients.

**Anne Foley Rauth** grew up in a small town in Northwest Missouri and received her MBA from the University of Kansas. She ultimately followed her passion by currently working in the nonprofit sector. Anne and her husband have three sons. Tell her what you've done just for fun at anne@annerauth.com.

**Jayna Richardson** lives in the beautiful state of Arkansas, where she often drags her husband and kids along on outdoor adventures. In addition to hiking and backpacking, she enjoys kayaking, biking, reading, and blogging.

**Melissa Richeson** is a writer and editor based in coastal Florida. Her creative writing has been seen in *Sunlight Press*, *WDW Magazine*, *The Washington Post*, *Florida Today*, the *Chicken Soup for the Soul* series, and others. When not writing, you can find her at the beach, preferably with her four sons.

**Vickie G. Rodgers** has a master's degree in nursing and is a former Professor of Nursing Education. She has a passion for the elderly and is currently the clinical educator of a senior community. Vickie has published a children's book that encourages intergenerational friendships, and she enjoys family time and being creative.

**Patricia Rossi** is an author, an avid runner, and a freelance artist. She is an active member of her community, serves on various not-for-profit boards and has facilitated, on a volunteer basis for almost two decades now, writing how-to-heal workshops for cancer survivors.

**Nikki Rottenberg**, a proud Canadian, started writing in 2009. She enjoys writing fiction and nonfiction stories and has received government grants and won a number of awards for her work. Nikki is a nature lover, hiker and photographer. Her beautiful daughters are her inspiration to live life to its fullest.

Before serving for two years in Ecuador, **Sandi Johnson Ruble** graduated with a B.A. in Journalism from Mississippi University for Women. She and Dan married in 1990 and have lived in eight cities, and have two adult children and a dog. Sandi enjoys visiting family, exercising with her friends and baking. She is writing a middle grade reader.

**Michelle Baker Sanders** is an adventure-seeking, food-loving, wine-sipping freelance writer with a passion for travel and a degree in psychology. Michelle lived in Europe for six years, splitting the time between Ireland and France. Today, she explores the U.S. as a full-time RVer, visiting the country's state and national parks.

**Jeannette Sanderson** lives in the Hudson Valley with her husband and two dogs. She has been bewitched by stories all her life and is always happy to hear or tell one. In addition to writing, Jeannette loves to read, run, and travel. She is the mother of two wonderful young adults. Follow her on Twitter @readwriterunmom.

**Mae Frances Sarratt** is married with two children and four grandchildren. She is a speaker, writing contest judge, podcast guest, and Sunday school curriculum developer. She has served as a staff member at The Carolina Christian Writers Conference.

**John Scanlan** is a 1983 graduate of the United States Naval Academy and retired from the United States Marine Corps as a Lieutenant Colonel aviator with time in the back seat of both the F-4S Phantom II and the F/A-18D Hornet. He is currently pursuing a second career as a writer.

**Bev A. Schellenberg** is a mom of three, an author (*A Prince Among Dragons* and *A Princess Among Dragons*), and a high school teacher in the Pacific Northwest. She received her Master of Arts degree in 2021 and wrote a novel manuscript as her thesis. She enjoys reading, attending comic cons, and playing hockey.

**Sally Schofield** retired from a career in advertising, where she traveled the world as an international sales representative. Her husband of thirty-seven years passed away and, after four years of being single, she met her current husband, a retired Presbyterian minister, online. Their relationship is the basis of the story that appears in this book.

**Joyce Newman Scott** worked as a flight attendant while pursuing an acting career. She started college in her mid-fifties and studied screen writing at the University of Miami and creative writing at Florida International University. She is thrilled to be a frequent contributor to the *Chicken Soup for the Soul* series.

**Kim Sheard** is the published author of many short stories and confessions, personal experience pieces, and Christian devotions. She got her start with a *Star Trek* story published in a Pocket Books anthology. By day, she owns a pet sitting company in northern Virginia, where she lives with her husband Henry and dog Scout.

**René Ashcraft Sprunger** graduated from Grace University, the University of Nebraska and Lesley College. She taught kindergarten and college. She was married to her soulmate, Mike, for thirty-seven years before he succumbed to cancer. Her favorite activities include spending time with her children and grandchildren and tending her flower garden.

**Jennifer Starr** is a Speech Language Pathologist, receiving her master's degree from Ball State University in Muncie, Indiana. She enjoys spending time with her family, traveling, creative writing, and cooking.

**Danielle Stauber** has been a wife and stay at home mom for the past twenty years. She and her family reside in Central New York. Danielle has loved to write since before she could barely even spell. That love has only grown over the years. She has written novellas, poetry, and children's stories for her own three kids. E-mail her at Daniellestauber84@gmail.com.

**Peter J. Stavros** is a writer and playwright in Louisville, KY. His work has appeared in literary journals, anthologies and magazines, including *The Saturday Evening Post* and the *Boston Globe Magazine*. When Peter isn't writing, you might find him on his skateboard at the abandoned basketball court down the street.

**Noelle Sterne, Ph.D.** publishes stories, poems, essays, and writing craft, spiritual, and academic articles. Her *Challenges in Writing Your Dissertation* helps doctoral students fulfill their goals. In *Trust Your Life*, Noelle supports readers in reaching lifelong yearnings. Thankfully pursuing her own, Noelle writes daily.

**Long Tang** is the pen name of William Tang, a Chinese historian. He has published five books and numerous articles as Long Tang. He co-authored his first book, *Pets Only*, with his dog, Shadow. He lives in Virginia with his wife, a dog, two cats, two birds, and a forest full of animals.

**Camille DeFer Thompson** lives in Northern California. After retirement, she began contributing feature stories to a local newspaper. Her short fiction and nonfiction work have appeared in a number of anthologies. Read about her trials navigating the 21st century as a baby boomer on her humor blog at www.camilledeferthompson.net.

**Terri Turner** is a retired elementary school teacher. She loves to cook, hike, write, read, and spend time with her family. She self-published a children's book, titled, *What Will You Do, Missy Moo???*, and hopes to one day publish more books for kids!

**Elizabeth Veldboom** is a writer, spoken word artist, and inspirational speaker. She writes and speaks from the perspective of a single Christian woman in her thirties and covers topics such as foster care awareness, relationships, career building, and loving Jesus. Learn more at www.30sandspillingthetea.org.

**Laura Vertin** holds a master's in social work. She lives with her husband and two children in Dublin, GA. This is Laura's second story published in the *Chicken Soup for the Soul* series. She enjoys writing short stories and poetry, gardening, and spending time outdoors.

**Samantha Ducloux Waltz** lives in Portland, OR where her family and friends, pets, writing, yoga and gardening keep her busy and happy. Her writings include anthologized and award-winning essays, her Seal Press anthology *Blended: Writers on the Stepfamily Experience*, and her novel *The Choice of Men*.

**Benny Wasserman** was an aerospace engineer for thirty years. After retirement he spent twenty-five years as an Einstein impersonator. He is the author of the book *Presidents Were Teenagers Too*. He has been published in the *Los Angeles Times*, *Reminisce Good Old Days*, and other titles in the *Chicken Soup for the Soul* series. He is a voracious reader and ping-pong player.

**Dorann Weber** is a freelance photographer who has a passion for writing, especially for the *Chicken Soup for the Soul* series. She is a contributor for Getty Images and worked as a photojournalist. Her photos and verses have appeared on Hallmark cards. She enjoys reading, hiking, and spending time with her family.

**Linda J. Wright** has been involved in animal advocacy and activism for over thirty years and is the founder of The Cat People, a cat rescue and rehabilitation nonprofit. An award-winning writer, she is also the author of the *Kieran Yeats* series of animal rescue novels and the owner of Cats Paw Books at catspawbooks.com.

# Meet Amy Newmark

**Amy Newmark** is the bestselling author, editor-in-chief, and publisher of the *Chicken Soup for the Soul* book series. Since 2008, she has published 199 new books, most of them national bestsellers in the U.S. and Canada, more than doubling the number of Chicken Soup for the Soul titles in print today. She is also the author of *Simply Happy*, a crash course in Chicken Soup for the Soul advice and wisdom that is filled with easy-to-implement, practical tips for enjoying a better life.

Amy is credited with revitalizing the Chicken Soup for the Soul brand, which has been a publishing industry phenomenon since the first book came out in 1993. By compiling inspirational and aspirational true stories curated from ordinary people who have had extraordinary experiences, Amy has kept the thirty-one-year-old Chicken Soup for the Soul brand fresh and relevant.

Amy graduated *magna cum laude* from Harvard University where she majored in Portuguese and minored in French. She then embarked on a three-decade career as a Wall Street analyst, a hedge fund manager, and a corporate executive in the technology field. She is a Chartered Financial Analyst.

Her return to literary pursuits was inevitable, as her honors thesis in college involved traveling throughout Brazil's impoverished northeast region, collecting stories from regular people. She is delighted to have come full circle in her writing career — from collecting stories "from the people" in Brazil as a twenty-year-old to, three decades later, collecting stories "from the people" for Chicken Soup for the Soul.

When Amy and her husband Bill, the CEO of Chicken Soup for the Soul, are not working, they are visiting their four grown children and their spouses, and their five grandchildren.

Follow Amy on X and Instagram @amynewmark. Listen to her free podcast — Chicken Soup for the Soul with Amy Newmark — on Apple, Google, or by using your favorite podcast app on your phone.

# Thank You

**W**e owe huge thanks to all our contributors and fans. We received thousands of submissions for this popular topic, and we spent months reading all of them. Laura Dean, Maureen Peltier, Susan Heim and D'ette Corona read all of them and narrowed down the selection for Publisher and Editor-in-Chief Amy Newmark. Susan Heim did the first round of editing, and then D'ette chose the perfect quotations to put at the beginning of each story and Amy edited the stories and shaped the final manuscript.

As we finished our work, D'ette continued to be Amy's right-hand woman in working with all our wonderful writers. Barbara LoMonaco, Kristiana Pastir and Elaine Kimbler jumped in to proof, proof, proof. And yes, there will always be typos anyway, so please feel free to let us know about them at webmaster@chickensoupforthesoul.com, and we will correct them in future printings.

The whole publishing team deserves a hand, including our Vice President of Marketing Maureen Peltier, our Vice President of Production & COO Victor Cataldo, and our graphic designer Daniel Zaccari, who turned our manuscript into this beautiful, inspirational book.

Changing lives one story at a time®
www.chickensoup.com